BLACK TENT, EASTERN SYRIA.

(Copyright by Underwood & Underwood, New York.)

P. 243

[GREEN FUND BOOK No. 16]

ORIENTALISMS IN BIBLE LANDS

GIVING LIGHT FROM CUSTOMS, HABITS, MANNERS, IMAGERY, THOUGHT AND LIFE IN THE EAST FOR BIBLE STUDENTS.

BY

EDWIN WILBUR RICE, Litt.D., D.D.

AUTHOR OF

"Commentaries on the Gospels and The Acts;" "Our Sixty-Six Sacred Books;" "People's Dictionary of the Bible;" "Handy Helps for Busy Workers;" "The Sunday-School Movement and the American Sunday-School Union," etc.

THIRD EDITION

PHILADELPHIA:
The American Sunday-School Union,
1816 Chestnut Street.

NOTE TO THIRD EDITION.

To present a yet more complete panorama and picture of Oriental life as it was two thousand years ago additions have been made in this Third Edition. The more important of the added topics are: Oriental Language Pictorial, Old Law Code, Terebinth Tree, Pachyderms, Tax Extortion, Cuneiform Writing. Additions made in the Second Edition were: Significance of the "Sop" to Judas, Family Customs, Circumcision, Naming of Children, and other Oriental habits and customs.

I trust these added lights on Oriental life two thousand to four thousand years ago will aid the Bible student in gaining a better knowledge of the Holy Scriptures and of the will of God.

E. W. R.

PHILADELPHIA, June, 1929.

CONTENTS.

CONTENTS.

CONTENTS.

FOREWORD.

THE Book through which the one great religion of the world has come to mankind is thoroughly Oriental. Every part of the Bible is saturated with the peculiar traits, modes of thought, customs, manner of speech, and imagery that characterize Eastern life. A knowledge of these is essential to a clear understanding and right interpretation of the Holy Scriptures.

Once it was common to speak of the "unchanging East," as scholars and explorers were wont to do in the last generation. For centuries there was indeed a persistence of the same manners and customs, partly due to the physical characteristics of the lands of the East, and partly to the indisposition of the people for change. That day has passed.

There is no portion of the globe where such marvelous and radical changes are going on to-day as in the Orient. In Jerusalem, in Joppa, and in Damascus one sees the railway locomotive, hears the click of the telegraph, and may talk to his distant neighbor through the telephone. Soon it will be impossible for a traveler to discover simple native Oriental Life. Even now it is difficult to find a village or people in any Bible land so remote as to be free from the influences of Western life, which are sweeping through all Oriental countries. Native Oriental customs are already modified by these influences to an extent little suspected by many even of the Orientals themselves.

Another common view among the "laity" and learned was that the early biblical narratives described human life in a primitive stage. But we now know that Abraham was "comparatively a modern man," scarcely midway between the present and the infancy of the human race. Early records of peoples in the Euphrates and in the Nile valleys show a high state of culture, civilization, and social life thousands of years

9

before Abraham.   The biblical books in their color fit in a wonderful way into these newly discovered historic facts.

Moreover, the strange manners and customs in Oriental life produced opposite modes of thought and idioms of speech from those of the West, and which find constant expression in the Holy Scriptures.

For years the author has had missionaries, travelers, and natives of Oriental lands gathering these characteristics of Eastern life (which would make many volumes) for the purpose of throwing light upon the Scripture narrative.   Distinguished specialists, as the late Prof. George E. Post, M. D., LL. D., of the Syrian Protestant College of Beirut, Frederick J. Bliss, Ph. D., explorer, who uncovered the site of Lachish, J. T. Haddad, a native of Damascus, and for years in the employ of the Turkish Government in Bashan-Land, the Rev. J. E. Hanauer, a lifelong resident of Palestine, and others have furnished results of their researches and knowledge of Eastern customs to the periodicals edited by the author.   Hundreds of books, narratives, and reports by missionary, consular, commercial, and educational residents and observers of the past century have been carefully gleaned to aid in presenting a clear idea of the customs and life in various lands of the East.   Due acknowledgments are made of the author's indebtedness to these several sources in the footnotes throughout this volume. All this material, published and unpublished, has now been classified and condensed into a convenient form in this book for use by the Bible student.

While we can no longer see the forms of living men in almost the same garb, and speaking almost the same language, as in the days of the old Hebrew patriarchs, it is still true that "native Oriental life is the only key that can unlock the sense of many a valuable text of Scripture and bring it clearly into our view."

1910.   EDWIN WILBUR RICE.

I.

THE ORIENTAL FAMILY.

1. *The Bible—Oriental Color.*—Every book of the Bible is highly colored with Orientalisms of thought and of expression. A right apprehension of the force and meaning of its teachings, and of its shades of truth, depends largely upon a familiarity with, or a good knowledge of, life in the East. For each sacred writer reveals his message from God through the atmosphere of Oriental life, manners, customs, and modes of thought as they existed in his time, two thousand to four thousand years ago.

2. *Overturned Customs.*—For Western people reverse, upset, and completely turn around the customs and habits of Oriental nations. How different must be the thought and expression of the East, growing necessarily out of these opposite ways of life and manners!

Occidentals entering a church take off their hats. But when an Oriental enters a temple, he reverently takes off his sandals or shoes at the door, but covers his head with his turban, and conceals his hands under his robes. In the Orient, women wear loose trousers and the men often wear skirts: the women wait on men and give them seats: the men often bare their arms and neck, but the women cover and conceal theirs: they paint their nails, while their Western sisters often paint their cheeks. Shaving the head is a fashion in the East, but a mark of prison-punishment in the West. To shave off the beard in the East is a disgrace. The Oriental shepherd never drives his sheep, but leads them: the carpenter pulls his saw and his plane toward him to cut and smooth the wood, never pushes them from him. The Oriental commonly sleeps with his head covered, and perhaps his feet bare: never the reverse. He refuses by throwing the head backward—not by shaking it: he beckons the op-

11

posite way to us by waving his hand, palm outward and down-ward, not by a wave toward him.   A girl in the East when married keeps her own name, and is often called after her father, not after her husband.   A wife follows her husband on the road at a respectful distance; it would be a shame for them to go arm in arm in the street.   In the West, people decorate their walls, and often leave the ceilings plain: the Oriental usually decorates the ceilings of his room and leaves the walls plain. Western people write and read from left to right of the page, the Oriental the reverse way, from right to left, or from top to bottom of the page.   The Oriental places his seal or signature attesting a document or letter at the top or beginning of the sheet, not at the end or bottom of it.   Love and courtship may follow marriage: not precede it.   An Oriental, finding him-self at the tent-door of his deadly foe, would not flee from it, but probably, boldly enter and claim and be granted brief hospital-ity and protection, the host defending the guest, though a bitter enemy, at any cost, even to that of his own life.   The Ameri-can in mourning puts on black, the Chinese wear white; in greeting he may shake his own hands, but not his friend's. About everything is done the reverse way by Orientals to what Occidentals do.

No study of the Bible, therefore, can be satisfactory that does not include some knowledge of life and thought in the East. In fact, we must transport ourselves into the conditions and spirit of this Oriental life, difficult as that may be, or often miss the intent of the divine message and sadly misinterpret it. To understand the working of the Oriental mind in religion is more difficult for us than in almost any other phase of his thought.   Fortunately, this study is attractive from its many remarkable contrasts, and will increase in fascination as new vistas of meaning and knowledge are opened to those who pur-sue it.   Let us ask, first of all:

What is the Oriental idea of the family?

3. *The " Father."*—To the Oriental, the family is a little kingdom in itself.   The "father," or head, is king—a su-

preme ruler in his realm. The Oriental requires a "father" at the head of every company, every band of traders and travelers, as well as for every tribe, community, and household. The Oriental cannot conceive of any such band or company without a "father," though not one in the band may be kith or kin to the so-called "father." They may be servants, stragglers, or strangers that are journeying together, yet one of their number must be "father" to all the others. Any other idea is unthinkable to the Oriental mind. Their idea of "father" also includes a wider range. What a man invents, makes, manages, of that, too, he is the "father." Thus, Jubal "was the father of all such as handle the harp and pipe," because he was the reputed inventor of these instruments, and Jabal was the "father of such as dwell in tents and have cattle," because he was the supposed pioneer in that mode of life[1]; not because either of these men was the natural father of all such persons. Even when one becomes the preserver, protector, or helper of another, he was called a "father," as Joseph says God made him "a father to Pharaoh." The young Levite became "a father and priest," to Micah and the Danites.[2]

4. *No Courtship.*—This idea of "a father" shows how deepseated is the Oriental conception of the unity of the family. Moreover, the Oriental always conceives of the family as of God's appointment, "God setteth the solitary in families."[3] Nor does he think of love and courtship as necessary *before* marriage. His idea is that love follows the formation of the family, and to his mind is as natural a result of the relation of husband and wife as of brother and sister. He has no conception of our artificial and modern process which we call courtship. The parents carry out God's purpose by selecting the bride, and arranging the betrothal and marriage for their children. The young couple acquiesce in what is done for them. The dowry is not in any proper sense to be regarded as the price of the wife. It is rather a wise provision, divinely

---

[1] Gen. 4 : 20, 21.　　[2] Judg. 17 : 10; 18 : 19.　　[3] Ps. 68 : 6.

sanctioned, for the highest good of the new-formed family. This conception prevails generally throughout the East. The divine appointment or idea may be obscured among other than Hebrew peoples, but the germ existed, though sadly perverted in development—a survival of the primitive Edenic state.

5. *The Son.*—From almost every point of view, the structure of an Oriental family is a puzzle to Occidentals. A son, when he is a child, in nowise differs from a slave, though he is lord of all.[1] This seeming paradox grows out of the structure of the Oriental family. Prof. Post points out that now in the Orient the women of a monarch's household are commonly slaves. Many of the women in the households of the pashas and sheikhs are also slaves. "Thus the children are in subjection." They must kiss the father's hand when they see him: must always stand in his presence with folded hands; eat apart from him; in a word, feel and act like slaves. This training fits the child (so they think) to appreciate the transition from subjection to the rights of a son, when his days of tutelage are over.

6. *The Father Rules.*—It follows from the Eastern conception of the unity and indivisibility of the family, that the father never ceases to have a responsibility for his son's conduct as long as he lives, even if the father is a hundred years old and the son eighty years of age. So, too, the family and tribal loyalty prevailing in the East overshadows patriotism. Thus, when a Copt or an Armenian settles in Syria, he does not become a Syrian, but remains a Copt or an Armenian. His sentiment of nationality is drowned in his absorbing affection for his family or his tribe. He refuses to become a patriot. He has no true national patriotism. Out of this Oriental idea of the solidarity and selectness of the family springs the desire to conserve it, and the social law binding on every member to defend the family and every other member of it. Thus, blood feuds, fierce and bitter and of long duration, constantly break out in the Orient.

7. *Patriarchal Rule.*—The prominence of the patriarchal idea

[1] Gal. 4 : 1.

SHEIKH AND WIFE, RAMALLAH.   P. 13

(Copyright by Underwood & Underwood, New York.)

JEW IN SYRIA.   P. 14

'Vester & Co.)

in the Oriental family-polity underlies their entire social life, an idea difficult for the Western mind to grasp, and more difficult to define. This accounts, in part, for the Jewish race maintaining a distinct type, though scattered, yet rarely becoming assimilated in any nation. The Oriental has a similar exclusiveness by nature, and hence is rated at his own estimate of himself and is not welcome in lands that seek strength through the homogeneity of its people. With him the patriarchal is largely at war with the national idea. The "organic unity of the race is held tenaciously by nearly all Orientals," and this idea is generally limited to the particular race to which he belongs.

8. *Semites and Hebrews.*—Thus, the tendency of the Japhetic race to colonization, involving the separation of families, by the migration of younger members, has been noted as in sharp contrast with the general practice of the Semitic race, which for past centuries clings to the old world. The Jews are an exception to the general social trend in modern history. The scattering of that people is a marked instance of divine providence, and a signal confirmation of divine prophecy. Their migrations have been generally due to compulsion. Yet, true to Oriental and their own constitutional habits, and their strong family and tribal instincts, they do not easily amalgamate with the peoples where they sojourn. Their peculiar racial and religious characteristics are tenaciously held. They live largely by themselves. There is a Jewish quarter in every great American and European city, a proof in itself of their Semitic racial character and of their Oriental origin.

But the Hebrews, in common with all Orientals, and with Western civilization, testify in their history and by their blood that the family is the unit of the social organism. In this the divine idea survives alike in all civilized races of mankind.

II.

9. *Love-making Unknown.*—No young man and maiden in the East would think of courtship, or in any way arranging for marriage of themselves. Love-making is an unknown pastime among Oriental boys and girls. Out of the theory of the East, that love comes after, not before marriages, arises customs tending to restrain this sentiment of the human heart. The irrepressible power of love is, in part, anticipated by the parents, who arrange for the betrothal of their children at a very early age. The selection is made by the parents on both sides, and the two parties themselves may never look into each other's faces until the marriage is completed.

10. *Girl's Gifts.*—The parents of the girl, by immemorial custom, see that she is prepared for a proposal of marriage. From early childhood she acquires necklaces, rings, ornaments, and gems, according to her station in life. These are gained in various ways—by gifts of parents, relatives, or guests, and are sometimes earned by the girl herself. To these she adds various kinds of embroidery and articles of needle-work, to wear on her person. These become her personal property, inalienable, and cannot be taken from her without her consent. Even her husband, who may divorce her, by law and custom, is forbidden to take from her any apparel or gems, necklaces or money, or anything worn or carried on her person, even though some of them were bestowed on her by himself. These are seen on the merest children in the East. Thus, Miss Whately tells of little girls in her school at Cairo, Egypt, who came daily arrayed in coin-necklaces, corals, and trinkets, which might be the only support of a girl should the husband, in some freak of temper, divorce one that had been betrothed as his wife. For the girl could retain without dispute all these, and they

might be absolutely necessary for her support and her only living.

11. *Wife-seeking*.—Moreover, the girl is married generally at twelve, and sometimes as early as seven years of age. She may be betrothed much younger, when a mere infant. It is rare that man or maiden marries outside the tribe to which each may belong. The father, parents, guardians, or elders are expected to arrange marriages, betrothals, and dowry contracts for the children.

The Oriental modes of wife-seeking vary widely in different tribes and countries, yet they are broadly alike in their general characteristics.   In Western Asia it may be the father, of his own accord, concludes it is time a wife be sought for his son. Or perhaps the father has not thought of it, and the young man says to his father, "I have enough for a marriage dowry." This means that he wants a girl-wife found for him.   The father approves. The mother, or near female relative, or a *Khatibeh*, professional "matchmaker," is employed and instructed to find a wife for the young man. He may describe his ideal maiden to them as a guide in the search.

12. *Matchmaking*.—With this commission, the women "matchmakers " make diligent inquiries among all the kinsfolk respecting suitable girls, and then start on a tour of personal inspection. The mothers of marriageable girls know very well the purpose of the visit, though they may affect indifference and ignorance. The women "matchmakers" call on the mother of some daughter. The salutations are profuse; the greetings prolonged and exceedingly complimentary. The visitors are invited to sit on divans or rugs, the servant brings coffee to sip, the conversation drifts around and into every subject but the one for which the guests really came.   Meanwhile the mother conveys a hint to her daughter, in another apartment or upstairs, to array herself in her best attire.

Having exhausted the topics of interest and neighborhood gossip in talk, and spent hours in dallying about many things of no interest whatever to either party, the guests venture deli-

cately to hint at the real business. The matron perhaps asks of
the hostess, "Do you happen to know or have you heard of any
kinsfolk having marriageable girls?" "None suitable for so
highly exalted a family as that of her caller," is the diplomatic
reply. Nothing daunted, the guest proceeds, "Might we have
the high pleasure to look upon the beautiful face of the lovely
Anîseh, Maryam, Haddeseh?" or whatever may be the name
of the daughter. With tactful diplomacy, the mother replies,
"Ah, Anîseh is very young and bashful." Pressed further, she
exclaims in well-feigned alarm, "My daughter would faint dead
away to look upon so distinguished a person as the mother of
Yakob Ibriham." But the guest is persistent, she will not be
put off, so the mother calls to her daughter. The daughter
hears, but appears not. She knows the custom too well to
make unseemly haste in such a matter. The mother urged,
calls again and again in vain. Finally, after five or six urgent
pleas, the daughter comes in, closely veiled, bearing coffee on a
tray, and shyly offers the customary second cup to the guests.
They courteously decline to accept it until they may see the
maiden's pretty face. If they accepted the second cup, custom
would require them to leave. Further diplomatic parleying
follows, but the veil is at last lifted and the personal inspection
begins. The girl's features, form, hair, eyes, nose, lips, cheeks,
and expression are carefully noted by the women "inspectors,"
the parting cup of coffee accepted, and the guests depart home to
report. If not satisfactory, other tours will be made to other
families, until the "matchmakers" are pleased. Then on their
return, with high-sounding Oriental phrases, they proclaim the
girl's beauty and marvelous charms and attainments to the
family and in the hearing of the young man. If the "father"
is satisfied with the report, the first stage toward betrothal
ends and the second begins.

13. *The Contract.*—The customary deputy, called "friend of
the bridegroom" [1] is engaged, and entrusted to make the nego-
tiations, arrange the contract, and pay the portion of the dowry.

---

[1] John 3 : 29.

DHOBI WASHMAN AND SIX YEAR OLD WIFE, INDIA.

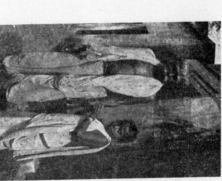

MAN AND CHILD WIFE WITH RED PAINT MARK ON HEAD, INDIA.

(C. A Tennant.)

MOTHER, FOURTEEN YEARS OLD, AND TWO CHILDREN, INDIA.

P. 17

Sometimes the son may ask his father to secure a particular woman for his wife, as Samson did.[1] So Shechem asked his father Hamor, "Get me this damsel (Dinah) to wife."[2] The deputy or "friend of the bridegroom" is fully informed of the stipulations or conditions of the proposed marriage contract; entrusted with the treasures or money to be paid as dowry, and usually given wide discretionary power in perfecting the contract. Thus Eliezer was deputed by Abraham to find a wife for Isaac, with full power even to choose the girl, bestow the ring, bracelets, and dowry, and bring the girl back from kinsfolk in far away Mesopotamia.[3] A well-known character in Palestine is the *Wasit*, deputy, or "go-between," in all business affairs. Sometimes the village *Mukhtar* or Sheikh may be chosen as the intermediary in business and family transactions. Similar agents are employed in India, China, and Japan. Sometimes the young man's mother has her mind upon a girl among their kinsfolk or neighbors, and watches how she is trained, how her daily duties are done, whether she is careful in housework, apt at sewing, embroidery, and what are her other womanly qualities, and especially her disposition and temper. The girl is presumed to be not of a higher family than the groom; she may be of an inferior class if she has rare attractions of person and disposition. What Western peoples would count blemishes of person, the Orientals often admire. Thus, a cross-eyed girl is often a beauty with them, and is lauded by their poets, especially when she has dark eyes. A man with no hair on the back of his hands, or on his chin, or his lip, is derided as ugly, and one with a bald head is hooted at, as Elisha was by the boys.[4]

14. *The Dowry.*—The amount of the dowry depends largely upon the position and possessions of the families. With the thrifty peasantry and villagers of Syria the usual dowry is equivalent to $150 to $250. The Mosaic law rates the dowry at fifty shekels—about $30.[5] The sum must be agreed on and paid in advance. Parents sometimes shrewdly make an exchange

---

[1] Judges 14 : 1-3.   [2] Gen. 34 : 4.   [3] Gen. 24 : 1-67.
[4] 2 Kings 2 : 2, 3.   [5] Ex. 22 : 17; Deut. 22 : 29.

of children, and thus evade or reduce the cash dowry. The father of a young man and a maiden proposes to the father of some girl and boy that their children be paired; his young man taking the other's girl to wife, and the boy from the other family accepting the maiden for wife. Where the parties belong to the same tribe the dowry is more easily settled, than where one family has sons only and the other marriageable daughters only. There often is, in that case, a wide difference in the ages of the couples, but it is no obstacle in the East. It is rather counted an advantage if their bride-daughter is considerably younger than the groom. Oriental custom still makes the parents strongly to insist on the marriage of the elder before the youngest daughter. Laban pleaded this in excuse for his deception in giving Leah to Jacob instead of Rachel.[1] Where the young man's family cannot pay dowry in money or treasures, he serves the girl's father a certain time in lieu of dowry, as Jacob served Laban. In any case the bride's trousseau or wedding costume is furnished to her by the groom or his relatives.

15. *How Settled.*—By custom, when the girl chosen by the mother pleases the father of the young man, they ascertain whether the father of the girl will entertain a proposal for the alliance. If so, a deputy or "friend" is sent, who, with the father of the groom or some male relative, plans a call on the other household, and as near meal-time as possible. In some lands of the East the rules of hospitality permit one to refuse to eat until he receives a promise that the favor he has come to ask will be favorably considered or granted. They are asked to "break bread." The deputy, however, politely refuses, and their mission is stated, the meal is then partaken of by all parties, but not until after it is over is the business begun. The father of the girl has a *wakeel*, or deputy, also to speak for the maiden. The presents for the bride are shown.[2] The two representatives get down to business in earnest. There is generally much haggling about the amount of the *Mah'ar*, or dowry. The

Gen. 29 : 26.   [2] See Gen. 24 : 30.

SERVING COFFEE, RAMALLAH. P. 18

groom's friend offers a sum, which is promptly refused as ridiculously small. The sum wanted by the other is extravagantly large. After much discussion and paring down of demands, and astonishingly large concessions, a friendly agreement is reached, somewhere between the amount asked and that first demanded. Then follows more bantering on other terms of the contract. The groom's "friend," who has hitherto lauded and praised his master, now assumes a deprecatory tone. In strong derogatory phrases, and Oriental hyperbole, he wants to be assured that the other party is in real earnest, and not fooling with his master. Would his master be truly accepted? He might be lazy, improvident, beating his wife, and bad. The girl's representative is fully prepared for this turn, and promptly answers that she wants him just as he is, will gladly be the young man's slave. Then the latter retorts in vigorous language. Does the groom mean what he says? He has never seen the girl. She may be deaf, blind, sick, worthless, good-for-nothing, and be no end of trouble by her ugly temper. Again, with Oriental exaggeration, the "friend" of the groom avers that he takes the maiden just as she is, as the companion of his life, the joy of his eyes, forever by his side. The affair is settled, the betrothal agreed to by the representatives of both parties, and confirmed and witnessed by all persons present (if Moslem by repeating a passage of the Koran), the dowry paid, and the betrothal is completed. If the groom is going on a journey the marriage contract may be written, formally signed, and delivered to the girl's representative. Usually, one-half or two-thirds of the dowry is paid to bind the contract and the remainder held in reserve to be paid the wife in case of the husband divorcing her or of his death. If the girl is of age, she may choose her own *wakeel*, and her consent to the alliance may be necessary, especially in Egypt. Sometimes the father may object to betrothing his daughter to a man not of the same profession or trade as well as of the same tribe with himself. When the betrothal is simply by oral consent, which is more usual among the peasants, it may be confirmed by the gift of a piece of money, coin, or a gold ring, as the deputy says, "See by this coin thou art set apart for me, according to the law of Moses and of Israel," or "Be thou wedded to me."

16. *How Paid.*—Sometimes the betrothal may be confirmed by a more formal ceremony, described by Lane. The groom and bride's deputies may sit upon the ground, face to face, with one knee on the ground, and grasp each other's right hand, raising the thumbs, and pressing them against each other. A *fick'ee*, or schoolmaster, instructs them what to do and say. Placing a handkerchief over their hands, he utters some words on the advantages of marriage, and adds a prayer from the Koran, then the bride's *wakeel* repeats after the master, "I betroth to thee, my daughter (Anîseh), the virgin (or Seyyib), for the dowry." The groom's friend then says, after the *fick'ee*, "I accept from thee her betrothal to myself, to afford her my protection; all present bear witness." This is repeated three times, all persons again repeat a passage from the Koran; each receives an embroidered handkerchief; the one given the *fick'ee* has a coin wrapped in it; the time is fixed for the marriage or coming together of the couple. The time between betrothal and coming together of the pair varies widely, according to tribal and national custom. The Talmud makes it a year for a virgin and a month for a widow. The reason for so long a time is that the girl may have her garments provided, says the Talmud. Meanwhile the girl is regarded as a wife from the day the betrothal is settled. Thus Jacob said to Laban, "Give me my wife." [1] So the betrothed maiden is called a "wife" in Mosaic law.[2] And the man that had a betrothed maiden, though he had not taken her home, is called "an husband." [3] And as the Scriptures imply, Joseph and Mary of Nazareth were regarded as husband and wife after betrothal.[4]

17. *Second Marriage.*—The mode of seeking a wife described above applies to the first betrothal or marriage only, that of a virgin. The second betrothal, or that of a widow, is much more

[1] Gen. 29 : 21. [2] Deut. 22 : 25, 26.
[3] Lev. 19 : 20. [4] Matt. 1 : 18–25; Luke 1 : 26.

simple, and the dowry is considerably less, and the whole proceeding attracts less attention of relatives, and the parents do
not attach such importance to it as to the betrothal of an unmarried daughter.

The dowry can be partly or wholly invested in bracelets, and
ornaments given to the bride to attach to her person, or, in some
cases, it is put out on the best security and rate of interest.
There are allusions in the contract letters and records of Ancient
Babylonia to the retention and returning of the *terhatu*, or dowry,
and many stipulations respecting payments of it, before the
days of Abraham, as we know from the laws of Hammurapi.

18. *Exempt From Duties.*—In some Oriental lands the father
of the girl presents her an amount equal to the sum given by the
bridegroom, and the two sums make the bride's dowry, the total
being called *Mah'ar*, and is her inalienable property.   The
betrothed man was exempt from military service and certain
public duties that he might be "free at home one year." [1]

The family asked that Rebekah might "abide with us a few
days, at least ten; after that she shall go." [2]   But Jacob waited
seven years for Rachel, then was given Leah, and served seven
more years for Rachel.   No fixed time between betrothal and
nuptials seems to have been customary in old Babylonia, but
the code of Hammurapi requires of a man who has taken a wife
that a "marriage contract" be executed, or the "woman is not a
wife."   Custom also excused these young persons from attending burials or entering tombs or cemeteries.   Between betrothal
and the "nuptials," or coming together, no private intercourse
was permitted the betrothed.   All communication must be
through friends or deputies. [3]

NOTE.—*Elder Brother as "Father."*—If the "father" dies, the elder
brother, or uncle, or eldest male relative becomes the head of the family
and "father."   If the "father" had more than one wife, the brothers
by the same wife are the proper guardians of their respective sisters, and
bound to protect, avenge, or punish them.   See story of Dinah and of
Tamar, Absalom's sister. [4]   Brothers with marriageable sisters could
exchange a sister for a wife.

[1] Luke 14 : 20; Deut. 20 : 7–24 : 5.   [2] Gen. 24 : 55.
[3] Ruth 4 : 9–11.   [4] Gen. 34 : 25 ; 2 Sam. 13 : 32

III.

MARRIAGE PROCESSIONS.

19. *Parades in Public.*—Unique features connected with betrothal and marriage in Oriental lands are the jubilant public processions. There are often three or more of these street parades in succession, for the Oriental takes great pride in display. Thus, the costumes and presents for the bride are the occasion of a street cavalcade, more or less conspicuous, in proportion to the tastes and station of the parties. When the bride goes to the home of the bridegroom, another public procession is necessary, while the largest and most brilliant of all is that of the bridegroom and his company.

20. *Bridal Costumes.*—Here again custom widely differs among various Eastern peoples, and among the same people, because of the wealth and circumstances of the parties. Thus, among the peasantry of Palestine, remote from the route of tourists, Elihu Grant witnessed a noisy procession of women and children in a village on the occasion of taking home the wedding costumes purchased for the maiden by the bridegroom. The garments were borne through the streets with shouting, beating of drums, and firing of guns, to attract attention to the bride's costume, a red striped dress displayed on a stick, a gay jacket on a cross-stick frame to hold out the sleeves, a girdle, a heavy coin head-dress, and three mirrors, one on each arm and one on the breast. This *Zeffeh*, or parade, was accompanied by crowds of women singing and dancing, adding to the gaiety of the occasion.

Lane witnessed similar processions in Egypt, called a *Zeffeh*. Early in the last century, among the middle-class families, the bride was escorted in state to the bath, headed by a party of musicians, with hautboys, drums, and persons bearing trays covered with silk kerchiefs, having the linen and utensils for the bath, ornamental bottles of rose-water, or orange flower-water, which was occasionally sprinkled upon the company, and a silver salver or vessel for burning aloe-wood or some odoriferous gum. The bride was sometimes under a canopy of some pink or gay color, and her person was entirely concealed by a Cashmere shawl, which was fastened by jewels of emeralds or diamonds. Two or three female friends were with her under the canopy, and sometimes in hot weather one of them, walking backward before her, was constantly fanning the bride. Among the lower classes the procession was much the same, the women often uttering shrill cries of joy, called *Zagarīt*, in which female spectators joined. This occurred usually two or three days before the nuptials, or wedding feast.

21. *Bride's Procession.*—The bridal procession on the eve of the nuptials is celebrated with demonstrations of joy, music, singing, and shoutings by the women. Thus Prof. Post describes this custom as observed in Northern Syria and the Lebanon: "When the time has come to bring the bride, for she is brought to her husband, he usually sends several of his best men to her house, who bring her on a sumptuously caparisoned animal (camel or ass) if she be rich, or walking if she is poor, attended by a crowd of the family friends, who howl forth their songs of welcome and their prayers for the happiness of the pair. The trousseau and household goods of the bride are often borne before her, especially in case of a bride of the lower class. Men of both parties play before the procession (which is usually at night) with sword and target practice, dancing, and with wild feats of horsemanship. The bride moves very slowly, and if walking, affects to be reluctant, holds back, and requires actually to be pushed along by the attendants. She is closely veiled, and it is a disgrace for her to smile, or to say a word, or appear to notice anything." "The women are received by the mother and sisters of the groom in an apartment quite separate from the men."

In Hauran.—A native Syrian, Mr. Haddad, also more fully tells of the bridal processions, as he saw them from his youth up, among the peoples east of the Jordan and elsewhere. "The bridegroom's parents and older relatives prepare his house for the marriage and invite his friends." "A few women, with some men, are selected to bring the bride; the women to make up the bride's procession; the men to act as escorts and helpers. The bridegroom never goes with this party to bring the bride. On reaching her home, the groom's delegates are welcomed and entertained by her father, brother, or head of her house, with his guests, who are his relatives and friends, invited to pay the bride a good-bye as a daughter in her own home. The bridegroom's party ask permission to take away the bride, and also invite her father's guests to go with them, the men making the request of the father, and the women of the mother. After many compliments and ceremonies, hesitations, and delays the requests are granted. The bride is made ready. Though all are invited from the bride's house, only a few are expected to go. The women go in the bride's procession first. The bride herself has a fine mantle covering her, and a bridal veil of rich embroidery and border. She may be on horseback; sometimes she walks. The procession moves very slowly; music sounding, lamps and candles lighted in the hands of every one, and long torches carried in front by hired men, or by those who give their services to the bridegroom."

"The party going to the bride's house would reach her home an hour or more after sunset. An hour or so later they would be ready to return with the bride to her new home. That may not be half a mile, but it takes about an hour and a half to go the short distance, because the bride, in her coyness, walks so slowly." "When the bride arrives at the home of her husband, the women of his household and the invited guests meet her with songs and the burning of incense and conduct her to the best room; the bride-chamber."

In Egypt and India.—Lane witnessed similar bridal processions in Egypt, having some added features of peculiar interest. Thus, on the return of the bride from the bath, her companions sup with her, singing love-songs. Later at night the bride takes in her hand a lump of henna mixed with paste, and receives gifts from her guests, each one sticking a coin, usually of gold, in the henna. When the lump is stuck full of coins, the bride scrapes them off in a basin of water, and selects another lump, until all her guests have had an opportunity to make their gifts. The henna is bound with linen upon her hands and feet until morning, when they will be dyed a deep orange-red. Her guests also dye their own hands.

The procession of the bride (*Zeffeh El-Anîseh*) may be preceded by two swordsmen, clad in drawers only, engaged in mock combat, or by some strong man carrying an extraordinary burden of two hundred pounds' weight, or one performing remarbable conjurer's tricks. In India, marriage processions at night, with torches, lamps, and vessels of oil, are common sights, noticed by various travelers, during the past century. Trumbull mentions a bride's procession in the Arabian desert, which he supposes ended by the bridegroom meeting the bride and lifting her over the threshhold of his home. But he did not witness this act.[1] Where the groom leaves his house especially to avoid meeting his bride on her first entrance to his home, and until after the nuptial feast, as native observers say is usual, the "threshhold greeting" would be exceptional, and by no means universal. Thus the author of "Scripture Manners and Customs" affirms that the bride and bridegroom do not meet at his arrival, each being engaged apart until the afternoon of the marriage day; this is affirmed as the custom in Eastern Syria also, as Haddad stated.

22. *Bridegroom's Procession.*—Whoever would see the splendor of an Oriental wedding, must attach himself to the party or procession of the bridegroom. If he is some great man, the rejoicings and proceedings are of the most magnificent kind. No cards or written invitations are sent, the man invites his friends by a personal call or through a servant. The invitation is repeated. "When the hour approached," says Prof. Post, "the guests, dressed in brightest colors, the married women loaded with jewels and flowers, and the girls more simply dressed, throng the house of the bridegroom. The men

[1] See p. 38.

are received in a room or court by the groom and his (male)
relatives; the women in the women's apartment by his mother.
These visits are continued one or more days before the actual
wedding feast. Each guest is received by all in the room standing. If intimate, the host kisses him on both cheeks and em-
braces him. The guest, on taking his seat, gives a wave of his
hand, and inclination of the head to each of the assembly.
Sweetmeats, sherbet, cakes, and coffee may be served. Gipsies
are usually hired to play during the days of festivity, and those
that dance and play with sword and shield. The music is over-
powering to Western taste, but seems inspiring to that of the
East." "In their apartment the women shriek and howl their
congratulations and improvise impressive rhymes, often of a
very obscene character."

The bridegroom's procession in Eastern Syria is thus described by Mr. Haddad, a native of Damascus: "Before the
procession of the bride reaches the house of the bridegroom
he will be taken out of his home, the young men taking him in a
procession around the town, out one way and back by another."
To go out and return the same way indicates bad luck or failure.
"To go in a circle" is a good omen. The bridegroom may
make as an excuse that he goes to prayer, to the mosque, to
church, to the barber, or to be robed in wedding garments.
The real purpose is "to busy him outside, so that the bride will
reach his home while he is absent from it." "If he were in the
house on her arrival, he must welcome her, which would lessen
his dignity. If she is in the house, she can welcome him,
as being herself the lady of the house. The bridegroom's procession is headed by persons with torchlights, a band of music,
men shooting guns, playing sham fights with swords and shields,
and singing, every man with wax candle or lamp, walking very
slowly. They pass a friend's house, where they may be entertained, sprinkled with perfumes, and receive congratulations. It is expected that every house of friends and acquaintances will have a supply of water of roses and other perfumes
and sprinklers for wedding processions."

ORIENTAL BRIDE AND GROOM.   P. 26

SWORD CEREMONY.

(Copyright by Underwood & Underwood, New York.)

MARRIAGE—WELL CEREMONY.   P. 26

SIGNIFYING WIFE IS TO SERVE HUSBAND.

(Copyright by Underwood & Underwood, New York.)

23. *The Midnight Call.*—As the bridegroom does not return until the bride and her procession have had ample time to reach there before him, his party will be coming in about midnight or later. As the procession approaches a cry is made ("*halil*"), and a band of maidens, with sweet voices (paid voices or relatives), rush out from his house to meet him, with lamps, songs of praise, congratulations, and welcome. Or, the band may be waiting by the way, as the ten virgins of the parable.

The bridegroom and all who properly belong to the procession enter the house, and immediately the door is shut. He may have expected ten virgins to greet him; five of them had gone to get oil; "he was indignant at their negligence, and kept them out."

Mr. Haddad notes, "In later times Christians have adopted Western ways: the bridegroom may meet the bride at the church, . . . may go with his party to the bride's house, and bring her either to the church or to his own house, . . . but many are sticking to the old custom," as described above, and "look upon the modernized people as misbehaving, and criticize them bitterly."

Henderson describes a Russian Jewish procession, where Western influence had changed the ancient Oriental custom. Thevenot witnessed a like procession many years ago at Surat, India, when the governor of the town married his daughter to a noted man. The cavalcade was at night; hundreds of men marched, carrying torches made of bamboo, at the top of which was an iron cup containing rolls of oiled cloth, made like sausages. Women, little boys, and girls each with a bundle of osier twigs, and fine little wax candles on their heads, were mingled with the two hundred men; baskets, vessels of oil for the flambeau, and music made up the crowd.

Lane also saw many such processions in Egypt, the men bearing torches, called *Mash'al*. This was a staff with a cylindrical frame of iron at the top, filled with wood or other inflammable material; one staff bearing three, four, or five of these receptacles on cross-pieces for this purpose. Sometimes a great frame lantern, having sixty or more lamps in circles, or one above another and made to revolve, were carried by two bearers; the bridegroom also having a lamp or wax candle.

24. *The Shut Door.*—Among the Hindus, Mr. Ward saw a like procession about a century ago, when at midnight the cry was made, "'Behold, the bridegroom.' He came from a distance to Serampore. All, who had been waiting for hours, now lighted their lamps, and ran to get their stations in the procession. Some had lost their lights and were too late. The bridegroom was carried in the arms of a friend to a superb seat, then went into the house; the door was immediately shut and guarded. I with others expostulated with the door-keepers, *but in vain.*" [1] Music, lamps, and torches are important features in true Oriental wedding processions. They illustrate many Bible passages: Laban asks of Jacob, "Wherefore didst thou . . . not tell me, that I might have sent thee away with mirth, and with songs, with tabret, and with harp?" [2] The Psalmist describes a royal bride, "The King's daughter within *the palace* is all glorious: Her clothing is inwrought with gold. She shall be led unto the king in broidered work." [3] The bride's costume and girdle Jeremiah uses in reproving the people: "Can a virgin forget her ornaments, or a bride her attire? yet my people have forgotten me." [4] So, again, the prophet says of one clothed with "the garments of salvation" "as a bridegroom decketh himself with a garland, and as a bride adorneth herself with her jewels."[5] The writer of the book of Maccabees mentions a marriage procession: "Behold, there was much ado and great carriage: and the bridegroom came forth, and his friends, to meet them with drums, and instruments of musick." [6] The shouting of these processions is repeatedly alluded to as "the voice of the bridegroom, and the voice of the bride" by the prophets of the Old and the New Testament.[7] Even "the holy city, new Jerusalem," is compared to "a bride adorned for her husband." [8]

---

[1] Matt. 25 : 5-10.   [2] Gen. 31 : 27.   [3] Ps. 45 : 13, 14, R. V.
[4] Jer. 2 : 32.   [5] Is. 61 : 10.   [6] 1 Mac. 9 : 39.
[7] Jer. 25 : 10; Rev. 18 : 23.   [8] Rev. 21 : 2.

IV.

MARRIAGE FEASTS.

25. *Great Feasts*.—The typical Oriental has no special marriage ceremony in the Occidental sense. An Oriental marriage culminates in a festival of great pomp, given by the father of the bridegroom. It usually lasts from three to seven days. The feast on the last day is attended with no little splendor. A preliminary invitation has already been sent to the guests, and as the time for the feast arrives or approaches, other messengers are sent to call the guests. So Esther invited Haman to a banquet, and "on the morrow" sent to bring him unto the banquet.[1] And in the parable of the King's Son's marriage, the king sent his servants "to *call* them that were *bidden* to the wedding."[2] So, too, in the parable of the great supper, the man "sent his servant at supper time to say to them that were bidden" perhaps twice before, "Come."[3] Sometimes, but rarely, the invitations are more widely given, so that a chief of a village and his people might attend, reminding one of the invitation —wisdom is represented as giving.[4] This will be further noticed under banquets and social feasts. In ancient Babylonia, the marriage took place at a house called the "wedding house" or "house of males." Later, it was the "father's house."

26. *Its Magnificence*.—Mr. Haddad tells how in Eastern Syria "the house is decorated, sheep and oxen slaughtered, great bonfires made, rockets sent to the sky, salutes of firearms continually heard, bands of music play, dancing and singing in the court-yard, crowds coming and going, congratulations offered to the parent of the groom, the guests bringing gifts of every kind, further to supply the feast,—sheep, oxen, chickens, milk, sugar, coffee, rice, fruit, incense, perfumes, even vegetables, wood, and charcoal." The West might discover some new

[1] Esth. 5 : 8; 6 : 14.   [2] Matt. 22 : 3, 4.   [3] Luke 14 : 16, 17.   [4] Prov. 9 : 1-5.

wedding gifts, and new ways of placing them on exhibition
from the ingenuity of the Orientals in these matters. Sometimes all the dresses, diamonds, jewels, and showy shawls are
loaded upon their slaves, who attend them, to show off the gifts.
When the guests have come, the "ruler" takes charge. The
"ruler of the feast" being before selected, usually a friend,
is in a conspicuous dress with wide girdle. He sees that every
one is provided with refreshments, and that proper honor is
shown to the bridegroom. Thus, in the marriage at Cana,
following their custom, Jesus directed the water that had been
turned to wine, to be first borne to the ruler or "governor of the
feast," that he might decide whether it was befitting the feast.[1]
He may also see that persons of note have a seat of honor given
them.[2]

27. *Its Variety.*—The feast is always very sumptuous in a
high-class family of the East. Prof. Post graphically reports
what he frequently witnessed in North Syria: "The meal is
served on vast platters or trays, five or six feet in diameter."
"The dishes consist of immense piles of *piláf*" [rice cooked
with meat or, as I have eaten it, with goat's butter], savory
sauces, stuffed sheep, fowls, soups, *leben* (curdled milk), cheese,
olives, pickles, and *Kibby*. Kibby is a compound of cracked
wheat and meat pounded together in a mortar, a layer of the
compound is spread on a copper tray, a layer of sliced onions,
pine seeds, and spices placed on it, covered with another layer
of wheat and meat, then baked in an oven and basted with fat,
"a rich, delicious, but unwholesome dish." "Besides these
there are vegetables, stuffed mallows, stuffed and fried egg-
plants, *Mejedderah* (Esau's pottage), sweets, and fruits of immense number and diverse flavors." "Orange flower-water and
rose-water enter into many of them and some are flavored with
musk." "The feast is served with much ceremony." "As
fast as one guest finishes his meal, he rises and gives place to
another." The conversation comes after the meal, and "over
the pipes and coffee which follow."

[1] John 2 : 8.   [2] See Luke 14 : 9.

28. *Congratulations.*—The courtyard is usually provided with rugs, mats, divans, and bolsters and pillows, while lamps and lanterns hang overhead, brilliantly lighted. The bridegroom has on his richest robes. "The Orientals love gay colors. They are specially skilled in striped and watered patterns. The sober dress of the West is not admired by true Orientals, both sexes dressing in as bright garb with as strong colors as possible." There are often "three distinct periods of congratulation" during the festivities. In families of Moslems, the merry-making is in the respective apartments of the men and of the women separately. Near the close of these festivities, the bridegroom is placed within the women's apartment or near the entrance facing the door. The bride, arrayed in her costume, veil, bracelets, bells, rings, and chains, is presented or seated where the bridegroom can view her. Sometimes she withdraws and comes again arrayed in a different costume, and this is done seven or more times. The last time she comes, the groom steps forward at a signal from his mother, lifts the veil from his bride's face, throws it over her right shoulder, and looks upon her face, perhaps for the first time of his life. It must be borne in mind, however, that all these customs, under Moslem influence have become more rigidly exclusive in regard to woman. Her condition has been steadily sinking in Oriental lands for more than a thousand years, except where Christianity has come in to better her position. Thus, the parading of the bride in successive bridal costumes is, by no means, universal or widespread among Orientals. The same is, in a measure, true in respect to some other marriage customs. In fact, they vary widely, as I have before intimated. Those given are common in some lands and tribes, and throw light on similar customs alluded to in the Bible.

29. *Unveiling the Face.*—The veiling and unveiling of the face, however, is a very old Oriental custom. Rebekah "covered herself" with "her veil" or mantle when she first saw Isaac coming to meet her. Yet when his servant met her at the well he probably saw her face, since it is said, "the

damsel was very fair to look upon." [1]   So Tamar "covered
herself with a veil" to deceive her father-in-law.[2]   And Boaz
said to Ruth, "Bring the " veil or " mantle that is upon thee,"
and he filled it with barley for her.[3]   Thus, the veil covering
the bride made it possible for the deception upon Jacob in
giving him Leah at the marriage instead of Rachel.   Similar
deceptions have been successfully practised in modern times
among Oriental families.   Thus, Hartley mentions one in
Smyrna, when a young Armenian asked for the younger daughter
in marriage.   The parents consented; the marriage festival
followed.   The festival or ceremony was perfected, the young
man was married to a closely veiled woman, and it came to pass
in the morning, behold, it was the elder daughter, as in Jacob's
case, and the excuse of the parents was precisely that of Laban,
"It is not so done in our place, to give the younger before the
first-born." [4]

The bridegroom is not only gorgeously apparelled and perfumed, but often he wore a crown or chaplet on his head.
Thus the king is represented as crowned by his mother "in the
day of his espousals." [5]   The joy and mirth of the companions
of the bride and the groom were used by our Lord in speaking
of the disciples, "Can the sons of the bridechamber mourn, as
long as the bridegroom is with them?" [6]

30. *Wedding Garment.*—There is another feature of interest
in marriage feasts.   Some state that proper wedding garments,
as an outer robe, were sometimes provided by the bridegroom
for guests as they came, when he was of a noble or wealthy
family.   Others deny that certain traces of such an Oriental
custom can be found.   Prof. Post affirms that it is not now the
custom to furnish garments to guests, and recent tourists in the
East fail to note any such custom.

On the other hand, history and travelers assure us that
Oriental princes and nobles had immense stores of costly apparel, and that these were often bestowed as marks of favor.

[1] Gen. 24 : 16, 65.   [2] Gen. 38 : 14.   [3] Ruth 3 : 15.
[4] Gen. 29 : 25, 26.   [5] Song of Sol. 3 : 11.   [6] Matt. 9 : 15.

Thus, Joseph gave each of his brothers "changes of raiment," and to Benjamin "five changes of raiment." [1] And Queen Esther "sent raiment to clothe Mordecai." [2] Naaman took "ten changes of raiment" among the gifts to be made to the prophet. [3] Some travelers in the Orient of a century or more ago found distinct traces of the custom of providing robes for guests at notable banquets. Thus, Olearius in his travels, says he and the ambassadors were invited by the Persian ruler, and were provided with splendid vestments to hang over their dresses. Schultz describes a garment furnished him as "a long robe with loose sleeves," to put on before appearing in the presence of the Sultan. And Chardin related a similar instance in which the robe was not used, and it cost the subject his life. [4] The evidence is that an outer mantle or garment was provided to cover the dress. It is also said that at the marriage of Sultan Mahmoud each guest was furnished a robe at the Sultan's expense. Other travelers and natives tell of feasts at which the generous host provided a *Kuftan*, or cloak, for the guest to throw over his dress. A native Syrian, Mr. Wad El-Ward, recently speaking of marriage feasts, says, "One of the main preparations, of which the expense is defrayed by the father of the bridegroom, is the preparation of outer garments made of some cheap material of any gay color he may fancy, so that a poor man having no clothes with which to deck himself is provided for, and if any are found without that garment among the guests the governor of the feast will reprimand him for his misdemeanor. Such a custom would be ground for the condemnation of the man without a "wedding garment" in the parable of our Lord. [5]

And Dr. Tristram tells of attending a feast at Orfa, in Mesopotamia, where, in an anteroom, there was a great pile of light cloaks, one of which was handed to each guest on entering, and it was delivered again to the servant on his departure. [6] The Persian merchant provides a robe for the guest he enter-

[1] Gen. 45 : 22.   [2] Esther 4 : 4.   [3] 2 Kings 5 : 5.
[4] Burder, Orient. Lit. I, 94.   [5] Matt. 22 : 12.   [6] Eastern Customs, p. 163.

tains, and this is left behind when the feast is over. Dr.
Tristram further states that he was once at a Jewish wedding-
feast in Hebron, where each guest was supplied with a cloak
as he crossed the threshold, and Dr. Tristram accepted one to
conceal his European dress. He adds, the custom of providing
an upper garment for each guest is not extinct, but is rarely
practiced now.[1] Earlier travelers, who went into Oriental
lands before Western influence had modified the habits, give
sufficient evidence that such a custom once existed. That
recent tourists find no traces of it does not overthrow the direct
testimony of those who had personal experience earlier of the
prevalence of the custom.

31. *Display of Gifts.*—Another feature of Oriental marriage
feasts is the manner of bringing the presents. This is done
with parade and great display. Expensive gifts that might be
borne on one animal, are spread out on four or five, and "jewels
that one plate would hold, are placed on fifteen." Thus,
Ben-hadad sent presents to Elisha borne on forty camels.[2]
So Jacob put a "space" between each of the several droves of
cattle that he sent as a present to Esau; each servant at the
head of the first, second, and so on was to say, "these are a
present."[3]

32. *Capturing the Bride.*—Another interesting custom connected with Oriental marriage has been called "Capturing the
bride." This appears to have originated with the primitive
peoples who were nomads of the desert. A maiden of such a
tribe, about to be betrothed, would sometimes flee to the
mountains when she knew her parents had betrothed her.
Then the young man was put upon his mettle, to pursue and,
if he could, capture and win her for himself. If she was unwilling
to marry him, he might fail in his pursuit. If she was testing
his sincerity or bravery, she might flee with coyness, and pretend to escape, until satisfied of her suitor's mind. Sometimes
the maiden was caught before escaping; one of this kind is
mentioned by Dr. Fish, in which the girl fought like a fury

---

[1] Eastern Customs, p. 84.   [2] 2 Kings 8 : 9.   [3] Gen. 32 : 16-19.

NOMADS OF THE DESERT.   P. 36

(Vester & Co.)

WOMAN WITH DOWRY.   P. 23

COINS ON HEAD-DRESS—JEWELS—RINGS—BEADS, SYRIA.

(Vester & Co.)

before yielding.[1]   Upon this primitive custom may have been
engrafted, perhaps, the later one of capturing a bride by strategem or in predatory excursions.   Such instances are given in
the history of Israel, as in Judges 21 : 21–23, where the young
men of Benjamin caught the daughters of Shiloh by the vineyards.[2]

33. *In Old Babylonia.*—The laws of old Babylonia, recently
recovered, throw much light on the structure of the Oriental
family and upon marriage customs before the days of Abraham.
Thus, it is clear that a wedded pair and their dependents were
regarded as the social unit.   But this unit might expand into a
clan or tribe.   The young man could not take a wife without a
bride-portion called *terhatu*.   His father provided this, or it
was reserved for him out of his father's estate.[3]   The woman
was given in marriage by her father; sometimes by the mother.
But a widow could remarry at her own will any man of her
choice, provided her children by a former marriage could care
for themselves.[4]   In early times there appears less seclusion
of women.   A suitor might not see his betrothed until marriage,
but this is unlikely in old Babylonian times, since the laws
anticipate his seeing another woman and wishing to abandon
his suit.   If this was brought about by the intrigue of the
suitor's comrade, the latter was excluded from marrying the
girl himself, by the law-code of Hammurapi.[5]

Moreover, the old Babylonian Code indicates that in early
times the prevailing idea of marriage was that of one man to
one woman.   Though polygamy was not unknown, it was excused on various grounds, but the cases were primarily regarded
as exceptions.   Nor was love wanting in the Oriental household.   It would take us too far afield to cite the legend of the romantic love of Ishtar, and the many thrilling stories of affection
and love with which the old literature of Egypt and Assyria
abounds.   The graphic portrait of the model housewife,
drawn by an old royal poet, King Lemuel, is not surpassed in

[1] Fish. Travels, p. 25.
[2] See Code of Hammurapi, § 166.
[3] See also Deut. 21 : 10.
[4] Ibid., § 172.   [5] Ibid., § 161.

any literature.[1] No modern love-song is so filled with the aroma of peace, joy, and ecstacy, springing from domestic life of conjugal love, as that which fills the antiphonal cadences of the Song of Songs, echoing down the ages in the old Hebrew Scriptures.

Lifting the Veil.—Since the issue of this book the Rev. J. E. Hanauer has written me that he was at a fellah-wedding in Artass near Bethlehem, where the bridegroom met the bride just outside the door of the house. A cake of dough was stuck upon the lintel. The bride put her hand over it, and he struck her on the back of the head thrice. Then a pitcher of water was placed on her head. The groom tried to knock it off, to prove his authority, but failed, for the young men present set on him with loud laughs, and beat him so vigorously with their fists on his back that, cursing them, he was glad to escape into the one-roomed house, dragging his veiled bride after him.

Then, standing beside his veiled bride, he drew his scimitar, and with its point raised the veil, " in the name of Allah (God), the Merciful, the Compassionate." His long right-hand sleeve had been tied to that of his bride.

This rite may have had its origin in primitive " capture of a bride " (p. 30) and reflect some threshold custom also (p. 27). Our Western custom of " throwing rice " after married couples may have sprung from this ancient rite also.

[1] Prov. 31 : 11–29.

V.

THE HOUSEHOLD.

34. *Training a Wife.*—The Oriental household is a complex institution. The bridegroom brings his bride to his mother's home. The theory is that the mother-in-law should train the girl-wife in her duties. Practically the young wife becomes the slave, doing the drudgery of the family, under the iron rule of the elder woman, who is the mistress. Thus, the household may usually comprise two or three generations, with children, grandchildren, and a retinue of servants and retainers. Abram could muster over three hundred, "born in his own house," to rescue his nephew Lot, taken captive by the predatory Eastern *sheikhs*.[1] In fact, his household seems to have become a clan, or wandering tribe, not unlike the Bedouins now sweeping over the Arabian deserts.

35. *Primitive Order.*—Was this the primal order of human society? The old law-code of Babylonia reveals wonderfully complex social conditions long before the days of Abram. It is held, by recent scholars, that this code points to a single pair as the normal early relation of the sexes and the foundation of the family.[2] Speculative and rationalistic theorists of the agnostic school of sociologists, I am aware, assume that promiscuous intercourse of the sexes was the primal relation, and that monogamy was a late development of the human race. This is pure assumption and unproved. It is contrary to some facts which they themselves advance to prove their evolutionary theory of steady progress rather than degeneracy in the race. For if this is so, birds have developed further than man. For the higher forms of bird life have advanced beyond the promiscuous stage, many of them pairing at least for the year. It would be difficult to prove that either Darwin or Herbert

[1] Gen. 14 : 14.   [2] Code of Hammurapi, see §§ 141, 148, 149, 162, 163.

39

Spencer ventured flatly to deny monogamy as the starting-point in the human family. The teachings of Christ seem emphatic on this point. The account of the first human pair in innocency in Eden shows clearly the Bible ideal of the family.

36. *The Social Unit.*—But whatever view is held respecting the relation of the sexes in the primal stage, there is now substantial agreement that in the moral progress of the race the family, where there is one wife only, is the social unit, and the comparatively even balance of the sexes, so far as known throughout the civilized world, seems to put natural law against polygamy and on the side of one wife only as nature's teaching, and in harmony with the divine ideal in human society.

That polygamy and concubinage widely prevail now, and have existed from time immemorial in many Oriental lands, may account, in part, for the degradation of woman, that being a penalty for the infraction of nature's law. These do not disprove the law, for nearly every law in nature's long code is frequently broken, and the penalties follow, though they are not always recognized as penalties. Nor are they completely deterrent when recognized; the law, however, is not thereby abrogated.

37. *Childless.*—Children, especially sons, are, and have been, ever the delight of Oriental families. The greatest calamity the Oriental can conceive of is to have a childless household.[1] It is counted a mark of the withholding of God's favor. The birth of a girl, however, is not an occasion of rejoicing. Natives avoid alluding to it in public or to the father.

Childlessness was, and is, a frequent excuse with Oriental people for taking a second wife or a concubine, who seems to be regarded as a wife for a limited time. Thus, Lane[2] tells of his exclusion from a certain quarter of Cairo (where he had engaged a room) because he was unmarried. He was urged by the sheikh to marry a young widow for a stipulated time, with the express understanding that he should divorce her at the end of the period. Yet he says it was "not very common for

[1] Gen. 21 : 6, 7; 30 : 1, 2, 23; 1 Sam. 1 : 11.   [2] Modern Egyptians, pp. 194, 225.

an Egyptian to have more than one wife or a concubine slave; the law (Moslem) allows him four wives." In ancient Egypt, according to Wilkinson, the practice, however, was unknown. Malcolm tells of similar limited marriages as prevailing or allowed in Persia.[1] The women who consent to such marriages are held in good repute, says Dr. Perkins. Polygamy existed in the patriarchal period, but Noah seems to have had but one wife.[2]

Childlessness was the plea made to persuade Abram and Jacob each to take more than one woman as wife. The earlier code of Babylonia permitted the custom, and the law of Moses sought to regulate and mitigate the obvious evils of the custom. In fact, it is held that both codes disapprove of it as a proper or ideal state, as shown by passages similar to Lev. 18 : 18.

38. *Divorce*.—In like manner, the law of Moses restricted and sought to check divorce by requiring the husband to "write her a bill of divorcement."[3] Christ condemned the custom of divorce prevalent in his day, based upon the Mosaic statute, and limited it to conjugal infidelity.[4]

Childlessness was also a ground for divorce under the Sumarian law, and in the code of old Babylonia. But the husband must pay to the divorced wife her marriage portion and the bride-price. Illness was not a ground for divorce under that old code. It required the husband to maintain her, but he might take a second wife. The wife could not get a divorce from her husband except through the courts in patriarchal times, and in non-Jewish lands, but a man could often put away a wife by a word. The most stringent of old codes, in other nations, shows how far in advance was the Hebrew legislation over that among heathen peoples. Even now in Moslem lands a woman may be divorced without legal process, at the freak of her husband, but she can carry away undisputed any amount of gold, silver, jewels, precious stones, or apparel that she has loaded on her person. So she usually wears all her treasures

[1] Van Lennep, p. 555. [2] Gen. 4 : 19; 7 : 7.
[3] Deut. 24 : 1–3. [4] Matt. 5 : 32.

and wealth on her person, not knowing when the fateful word may be spoken. The men likewise had their wealth in portable gems or treasures. This throws light on the remarkable story of Gideon and his ephod.[1]

While the Oriental household now generally comprises so many persons—sons, sons' sons, and son's sons' sons, children and servants, all under one head or "father"—the early and primal condition implies separation from the patriarchal home, the new couple making a household for themselves. The old record runs: "Therefore shall a man leave his father and his mother, and shall cleave unto his wife: and they shall be one flesh." [2] Whatever may be or have been the customs, this is the Bible ideal.

Divorce Among Modern Jews.—In Oriental lands some rabbis allow a man to divorce his wife if she spoils his dinner. A bill of divorce, however, must be given to, and *held* by, the wife to be valid. Mr. Hanauer tells me of a man who used stratagem to get such a bill into his wife's hands. He sent her from Jerusalem to Jaffa on pretext of her health. Soon after he sent her a letter, which she opened, unsuspectingly. It was a bill of divorce and valid, against her will, for she had held it in her hand.

Some Jews *pretend* to be converted to Christianity, and persuade their wives to accept a divorce. The wife discovers, too late, that it was a trick, for her rascally husband never became a Christian, and was as "good" an Orthodox Jew as ever.

[1] Judg. 8 : 24–26.   [2] Gen. 2 : 24.

VI.

ORIENTAL CHILDREN.

39. *Joy Over Children.*—Orientals still have a great desire
for large families. The birth of a son is the occasion for an
outburst of rejoicing and congratulations from all the neighbors
and friends, and often of a feast. Servants and members of
the household vie with one another in being the first to announce
the news to the father, with more or less formality and ceremony, and are sure to be rewarded by some customary or special
gift.

But the birth of a daughter no one wishes to mention.
Every one avoids telling the father of it. The strong contrast
of the prophet in view of this custom increases to a startling
degree the force of his expression.[1] Yet to have no children
was the bitterest reproach upon the wife. So Rachel rejoiced
when Joseph was born, for "God hath taken away my reproach." [2]   Elizabeth gives the same reason for abounding joy.
"The Lord . . . take away my reproach among men."[3]
When the first son is born into the family, so great is the joy
and so notable is the event, it is heralded through the community.

40. *The Son-heir.*—One reason for rejoicing when a son is
born, and for no congratulation over the birth of a daughter,
is because the Oriental expects a son to be a help to his parents;
to follow the father's profession or trade, to continue the
family name; when married, to live in the same home and keep
the inheritance within the family. But a daughter is separated
from her parents, and when married goes to build up a house of
another, and takes her inheritance away from her father's
household to another's. The Oriental sentiment for large
families and pride in long continuance of lines of posterity
amount almost to a passion. It is forcibly illustrated in the

[1] Jer. 20 : 15.   [2] Gen. 30 : 23.   [3] Luke 1 : 25.

custom of the Hebrews for a man to marry his brother's widow to raise up children to his brother.[1] The farther back a family can trace its lineage, the greater is the honor, even to one hundred generations. It was because Abram had no son, at the time of Jehovah's promise that his seed should be as the stars in number, that Abram could not understand the promise.[2] An Oriental holds to the unity of the race and the indivisibility of the family. A grandfather rejoices to build a house and to plant a tree, for his kindred will dwell in the one and eat of the fruit of the other, and that is the same to his mind as if he shared the house and ate of the fruit himself.

41. *Family Names.*—The Orientals do not now usually have what we term a family name. A boy's personal name may be *Yakūb*, and if his father's personal name is *Ibrahîm*, he may be known as *Yakūb Ibrahîm*, that is, Jacob, son of Ibrahîm; and Ibrahîm's father's personal name may have been *Yakūb*, so that the grandfather and the grandson would both be known by the name *Yakūb Ibrahîm*. In Egypt, among the Moslems, boys are named often Muhammad, or after some of the Prophet's family, *Hhasan*, *Ali*, or *Omar*, or after some of the patriarchs or old prophets, as *Ibrahîm*, *Isma'il*, *Yakūb*, *Yūsif*, *Daūd*, or *Sulāimān*. The girls are also named in like manner, *Fatimeh*, *Azizeh*, or *Zeyneb*. Some names might not indicate the religious belief, as *Khalīl*, *Aziz*, *Ghanim*, and feminine ones, as *Anîseh*, *Habibeh*, *Halwah*.

There are several ways of forming names in Syria, for example: *Yuhanna abu Daūd*, John the father of David; *Yuhanna el Haddad*, John the blacksmith; *Yuhanna el Khuri*, John the priest, and John Mark, meaning John the son of Mark. This suggests the significance of Oriental names, common in Old Testament times as now. Thus Selim is safe, Aruad is happy, Anir is age or life, Muhammad is praised.

42. *Why Given ?*—Sometimes boys weak at birth are called by the name of lion, tiger, or wolf, thinking they may gain some of the strength of these animals. A boy born during an epi-

demic of that disease was named Small-pox. Girls are given names which signify, Pretty, Mild, Mercy, Sugar, Happy, and the like. Some boys may be named from trades prevailing in the family, as *Bannâ*, mason; *Bustâny*, gardener; *Hajjar*, stone-cutter. The birth of a son may be marked by a change of name of the father, as well as by great rejoicing. Thus a man's name may be *Yohanna*, but when he has a son born to him, named *Daūd*, the father may ever after be known by *Abu Daud*, the father of David, and the mother may be named *Umm Daud*, the mother of David. Joseph's name was changed by Pharaoh when he was introduced into the royal household.[1]

Mr. Baldensperger, a native of Jerusalem, states the *fellah*, or country woman of Syria, is not called by the name of her husband, but by her own name and the name of her father while she has no children. Thus, her name may be Fatme and her father's Ali, and she will be called Fatme Ali. When she has a son, she will be named after him. Thus, if her son is called *Eh'mad*, she will be known as *Im Eh'mad*, "the mother of Eh'mad." Or, a more polite way of calling a woman if she has no children, is *Im Ali*, "Mother of Ali," after her father's name.

43. *The Babe.*—Among Orientals it is not common to call a male physician at the birth of a child. Midwives only were permitted to attend women at such times. The midwife in the East is a stern autocrat, and will brook no interference with her orders from mother, husband, or any other person. Morier states that it was not uncommon for a peasant's wife, working in the vineyard, to go aside behind a rock or a shrub, give birth to a child, and take it home in the evening, wrapped and slung behind her back.[2] The new-born babe is usually washed in salted water, sometimes now mixed with oil, wrapped in a cotton or woollen bandage, or a swaddling cloth, about ten feet long, wound tightly around the body from the neck downward, and pinioning the arms and hands to its sides, so it cannot move hand or foot. Some think this wrapping will tend to make the child strong and healthy. The hands are bound to keep it from

[1] Gen. 41 : 45.   [2] Vol. 2, p. 106; compare Ex. 1 : 15-20.

hurting its eyes with its fingers. It is easier for the mother to carry the babe slung on her back when wrapped, and she feels it is safer if left thus in the cradle.

Among the lower and middle classes mothers usually nurse their own children; among the rich a wet-nurse may he hired, as Pharaoh's daughter engaged one for the child Moses.[1] Oriental women in some lands in early times were not allowed to wean their babes without the consent of their husbands. The babe, therefore, was usually not weaned until it was two years or two and a half years old, and now in Central Syria, the last baby is often not weaned until four or five years old.[2]

44. *How Carried.*—In Egypt, and often elsewhere, infants of both sexes are carried naked by their mothers, not in their arms, but astride on the shoulder, or sometimes deftly seated on the hip. When old enough to run about the children look out for themselves, and are seldom washed "for fear of the evil eye" if made too attractive. Hence they are naked or scantily clad, they are very dirty, their eyes sticky with filth from acrid discharge and from flies, it being counted injurious to the sight to wash them. Sometimes silver chains or bands with little bells are put on the ankles of the creeping child, the tinkling telling the mother where to find her babe.

45. *Child Growth.*—Orientals took note of the successive steps in the growth of children, since they applied different terms to designate the stages of development. Thus the Hebrews had ten or twelve terms designating children and child-life. These were mainly used to distinguish successive fresh stages in the child's development from birth to adult age. The newly born infant was *veled*,[3] as "unto us a child is born." The prophet ridicules the chosen people for their silliness: "they strike hands" (or "make bargains") with the *Yālde*,[4] new born babes of strangers.[5] The second stage of child-life was designated sometimes by *Veled*[6] and by *Yonek*, a suckling. So the writer in Deut. 32 : 25 tells of how the sword will sweep away all ages,

[1] Ex. 2 : 7–9.
[2] Grant, p. 66; see Ps. 131 : 2.
[3] Ex. 1 : 17–22 ; 1 Sam. 1 : 23, 24; 2 : 11.
[4] Is. 9 : 6.
[5] Is. 2 : 6.
[6] Gen. 21 : 14.

"the suckling (*Yonek*) with the man of gray hairs." Moses asks concerning rebellious Israel, if Jehovah should say to him, "carry them in thy bosom, as a nursing father beareth the suckling child," *Yonek*.[1] So a "tender plant" is *Yonek*, "a sucker." [2] Again, when the child began to eat and drink as well as to suck, he was then *olel*, as the mourning prophet graphically describing a famine says, "The tongue of the suckling child, *Yonek*, cleaveth to the roof of his mouth for thirst: the young children [*olalim*] ask bread, and no man breaketh it unto them." [3] Perhaps the next stage in child development is marked by *gamul*, "the weaned one." [4] For one must be past this stage to be taught.[5] The fifth stage shows an advanced step, but the child is still clinging to the mother, and counted "little children"; *taph*, which may point to children of both sexes at play, and in games together, as noted by the prophets,[6] "little ones," [7] or *pirchah*, young ones.[8] A sixth stage marks the foregleams of adolescence, the *Elem* and feminine *almah*, indicating growing large, or firm and strong.[9] And again, the lad or youth is *naar* (though this is doubtful),[10] one who breaks loose or frees himself from childish things, similar to *Elem* or "*alam*." [11] To the eighth stage more than one term applied (as indeed to some others), beside the general designations *ben*, son, and the Chaldaic form, *bar*. He now was *bachur*, a warrior, a young man.[12] They also had a special term for a child when he became "a son of the law." Then there were terms signifying peculiar ways of growth or conditions, thus *yachid*, an only child; [13] *neurim*, boyhood; [14] *neked*, a successor; [15] and *zera* [16] and *yalduth*, childhood.[17]

46. *Steps and Grades.*—Nor were the Hebrews singular in their discrimination and close observation of the stages of child-growth. The old Assyrian code reveals a similar if not as

[1] Num. 11 : 12.   [2] Is. 53 : 2.   [3] Lam. 4 : 4.
[4] Ps. 131 : 2.   [5] Is. 28 : 9; see also Hos. 1 : 8.
[6] Deut. 20 : 14; Jer. 40 : 7; Ezek. 9 : 6.   [7] Josh. 1 : 14.
[8] Deut. 22 : 6; Job 30 : 12.   [9] Is. 7 : 14.   [10] Comp. Ex. 2 : 6.
[11] 1 Sam. 17 : 56.   [12] Is. 31 : 8; Jer. 15 : 8; 18 : 21.
[13] Judg. 11 : 34.   [14] 1 Sam. 12 : 2,   [15] Gen. 21 : 23.
[16] Lev. 22 : 13; see also Talmud.   [17] Eccl. 11 : 10.

minute a subdivision of the periods of development in the children. And they wisely aimed to adapt their instruction and training to these successive steps in physical and mental growth. They held to *graded* instruction and lessons four thousand years ago.

The children were theoretically under the care of the mother until of an age for their education seriously to be undertaken. Then the boys were under the father's special oversight. The girls are left to aid the mother in the care of the younger children or infants, and to be trained in household duties, including bringing of water from fountains, grinding of flour in hand-mills, gathering fuel for cooking, making articles of personal apparel, including embroidery, and all kinds of fancy and needle work.

Jewish Circumcision.—Boys are usually named at circumcision; girls, when weaned. Circumcision is performed by the father, or by a "Mohel," a qualified circumciser, who must be a Jew of spotless reputation, rarely a surgeon, and take no fee for his services. The father or friends watch by the bedside of mother and babe the night before the ceremony, lest a she spirit of devils strangle them. A hired rabbi gathers the family and neighbors, and recites the "Shema."[1] A "Baalath Berith," or woman friend, takes the child to the room, or synagogue, which is received by a "Sandek," or male sponsor, who sits with an empty seat beside him, reserved for Elijah, supposed to be invisibly present. After prayers in Hebrew the child is named, circumcision performed, and a feast held.

In the rite, blood must be shed, the operator sucking the wound to promote it. Excess of blood is checked by squirting wine from the mouth upon the wound. The Jews often tear off the inner skin with the thumb-nail when the outer is cut, a mode ascribed to Joshua.

Christian Copts and Abyssinians practice circumcision; Moslems also at 13, the age Ishmael was circumcised. They thus recognize the bodies of "believers" slain in battle.

[1] Deut. 6 : 4–9; 11 : 13–21; Numb. 15 : 37–41.

VII.

ORIENTAL CHILD'S PLAYS AND GAMES.

47. *Shy and Actors.*—Child-nature has many character-istics in common the world over. The child of thousands of years ago and in Oriental lands was fond of play and loved games. Children are taught to hide from strangers, lest they be smitten with the "evil eye." When the foreigner appears the children suddenly disappear. They see him long before he catches a glimpse of them. When he departs, they reappear, with high glee over his absence. Or, if the stranger meets them, they will strike an attitude to excite pity, and cry for *backshish*, gifts. Or, they may shy a stone at some tourist who has ventured out of the customary route into the native children's domain.

48. *Kinds of Play.*—Children in the East now play around pits, cisterns, in gardens, on threshing floors, and upon the flat roofs of houses. They sling and throw at a mark, play house, peggy, and with sticks resembling stick-knife. They have games of ball, quoits, a native play called wolf, hide and seek, and play something like golf, marbles, leap-frog, blindman's bluff, swing-ing, see-saw, checkers, and draughts, similar to chess, though the manner of playing all these is thoroughly Oriental, and different from that of children of the West. The girls have dolls, toys, something like grace-hoops, and a great variety of other amusements. The little girls and boys usually play to-gether when very young, but at six to seven years of age the boys separate from the girls to play by themselves.

49. *Toys in the East.*—In patriarchal times the children had dolls and toys and much the same objects as amuse Oriental children now. For many ingeniously formed toy horses, goats, sheep, and elephants of burnt clay have been found in ancient Nippur and dug from other cities of old Babylonia. Even baby-rattles shaped like a chicken, a doll, or a drum were found with a small stone in the hollow body, that made a noise when the object was shaken, similar to the baby-rattles

4

of our times.   Similar toys for children were common among
the ancient Egyptians, as we know from specimens found in the
tombs and ruined temples of that wonderful land.   The little
Egyptian children before the days of Moses had painted dolls,
the hands and legs moving on pins, that could be made to assume
queer positions by pulling a string.   Miriam, Moses' sister,
may have played with such a doll.   Miniature models of the
human body and of animals were made as toys.   A man or
woman washing or kneading dough was imitated in motions
by the similar pulling of a string.   Or a small crocodile was
made to open and close its great mouth, to amuse a child.
Many kinds of plays with ball and hoop were known in very
early times in the Orient.

50. *Ball Games.*—The game of ball was played by children
of both sexes, though in Egypt it was more common for girls.
They would play it by hurling three or more balls into the air
and catching them in succession or leaping into the air and
catching a ball before the feet struck the ground.   In one form
of ball-game the one who failed to catch the ball would be
required to let her competitor ride on her back until she too
missed the ball.   The ball would be thrown by the opposite
party, also mounted on another girl's back, and each must play
from that position.   Balls were stuffed with bran or chaff,
covered with leather, some of them three inches in diameter.
Others were smaller and made of rushes, and covered with
leather also, in eight rhomboidal sections.

51. *Athletic Games.*—Dice and draughts, similar to chess,
wrestling, boxing, leaping, running and numberless other amusements, as odd and even, and *mora*, some of them unknown to us,
were the delight of the little people of five or six thousand
years ago.   All the games and plays of children in those lands
and times were intended to promote health and strength.

52. *Children Happy.*—Peasant children in the East are never
burdened with clothes.   They are usually barefooted, bare-
headed, and make up in dirtiness for any lack of garments.   To
conceive of all children in the East as sad and chronically un-

happy is a Western fiction. The prophet's bright picture of children playing in the streets of Jerusalem,[1] as they played in the streets of great cities on the Euphrates thousands of years ago, is fully understood by Orientals. The period for children's plays and games there is shorter than in the West, because the children mature much earlier.

53. *Japanese Children.*—The Japanese are conspicuous for the number and variety of games and amusements they have invented for children. Some of them have a high educational value, such as cards with bits of poems, or proverbs in two parts to be matched, or names of cities or towns and bits of wood cut in geometrical figures, to be put together, called wisdom boards and puzzles. In no country are the variety, colors, fantastic shapes, and novelties in kites so numerous, ingenious, and striking as in Japan. The childrens' toys also display great ingenuity, and suggest an amount of thought given to the amusement of children that would do credit to the great toy factories of Nuremberg. The girls have dolls and images in abundance. The boys have balls, stilts, pop-guns, slings, and blow-guns. As they advance in years, they practice as flute-players and in charades, as conjurers, dancers, song-singers, raree shows, and sometimes with genii or ghostly figures lighted in the dark to startle or frighten others or to give them courage. The Chinese also play foot-ball and shuttle-cock with their feet, and fly kites shaped like fishes, animals, butterflies, insects, and birds. The bird kites also have holes in them, with fine thread across, making them into Æolian harps, so that a bird-kite not only looks quite like a real bird in the air, but sings like one too. Oriental children also enjoy feats of wrestling and of acrobats, jugglers' tricks, dice, fortune-tellers, and magical arts, similar to those frequently mentioned in the Bible. The children have a play called *jang*, with wooden shoes, the game being to throw one shoe from a distance so that it will be inserted inside the other. These illustrate the wealth of Oriental thought and interest devoted to child development.

[1] Zech. 8 : 5.

VIII.

EDUCATION OF ORIENTAL CHILDREN.

54. *Child Culture.*—Schools for the education of children existed in the East thousands of years before Socrates questioned Alcibiades, or Confucius taught disciples and before Moses even "was learned in all the wisdom of the Egyptians."[1] Systems of public education, however, such as are now common in highly civilized countries, were not known. But specimens of school exercises in great variety have been found in the buried cities of old Babylonia, indicating the educational methods in the era of the patriarchs, and before Abram's childhood days in old Ur. And these methods are further illustrated by the peculiar education of children in Oriental lands as observed in the past century.

55. *Religious Motive.*—The methods vary widely among different peoples of the East, and sometimes among the same peoples, when they are of different religious faiths. Thus, instruction among the Moslems, usually, if not always, centers about the Koran; among the Buddhists, it is around their religious rites and in their sacred books, and among the Confucians about the traditional teachings of the Chinese Sage; yet in them all there are features distinctly Oriental. Thus, an Oriental school may be connected with a mosque, a temple, or a place of worship, house of some priest, or a public fountain, or public building, where children can be instructed at a trifling expense.

56. *Oriental Schools.*—Wilkinson, Lane, Van Lennep, and others have given us pictures of these schools. In Egypt the *fick'ee*, or Master, says Lane, received from the parent of each pupil half a piaster (about three cents) more or less, each Thursday, that day being the end of the Moslem week, as

[1] Acts 7 : 22.

Friday is their Sabbath or holiday. The teacher usually receives also a present of muslin for a turban, a piece of linen and
a pair of shoes, once a year, in the feast-month of Ramadan.
Their "blackboards" were wood-tablets painted white, written
upon with thin colored inks. When one lesson was learned,
the tablet was washed and another lesson written. The children
drop off their wooden shoes, if they have any, at the door;
squat on the floor, on a mat, a rug, or a bit of old carpet, holding
a tablet in hand. The master sits on a mat or small mattress,
and leans upon a cushion. The scholars study their lessons
aloud, the one that shouts the loudest being counted the most
studious. The din and noise can hardly be imagined. Books
are rare, says Van Lennep. The lessons to be memorized are
chiefly prayers and formularies of their religion. Reading and
writing are taught by letters, signs for syllables, and words on
the tablets, as they were many thousand years ago in Nineveh
and Nippur.

57. *Trained in Manners.*—The chief early training of the
Oriental child was and is to make all his gestures, looks, and
movements decent and graceful. Plato commended the ancient Egyptians for permitting their children to learn only
songs and verses that inspired to virtue. They diligently in-
culcated respect for the aged and toward strangers, and
reverence to parents. The young were to defer to superiors
in age and station. The son is early taught that he is not to sit,
eat, or smoke in the presence of his father unless he is bidden to
do so. He must stand quietly with folded hands, not speak unless spoken to, wait upon his father, and upon any guest.
This he is expected to do even after he has grown to be a man.
Disobedience to parents is one of the greatest sins. Muham-
med required children to be taught to say their prayers, and
were to be beaten if they neglected to say them. But Moslem
girls are seldom taught among the peasantry to read, write, or to
say prayers. The higher class of Egyptians often employed
a woman teacher to teach needle-work, embroidery, and sometimes reading and writing. An Oriental child is an example of

meekness with its parents. A child is not usually required to attend religious service or to fast until thirteen or fourteen years of age, depending partly on size and appearance. His father may permit him to sign documents, but after eighteen years of age he may transact business for himself, and is responsible before the law, and may wear a turban. "No son is dearer than a grandson" is an Eastern proverb.

58. *Oral Teaching.*—Where there is no school or teacher for the community, the mother teaches the little children as best she can orally. She sits on a mat or rug, with a cushion to her back, and holds the child for hours, as the Shunammite held her sick son.[1] The father takes charge of his son's education as soon as the latter passes from the mother's sole care, say at six or seven years of age. They are taught to kiss the hand of a superior, and to place the back of it against their foreheads in token of respect and obedience. The higher schools now in Oriental countries are adopting many features similar to Western institutions of learning, but these are not distinctly Oriental in origin or in character.

59. *Hebrew Graded System.*—The Hebrews had a somewhat systematic method of education, roughly adapted to their idea of the periods in child-life. Thus Rabbi Jehuda is cited in the Mishna [2] as fixing the subjects of study at different periods. "At five years of age, reading the Bible (Leviticus), at ten years, learning the Mishna; at thirteen years, the commandments; at fifteen years, the study of the Talmud; at eighteen years, marriage; at twenty, engaged in trade or business." Other views, however, were held; strong children only were set to regular study before six years old. Yet the infant even shared in the domestic worship on the Sabbath, and pointed to the house phylactery, having the small parchment on which were Deut. 6:4-9 and 11:13-21. The child in arms was often taught to touch this case on the door-post, and kiss its finger. Private prayers were early fixed in mind, the Psalms chanted in worship, and also the great Hallel [3] made familiar in childhood. The

<hr>

[1] 2 Kings 4:20.   [2] Aboth V. 21.   [3] Ps. 113-118 and 136. See ¶ 45.

youngest child asked the meaning of the passover feast.[1] The father was required to teach the religion of Jehovah to his child from the earliest time. God said of Abraham, "I have known him, to the end that he may command his children and his household after him, that they may keep the way of Jehovah."[2] To the devout Hebrew the law of God was the substance of all learning.

60. *General Knowledge.*—The sciences, civil laws, even medicine, were aids to the knowledge of God. "Astronomy was studied to make computations in the Jewish calendar," and to throw light on remarkable providences. History, geography, and the study of nature were all incidental to the chief subject, the national religious faith. The earliest lesson was the words of Jehovah,[3] beginning with Leviticus, rather than Genesis, if we may trust the Mishna, followed by other books of Moses, the prophets, and finally the *Kethubim*, holy writings, as Psalms and later books of the Old Testament.

61. *Teachers.*—The girls were not given the same kind and amount of instruction by rabbis as the boys. Having been taught the religious observances, the commandments, and the prayers at home; boys were sent to school, and if apt and promising, to an academy or to some learned rabbi. If the father was removed or unable to teach, the mother or some other relative might supply the instruction. Thus, Timothy who had a Gentile father, and a home in the heathen city of Lystra, was taught by his Jewish mother and grandmother from "a babe" the "sacred writings."[4] Before the destruction of the temple the rulers had provided every Jewish village with a teacher to instruct boys over six or seven years of age, as commanded in Isa. 2 : 3. The children were not to company with the vicious, were to suppress bitterness, be silent to those cursing them, see sin as repulsive, and as sure to bring penalty. Married men only could be teachers of schools. About the Maccabean period all gymnastic exercises were forbidden in Jewish schools, because of their corrupting tendencies to Grecian worship.

[1] Ex. 12 : 26, 27.   [2] Gen. 18 : 19.   [3] Deut. 11 : 19.   [4] 2 Tim. 3 : 15.

Every synagogue might have a school, and Maimonides affirms
that every place, where there were twenty-five Jewish boys of
suitable age or 120 families, was bound to appoint a teacher.
If there were forty boys, an assistant was required, and if fifty,
the rulers must appoint two teachers connected with a synagogue. The traditional account of 480 such schools in Jerusalem at the time of its destruction, is probably an exaggeration or
misunderstood reference.

62. *Subjects of Study.*—As a further testimony respecting the
subjects of study in Jewish Oriental schools, Philo refers to
synagogues as "houses of instruction," and affirms that "by
their parents, tutors, and teachers " the Jews were instructed,
from their earliest youth, in the knowledge of the law, so that
they bear the image of it in their souls. And Josephus quite
boastfully exclaims, "if anybody do ask any of us about our
laws, he will more readily tell them all than he will tell his own
name, having learned them as soon as we became sensible of
anything." [1] The writers of the Talmud indicate that the
earliest course of lessons were passages of the Bible. These
selections were nine chapters or sections of Leviticus, ten of
Numbers, the record of the Creation and the Flood in Genesis,
portions of Deuteronomy and Numbers 15, called the *Shema*,
and the Hallel.[2] Then followed lessons in Jewish traditions
and in the Gamara or rabbinical commentaries on their traditions.

63. *Value of Training.*—The schools sometimes had a recess
from about 10 A. M. to 3 P. M. during the heat of the day. The
high estimation placed upon their education, however narrow
and defective it may seem to us, is shown by some Talmudic
proverbs: "The world continues to exist only by the breath of
the children of the schools." "If you would destroy the Jews
you must destroy their schools." "Who teaches the child,
shall have a place with the saints above." And in Daniel it is
said, "They that are teachers shall shine as the brightness of
the firmament." [3]

[1] Contra, Apion, II. 19.   [2] Ps. 113-118.   [3] Dan. 12 : 3, margin.

64. *Hindu Education.*—Education among the native Hindus, before the British rule, was limited to Brahmins and two castes below them; the Brahmins alone were allowed to explain the Vedas, or sacred books, to the two castes. The larger and lower caste of Sudras—laborers—were forbidden to learn to read or even listen to the reading of the sacred books. It was a disgrace in India for a girl or a woman to know how to read.

65. *Purity Taught.*—There is another kind of education or training for Jewish children that must be noticed. The Mosaic laws were very strict and minute in respect to purity and keeping ceremonially clean. Every child was taught from infancy not only to regard the texts on the door and like things as holy, but also that multitudes of things amid which he moved were unclean and to touch them would defile him, and require him to be secluded from others until he could be made ceremonially clean again.

In running about, he must be careful not to touch any dead body or thing, any tomb, or receptacle where dead had been. He must never eat ham, bacon, pork, or any kind of swine's flesh, or of birds of prey. He must not taste or touch a drop of blood or certain fats, nor any one of a hundred things, that by their laws would defile him. When he passed certain things or persons in the street, he must carefully take up the skirts of his clothes, lest they touch and defile and render him unclean. The hands must always have clean water poured over them just before eating. The child must learn not to touch certain creeping things without wings. He must avoid a mouse, a weasel, several kinds of lizards, and the chameleon. If he should touch any dead person or animal or any person sick with certain diseases, as leprosy, or any one with morbid fluxes, or issues of blood, he was "unclean" and must have a sacrifice offered to make him clean. He must keep away from other children or persons often for seven days. For if one touched other children they too became unclean. They must be careful, therefore, not to pick up the bone of an animal, not to allow even their clothing to touch any of these objects, nor to enter any place where they had lain or been, lest they themselves be excluded from society of others, and looked upon as we look upon persons ill with small-pox. They must go through a process of purification to be admitted into company with others freely, even to those of their own household. This was a serious educational discipline for a Jewish Oriental child.

Many native Hindu rites required by their sacred books or practiced from law or custom about touching dead bodies, the leprous, the ceremonial impurity of men and women, their separation, and the modes of purification, bear a striking resemblance to the Mosaic laws in respect to uncleanness and their modes of purification.[1]

65a. *Oriental Language Pictorial.*—In the East primitive modes of intercourse and speech are notable. They talk in pantomime, gesture, and figurative words. Thus after the flood they spoke of a tower "whose top may reach unto heaven."[2] In my childhood children of the West thought that statement meant that those who survived Noah's flood hoped to build a tower so high that the people could climb into heaven, and so escape any future flood. But that was merely their way of describing a "very high tower." We have caught and imitate their idiom, when we speak of "skyscrapers." Not that the buildings "scrape the sky" or the clouds, but only that they are very high buildings. Again, it is said that "Nimrod was a mighty hunter before the Lord."[3] Not that the Lord had any connection with his hunting, but only that this was their way of saying he was the greatest of hunters. So of Saul his servants said, "an evil spirit from God," or from Jehovah, "troubled him."[4] Not that God sent "an evil spirit," but it was their way of saying that he was "very nervous" and "very irritable." It was their mode of expression of the superlative degree as we use it in our modern speech.

[1] See Allen's India, Ancient and Modern, p. 400 ff. Compare also Lev. chaps. 5, 14, 15, 22.
[2] Gen. 11 : 4.   [3] Gen. 10 : 9.   [4] 1 Sam. 16 : 14, 16, 23.

IX

RELATION OF PARENTS, CHILDREN, AND SERVANTS.

66. *Obedience.*—The Oriental idea of the relation and duties of parents and children and servants springs from their conception of the structure of the family.[1] Orientals are not always model parents, nor are their children specially noted for docility and good behavior, even though a son who should cease to reverence or obey his parents would be publicly outlawed as a monster. The Fifth Commandment appealed to the Oriental mind as reasonable and the only proper attitude of the child. The Christian interpretation of it, "Children, obey your parents in the Lord,"[2] has "a deeper meaning than either parents or children are apt to discover." Parents "not in the Lord" expecting obedience, may break the old command and forfeit obedience. And yet this may not, and in Oriental lands does not, usually relieve the child. The child's question is not: "Is my father a Christian?" "Is he worthy to be obeyed?" He may ask, "Can I comply with his command and not dishonor the Lord?" If he disobeys, even then he must be ready to accept any penalty that may follow. The Orientals assume that the father is to be obeyed, and that obligation goes on after maturity of the son, and practically never ceases. The Western caricature of the Fifth Commandment, "Parents, obey your children in the world," would shock the most debased heathen Oriental.

67. *Son Seeks Advice.*—The *principle* of the Mosaic command is ingrained into Oriental life. It may not be practiced or fulfilled in the spirit, but it is profoundly accepted in theory, and generally conformed to outwardly, to escape public odium. This reverence for parents among Orientals often amounts almost, or quite to, worship, as with the Chinese. Every

[1] Sec. I.   [2] Eph. 6 : I.

true Oriental honors father and mother in youth and old age, and after their death. On rising, each day, a man offers his prayers, and then goes to his father and mother to kiss their hands and ask their blessing. When he begins a new business, he asks the favor of God on his enterprise, and ends with a desire that his parents will approve of, and bless him, in this matter. He believes that if he honors his parents it will tend to shield him from loss and harm and bring him success.

68. *Slaves in the East.*—Servants in Oriental families are often slaves now, as they have been from time immemorial. Moslems, non-Protestant Christians, and, indeed, nearly all of Oriental religionists have slaves in the East. It is generally supposed to be of a mild type, and that slaves can buy their freedom. Domestic slaves born through the master in the house are not commonly sold. The domestic households of chief persons of Islam are largely made up of slaves, and hence slavery is not likely wholly to disappear in the East so long as Moslem power controls any state.

69. *Children as Slaves.*—Then, too, the children in an Oriental household differ practically in nothing from servants, domestic slaves, a condition Islam everywhere accentuates in the East. Their privileges in the home, their education, the seclusion of women, and the children often permitted in the women's apartments only, make them little better than household slaves, though they are heirs of the master. When his tutelage is over, and he enters maturity, then he becomes lord of all.[1] Until then he may be required to wait on his father like a common servant. The faithful servant stands at a distance in the room and keeps his eyes on the hands of his master and on those of his guest. For when the master wishes any service he signifies it by a gesture or motion of his hands, an Oriental custom of great antiquity. Thus the Psalmist says, "As the eyes of servants look unto the hand of their master, and as the eyes of a maiden unto the hand of her mistress; so our eyes wait upon the Lord our God."[2]

[1] Gal. 4 : 1.   [2] Ps. 123 : 2.

70. *Mixed Classes.*—A household now in Egypt and in other Bible lands, where the Moslem religion prevails, will be made up of several classes of persons besides the master, the mistress, and the children. There usually are several servants, some free and some slaves. The male slave, usually black, has more responsibility than even the free servant. He is often a great fanatic, quite ignorant, but with certain native aptness to execute the orders of his master. The female servants and slaves may, some of them, be white or Abyssinians, and are usually secondary wives, while others are black slaves, kept as cooks, waitresses, and for domestic service. But *free* servants cannot legitimately become concubines or secondary wives. The male servants may include a slave to wait personally on the master, a general servant, *sackka*, water carrier, a *bowwab*, or door-keeper, and a *Seis* or groom, or "coachman," as Europeans would say.

71. *Women Secluded.*—The women are secluded by a religious sentiment, which is thus stated, "Speak unto believing women (Moslems), that they restrain their eyes, preserve their modesty, and discover not their ornaments. Let them throw their veils over their bosoms, and not show their ornaments unless to their husbands or their fathers." It is counted indecent for a woman who is a Moslem to uncover her face (lift her veil) before an infidel. The Moslem regards all Christians as infidels. In earlier times women were not so rigidly secluded. This seclusion has tended to deteriorate woman, and to degrade her, as elsewhere stated.

72. *Women, Slave Companions.*—That women and children are forced to find companionship with slaves so large a part of their time, must make them craven in disposition and produce low types of character.[1] Slavery in some form existed in the days of Abraham, and two or more thousand years before the Christian era.[2] Even children were sold as slaves by their parents.[3] The penalty for offenses committed by

[1] See Gal. 4 : 1.
[2] Gen. 9 : 25; 15 : 2; 24 : 2, 34; 26 : 19, 32. See Code of Hammurapi,
[3] Ex. 21 : 7 ; Lev. 25 : 39.

slaves was half or less that put upon others.[1]   Under Moslem
rules, neither a Jew nor a Christian is allowed to make a
Moslem slave his concubine.   But a Moslem may have a second
wife of any religion.   The husband may have no control of his
wife's female slaves unless the mistress consents.   This is an
old Oriental custom, as seen in the case of Hagar and Sarah.[2]
See also Leah and Rachel, and their slave maids, Zilpah and
Bilhah.[3]

73. *Retainers*.—Another class, designated as retainers, do not
receive wages, but their living only and presents.   The gifts
to these retainers in the household may depend upon the number of visitors and persons calling on business.   These
retainers have a better social position than hired servants or
slaves, though otherwise it would be difficult for us to detect
the difference of these classes in their relations to the household.

A traveler in Syria during the last century says, " we had a
striking instance of the way ' the eyes of servants look to the
hand of their masters.'   Standing at the bottom of the room,
near the door and in a lower space, the youth who waited on
us watched every motion of our host with closest attention,
whilst he commanded or directed him by signs."

73a. *Son-Counselor*.—The son was ever waiting on his father as
a servant would.   Yet he was, also, in Oriental households a
counselor to his father.   In this respect he was always superior
to a servant.   He was part of the household, not only knowing
what was done as a friend might,[4] but sharing in the plans of the
household as the father's counselor, and entitled to a reasonable
part of the father's estate.   The eldest son was entitled to
double what would be the share of the other sons.

---

[1] Lev. 19 : 20.   [2] Gen. 16 : 1-14.   [3] Gen. 30 : 3-13.
[4] John 15 : 15.

VILLAGE WELL, NAZARETH.   P. 66

(Copyright by Underwood & Underwood, New York.)

CISTERN—WELL FOR SURFACE RAINFALL.   P. 66

(Vester & Co.)

X

WOMAN AMONG ORIENTALS.

74. *Woman Degraded.*—The degraded position of woman in the East now varies only in the relative extent of her degradation. Her social condition is generally worse to-day in Oriental lands than it was three thousand years ago. The only exception to this is in communities where Christianity has influenced home life. She is more a drudge, a slave, or a plaything for man than his companion. The rigid seclusion of women required by the Mohammedan religion, the inhuman custom of self-immolation of the widow on the funeral pyre of her dead husband under Brahminical rule, the utter lack of a moral code, and of a decent regard for her purity among the worshipers of Shinto, are simply indications of the almost universal degradation of woman in Asiatic lands.

75. *Examples in Orient.*—The exceptions to this are so rare as to prove the rule. In Burmah women have some freedom, and are not rigidly secluded, as in India. "They may freely mingle with men and attend to business matters of the family." But the marriage tie is loose and concubinage is common. Drunkenness and opium smoking prevail, the use of tobacco and the betel nut is almost universal by women and children.

In Korea, to a modern missionary's plea to send her daughter to school, the woman bitterly replied, "What is woman? After dogs and pigs were made, nothing was left, so woman was created out of the refuse." [1] Pagan and Mohammedan literature is so saturated with licentious thought and coarse, vile expressions that whole sections are untranslatable. The corrupt conversation among Moslem Asiatics, even women and children, is so foul as to be almost incredible. The Moslem seclusion of women has lowered her to the lowest—so degraded

[1] See Dr. Arthur J. Brown, "Near and Farther East," p. 264.

and vile that the sensuality is too utterly vile and lascivious to be mentioned.[1]

76. *Hebrew Women.*—She was in a better state among the Jews, but it cannot be forgotten that Jewish women were little removed from servile conditions even among them. Women were not admitted beyond the outer court in the temple at Jerusalem; they must worship by themselves, be screened from men in synagogues, and had only a partial share in religious privileges and blessings.

In ancient times she was not rigidly secluded or compelled to cover herself or her face with the veil. Nor was it "folly to teach women to read." Thus, the old Egyptians saw the face of Abram's wife,[2] and the young woman Rebekah was seen to be "good of countenance," by Abraham's man-servant.[3] And the young man Jacob saw the maiden Rachel and kissed her— an early example "of love at first sight."[4] The young women then were not counted bold or immodest if they conversed with strangers. But now women in that same land, seeing a man coming, turn their backs toward him, and though they are asking for bread, will not turn their faces nor take anything in their hands. If the stranger answers their requests, he must put the article near them and go away. Then the woman will pick up the gift.[5]

77. *Moslem Women.*—The Hon. Justice Ameer Ali affirms that the degradation of Moslem women is of comparatively recent date. "Almost to the end of the twelfth century (of our era) women mixed with men with dignity and self-respect, held reunions, gave concerts, and received visitors." Of a grand-daughter of Fatima, the lady Sakaina, he says, "she gave the tone to the cultivated society of her age. The reunions in her house of poets, scholars, jurists, and other distinguished people of both sexes, became the model for similar social gatherings at the residences of other ladies of fashion." Ali further states that Kădir, the Abbasside, promulgated the edict

---

[1] See *Mohammedan World of To-day*, 117, 139, 284 ff. [2] Gen. 12 : 14.
[3] Gen. 24 : 15, 16.   [4] Gen. 29 : 10, 11.   [5] See Burckhardt, 1, 352.

forbidding women to appear in public without the burka (veil) and adds, "with that commenced the decadence of Islam." [1]

The fellahin women of Palestine have the same contempt for Egyptian women as Miriam and Aaron had for the wife of Moses; "for he had married an Ethiopian woman." [2]

78. *Eating with Men.*—In ancient times women ate with the male members of the family. Thus, Job's sons are represented as calling their sisters to eat and drink with them. [3] Though the case of Elkanah may imply the modern custom of setting aside a portion of food for the women, after present day Oriental habits, [4] yet Queen Esther not only ate with the King, her husband, but also with Haman, [5] and the women were sharers in Belshazzar's feast. [6] The code of Hammurapi indicates that women before the era of Abraham were carefully protected in personal rights, and that their condition was higher and better than in most Oriental lands to-day.

79. *Queens.*—In ancient Egypt the law secured the right of succession to the rule of Egypt, and queens swayed over that land as well as kings. There may be much fancy and glamour gathered about the classic stories of Semiramis, and Dido of Carthage and of the Cleopatras of Egypt, and of Zenobia of Palmyra, and of Candace of Ethiopia. That they were women exalted to the highest place of power in the gift of their respective peoples proves the high respect which woman did command in that olden time. In the face of customs now universal in the East, tending to degrade woman, these notable instances show that woman has a royal supremacy of character, which at times rises above and defies the iron law of custom. Similar cases are given in the sacred Hebrew records of Miriam and Deborah, interpreters and prophetesses in Israel. Nor were women gifted and ambitious in evil, wanting in the qualities of leadership and popularity, of which Jezebel and Athaliah were notable examples among Israel's historic rulers.

80. *Peasant Women.*—The deep degradation of the peasant

---

[1] Pal. Fund Q., 1901, p. 69.   [2] Num. 12 : 1.   [3] Job. 1 : 4
[4] 1 Sam. 1 : 4.   [5] Esth. 7 : 1.   [6] Dan. 5 : 2.

5

women of the Orient is graphically pictured by Layard. "These poor creatures, like all Arab women, were exposed to constant hardships. They were obliged to look after the children, make bread, fetch water, and cut wood, which they brought home from afar on their heads. . . . They wove their wool and goat's hair into cloths, carpets, and tent-canvas; were left to strike and raise the tents; to load and unload the beasts of burden, when they changed camping-ground. . . . They had to drive the sheep and cows to the pasture, and milk them at night. . . . They carried their children on their backs during the march, and even when employed in domestic occupations." They brought water from the river, in large sheep or goat-skins filled and hung on the back by cords strapped over the shoulders, and, in addition, upon it was frequently seated the child who could not be left and was unable to follow its mother on foot "The bundles of fire-wood brought from a considerable distance were enormous, completely concealing the head and shoulders of those who tottered beneath their weight. . . . The men sat indolently by, smoking their pipes or listening to a trifling story from some stray Arab of the desert." [1]

The Palestine woman generally carries her child of two or three years old on the shoulder astride, but the Gipsy woman carries her child on the hip, a custom which Prof. Conder regards as coming from India, and their language as the Scinde dialect, from the original Sanscrit.[2]

81. *Wife Divorce.*—Again, the multitude of flimsy pretexts upon which a woman may be divorced add to the deplorable degradation of her condition in most Oriental lands. From his long residence in Syria, Prof. Post declares, "Moslems and Druses put away their wives at the merest caprice." [3] "It requires but a *word* to send away a wife of many years and the mother of a large family. Moreover, the injured woman cannot take her children with her. She may take whatever property she brought with her, and did not make over to her husband. There is no legal redress for her. The act of di-

[1] Nineveh, vol. I., 360, 361.   [2] Pal. Fund Q., 1901, p. 269.   [3] Compare Mark 10 : 2.

vorce is not an offense against Moslem law." "The Moslems write a form of marriage contract, but require no bill of divorcement.[1] . . . If the wife has no money of her own, she may thus suddenly be transferred from affluence to poverty."

82. *Growing Odious.*—"It is a fine testimony to the value of the principle of the Christian law that divorce is not favorably regarded unless there be some decided ground for it. A Moslem who sends his wife away for incompatibility gets talked about, and few care to face the odium. . . . It is especially unpopular to dismiss the mother of a family, particularly if she have sons. Thus the detestable *law* of Islam has had to bow to *custom* founded on the principles of Christ's gospel."

The general testimony of the best observers is that woman is degraded to a lower condition among the Moslems than among native Hindus and pagans. Lying and licentiousness are so common as to be utterly shameless. Illiteracy, ignorance, and immorality go hand in hand, plunging woman to the lowest of low depths. In Egypt 95 per cent. of the marriages are followed by divorce. It is a disputed question whether the prophet Mohammed could read or write. He is still boastfully called the "Illiterate." [2]

83. *Divorces One-sided.*—Worse still, "there is no such thing as a wife getting a divorce from her husband. She may procure a legal separation and support, but not divorce and freedom. . . . Oppressed wives often flee to the protection of their parents or brothers. The husband can compel her to return if he wishes. . . . A woman may torment her husband until he pronounces the desired and decisive words, which are as binding on him as on her. She seldom does this unless she has independent means." Of their servile position, as seen by Lane in Egypt, he says, "women prepare the husband's food, fetch water, spin cotton, linen, or woolen yarn, and make the fuel, which is composed of the dung of cattle, kneaded with chopped straw and formed into round flat cakes. When a poor woman goes out with her husband, she generally walks

[1] Mark 10 : 4.   [2] See Zwemer, "Moslem Lands."

behind him, and if there be anything for either of them to carry, it is usually borne by the wife."

84. *Woman a Drudge.*—Among the peasants of Palestine "men never carry anything." While a woman may rarely be *yoked* to the plough, yet Dr. Chaplin and Dr. Conder say they have seen a woman pulling a plough, side by side with a donkey, on the plain of Sharon or elsewhere in modern Palestine. Sacks, bundles, saddle-bags, baby-sacks, in which they carry their babies on their backs, and almost every other conceivable burden do the women carry in the East; this is the common testimony of explorers.

Even the wife of an Arab sheikh prepares the dinners, sees to the sacks of rice, corn, barley, coffee and supplies, directs the grinding of the mills, baking of bread, churning of butter, lighting of fires, and distributes the supplies asked for. Everything passes through her hands. Her children, "little naked urchins, black with sun and wind, with a long tail hanging from the crown of their heads, roll in the ashes or on the ground" near her.[1] The meal she has prepared for her husband with her own hands she may not eat with him. A man bringing his wife to a feast is now quite unknown to native Orientals under Moslem rule. Women may look on at a feast through a lattice, so arranged as not to give a semblance of a human being behind it. She is not the friend and companion, but the slave of her lordly husband. Women do the field work in the East. She may have fine taste and skill in embroidery, and may spend her time on it, but whether peasant of the poorest, or wife of the favored class, both are alike, servile and generally ignorant. Some Orientals count it a sin to teach a woman to read or write.

85. *Women Concealed.*—The modern Oriental custom of the seclusion of women is not easily overcome by protestant Christianity. Church buildings are divided by a curtain or lattice or there is a gallery reserved for women. "In many of the Protestant Churches the building is divided by a veil and the women are concealed from the men. . . . Where the veil is abolished the

[1] Layard, Nineveh, vol. I., 102.

TÁ AMIRAH WOMEN COOKING.   P. 6?

(*Pal. Exp. Fund.*)

WOMEN AT MILL.   P. 68

ROWS OF COINS ON HEAD-DRESS OF ONE ON THE LEFT.

(*Vester & Co.*)

women occupy one side and the men the other." This custom is common also in the meeting-houses of the Friends, both in England and America, though they are very careful to avoid other heathen customs, such as the names of the days of the week. "A public assemblage in the East," says Prof. Post, "is generally altogether a gathering of men. Even when women are present, sheeted like ghosts, an allusion to them in an address would sound strange to the Oriental ears." To begin an address in our customary way, "Ladies and Gentlemen," would shock the Oriental mind. If under polygamy woman is not deprived of her influence, "she has not much influence for good, but retains a vast power of evil." The wives and daughters of Emirs and rulers secretly sway a terrible influence through their political schemes and intrigues. They have no conscience and often no mercy. The refinement of true Christian love is impossible in such a community, but the devotion and faithfulness of woman exist even in Turkey and India. Christianity gives a new position to woman, and is laying the foundation for a new civilization in all Oriental lands.

XI.

SOCIAL INTERCOURSE—NEIGHBORS, KINSMEN.

86. *Social Basis.*—Social intercourse in the East springs from kinship, religion, and neighborly residence. The families of a tribe by intermarriage become so closely related that practically all of a tribe are kindred. This is characteristic of the nomads of the desert and in most of the villages, though families of two or more tribes may reside in the same village. Thus kinship is the basis of social life and of fellowship.

Religion and proximity tend to strengthen the social relations primarily formed by kinship. The stranger coming within the territory of the tribe is treated as a guest, because by an ingenious and necessary Oriental fiction, he is regarded temporarily a kinsman. The law of hospitality is founded on this pretty fiction—if it is a fiction. Is it not rather a significant survival of the deeper fact, and a recognition of the great brotherhood of the whole human race?

87. *Social Visits.*—Social intercourse among Orientals is marked by studied courtesy, great urbanity, and no little familiarity. Even what seem to us their tedious formalities have a fervor of sincerity and national dignity of deportment thrown into them that command respect.

Calls of courtesy are usually made on gala days, festal or birthdays, or times of sickness and affliction. Ordinary visiting-calls are scarcely known in native Oriental communities. The men meet daily in the market and the women at the well or around the village oven, so that news passes from one to another with marvelous celerity. Visiting is a real business when it is done by Orientals. Prof. Post, out of his experience, declares. "Visitors must always be received. To send word that you are engaged or at dinner would be considered a wanton

insult. Even sickness is not a reason for refusing to see friends.
In fact, they walk right in where a meal is being served or into
a sick chamber. . . . Visitors often sit for hours, sometimes all
day. They generally spend the whole evening." One of the
greatest difficulties of a physician in the East is to keep the
sick free from such intrusions. Orientals will keep coming
and going, not giving the host time even to eat. So our Lord
and his disciples were thronged with visitors, and were forced
to slip away from the house secretly, into a desert place, to rest.[1]
Sometimes when the visitor comes suddenly he may be obliged
or desired to stand outside until the room is put in order to
receive him. Or, if a man meets a friend whom he wishes to
take home with him, he hastens to his tent or house in advance,
to have the room made ready, and then goes back to bring his
friend. This may be alluded to in the saying of Jesus, "I go
to prepare a place for you."[2]

88. *Guests.*—In Jerusalem, pilgrims to feasts may be guests
with the same family, year after year. Mr. Haddad gives an
illustration: "When visiting Jerusalem at Easter, I used to send
word by post from Damascus or by messenger from Beerah,
three hours' journey from Jerusalem, to the family I was accustomed to stay with on these occasions." So Jesus sent word
when he was to keep the passover with a family in Jerusalem.[3]

Assemblages or visits of neighbors, for congratulation and
sympathy, are frequent and prolonged in the East. It is no
exaggeration of daily life in the Orient to say that men sit with
the afflicted, the sick, or the distressed for the entire day.
So Job's friends are represented as sitting silent with him for
seven days and seven nights.[4]

89. *No Privacy.*—Orientals are gregarious and, therefore,
social. Villages and hamlets consist of houses crowded together. Houses there are rarely isolated. The Eastern house
itself is not arranged for privacy, except upon the flat roof.
Among the peasants the house consists of one room, with a
curtain across a corner, or if there are several rooms, these

[1] Mark 6 : 31, 32.   [2] John 14 : 2.   [3] Mark 14 : 13-15.   [4] Job. 2 : 13.

open into a central court, so that when one has entered the common enclosure he can see into all the rooms of the house. A single house may be hive-like, the abode of many branches of the same family, so that privacy and domestic seclusion in the Western sense are impossible. They enjoy, however, social conditions to which we are utter strangers. Each household shares their joys and sorrows. One who has spent a life-time among them testifies: "What is lacking in depth of feeling is made up in breadth. Childlike, the whole commune swings easily from the extreme of sorrow to the extreme of joy. An assembly for congratulation with the shepherd, who had found his lost sheep, was as natural to the Orientals as it would be unnatural to us.[1] It is a question whether the Oriental has not more of common humanity in this phase of life than there is in the cold isolation and intense individualism of the Occident."

90. *Greetings.*—The Orientals upon entering one another's dwellings have customs and courtesies of their own. These vary widely. In coming to the house of a Moslem a man makes his coming known by a peculiar call, in order that the women inside may retire to their own apartment before he enters. The neighbor would enter without further formality. The host would greet the caller with "enter" or "welcome." The man may drop his shoes or sandals outside the door. Old friends or persons of equal rank, when thus meeting, warmly embrace each other. They seem almost to fall upon one another. "Each places his right hand upon the other's left shoulder," and kisses him on the right cheek, then, "putting the left hand on the other's right shoulder, again kisses him on the left cheek." So Jacob received and kissed his father Isaac, and Jacob embraced and kissed Joseph's sons.[2] Thus, Absalom treacherously stole the hearts of the people, and Joab slew his brother while pretending to greet him with a kiss.[3] And Judas betrayed his Lord with a kiss of greeting.[4] There

Luke 15 : 6.   [2] Gen. 27 : 27; 48 : 10.
[1] [3] Sam. 15 : 5; 20 : 9.   [4] Matt. 26 : 49; Luke 22 : 48.

are about forty allusions to this mode of greeting in the Scriptures.

"Intimates greet one another with a kiss, without regard to sex. Esau embraced his brother Jacob, and 'fell on his neck and kissed him'; Jacob kissed Rachel, and Laban ran to meet and embrace Jacob, 'and kissed him,' Aaron met his brother Moses and 'kissed him.' "[1]

A Bedouin camel-driver met a friend, says an old traveler, "when they kissed each other five times on the cheek, holding the hand, and asking questions at the same time." And Dr. Tristram observed that "ordinary acquaintances touch each other's hand, and then kiss their own, and apply it to their forehead, lips, and breast. . . . The kiss on either cheek is a sign of close intimacy. . . . It is the mark, not of gratitude nor of homage, but of unselfish love and esteem."[2] The betrayal of Judas was thus intensified as the blackest of treachery.

91. *Sitting and Conversation.*—After this act of greeting, other acts of welcome would follow. The salutation might be briefer between familiar neighbors than between others. The seat of honor is farthest from the door and at his right hand. So the King's mother sat on the right hand of Solomon.[3] To this seat the host would point, and by expostulation and entreaty persuade his caller to occupy it. They sit on the floor, on a mat, or rug, with their feet curled under them, to conceal them, tailor-fashion. The conversation is rapid and lively, all talking at the same time. The exclamations might run thus: "Hundred welcomes"; "May God preserve you"; "Peace be upon you"; "Your day be happy"; "May your day be blessed"; "Peace to your family"; "God preserve your health"; "Peace to this house." These throw light on our Lord's directions in sending out his disciples.[4]

92. *Topics Tabooed.*—In a Moslem, Buddhist, or non-Christian dwelling the Oriental would not ask about his neigh-

---

[1] Gen. 29 : 11–13; 33 : 4; Ex. 4 : 27.   [2] Eastern Customs, 205.
[3] 1 Kings 2 : 19; see also Ps. 16 : 11 and 45 : 9; Mark 14 : 62 and 16 : 19; Acts 5 : 31 and 7 : 56.
[4] Compare Matt. 10 : 12, 13 with Luke 10 : 5.

bor's wife. If the families are not so familiar in their friend-
ships, the greetings may be carried to what would seem to us
an absurd extent; good wishes and overflowing compliments
being repeated again and again, thus, "Peace of God upon you";
"May your day be enriched"; "By the blessing of your face";
"Your presence is the sun of my house"; "May you be happy";
"In your presence, 'happy'"; "You are comfortable—I am
comfortable," which means, "I am comfortable if you are."
After a pause, these same courtesies may be repeated, and gone
over many times. The Persian would say: "Is thy exalted
high condition good?" "May thy shadow never be removed
from my head!"

93. *Refreshments.*—Following these prolonged courtesies of
welcome and inquiries as to health, and profuse and hearty
good wishes for future health and prosperity, a servant, or the
host, may present a dainty sip of sweetened water, flavored with
orange blossoms or preserves, followed by cold water to wash it
down. Meanwhile a basin has been brought and a pitcher of
water to wash the feet, if that was necessary. In village houses
the guest may be delicately sprayed with some deliciously perfumed rose-water, or sweet-smelling aromatic spices may be
scattered about him. This, it is said, is to show what sweet
thoughts the family has toward the guest.

94. *Politely Detained.*—Should he rise to depart, he will be
pressed to stay. Some simple sweetmeats will be brought, with
further social chat. If he again rises, again "stay, not yet, not
so soon" greets him, and other refreshments appear, without
apparent end. After a prolonged entertainment, consuming
most of the morning or the day, finally a tiny cup of coffee may
be brewed and offered. The tiny cup, without a handle, is
placed within another cup, for the inner one is too hot to touch,
and he is warned to let it cool before venturing to sip it. This is
done still further to prolong his stay. The "courteous host
continues to dissuade his guest from bringing the visit or call to
a close," says Prof. Grant. When the parting finally comes,
the departing Syrian guest may say, "*A Khatrak*," "By your

leave," and the host, finding that he cannot longer detain the friend, replies, *ma' Salameh*, "with peace," that is, "Go in peace," and again the friend responds, "Peace to you." So the Bible story makes the old man say, "Peace be with thee."[1] Thus Amasa responded to David, "Peace, peace be unto thee, and peace to thy helpers."[2] See other instances, as the spies,[3] and of our Lord to his disciples.[4]

95. *Going with the Guest.*—It is quite in keeping with Oriental politeness to accompany the departing guest a certain distance on the way, depending upon the rank or character of the friend. If of a lower rank, the host rises and goes toward the door; if equal, he accompanies him to the door, if superior, the host goes to the gate and a distance, sometimes for several hours. This is a high type of politeness, and is called "bringing the guest on his way." So Paul was accompanied from Tyre and from Cæsarea by Mnason and others.[5] Mr. Haddad, out of his experience as a native Syrian, says, "When a person is going away, friends will go with him a few miles, and kiss at parting." "When I was leaving some Mt. Lebanon friends, they followed me for two hours until I was obliged to tell them that they must go no further." Compare the case of Naomi and Ruth.[6]

96. *Greeting and Parting.*—Other residents of the East tell of embracing as characteristic of Oriental greetings and partings. Men as well as women throw their arms around each other's necks and kiss each other on both cheeks. In Syria, embracing is not clasping in the arms, but grasping the shoulders, as before described, and placing the head over one shoulder, and then over the other, often without kissing. This resembles the ancient mode of "falling on the neck." So Paul embraced his disciples.[7] In like manner the father welcomed his prodigal son.[8]

In Syria, Prof. Grant observed a very graceful greeting, the right hand sweeping downward toward the ground, or touching

---

[1] Judg. 19 : 20. [2] 1 Chron. 12 : 18. [3] Judg. 18 : 15.
[4] Luke 24 : 36 ; John 20 : 19. [5] Acts 21 : 5, 15, 16. [6] Ruth 1.
[7] Acts 20 : 1, 10, 37. [8] Luke 15 : 20.

the breast, then the lips and forehead. The response was prompt and by the same set of gestures. Kissing is more frequent among women friends, meeting after a separation, than among men. It is still true, as in our Lord's day, that some love public greetings, as in the market-place.[1]

Greeting an Enemy as Brother.—Oriental greeting, sometimes unwittingly, gave protection to a bitter enemy. By the Oriental law of "*dakheel*," a foe might gain refuge and his life. Thus, by a shrewd stratagem, Benhadad's servants brought him *dakheel* or protection; for the king of Israel spoke of him as "brother." This would entitle the greatest enemy to protection; nor could the law be broken. See the story in 1 Kings 20: 28–34. An Arab once received and fed the murderer of his own son, unawares. When the pursuers of the murderer arrived, the father and host refused to let them kill his son's murderer, not only, but because the man had entered his tent and taken bread and salt with him, the father actually aided the criminal to escape from the blood avengers. He was bound to do this by the law of *dakheel*, or "entrance into protection." But compare the case of Sisera, which looks like treachery under Oriental custom.[2] See page 82, on "Foe-Guest."

[1] Matt. 23 : 7.   [2] Judg. 4 : 18–22.

XII.

SOCIAL INTERCOURSE—SALUTATIONS.

97. *Salutations Important.*—Salutations among Orientals precede and follow all intercourse. Half and sometimes nine-tenths of many of their letters consist of salutations. Notice the many in Paul's letter to the Romans, 16th chapter.[1] In some business letters the greetings may be spun out over one or two pages, and the business put into a single sentence. "Men will stop in the midst of conversation and exchange a series of complimentary expressions. A necessary prelude to intercourse between master and servant or monarch and subject is the salutation. As showing how rude the omission of it is regarded by Orientals, Prof. Post tells of a Caliph on a hunting expedition calling out to a shepherd lad: "Boy, fetch me that gazelle." The youth raised his head and replied: "You are ignorant of well-born men when you speak so contemptuously to me. Your words are the words of a giant, but your manners are the manners of an ass!" The Caliph, in anger, answered, "You wretch! Do you not know me?" The youth retorted, "Your want of manners has caused me to know you, but you began to talk to me without first saluting me!" This lack of salutation of Naaman by Elisha greatly angered the Syrian general. For the prophet merely sent a messenger to tell him what to do to be cured.[2]

98. *Makes Bonds.*—On the other hand, the customary salutation puts even the stranger within the charmed circle of kinship. Dr. Trumbull relates how he unwittingly brought himself and his whole party within the bonds of hospitality of a Sheikh and his tribe by politely saluting a passing Bedouin woman. He and his companions were compelled by the Sheikh to halt, dismount, wait for a fire to be kindled, coffee to be made

[1] See 1 Cor. 16 : 19–21; Gal. 1; Eph. 1; Col. 1.   [2] 2 Kings 5 : 10.

and served, and the Sheikh urged them further to remain until a lamb should be slain and cooked, and bread baked for the party. After all this trouble, the Oriental was profuse in his thanks for the opportunity to entertain them, he would take no payment of the chance stranger, but helped him to mount his horse and kissed the hands of the mounting guest, and blessed him with a parting *Salaam*, "Peace," as he departed.

99. *Salaams.*—These *salaams* and salutations take time, but time is of no value to the Asiatic. Business can wait, as of secondary moment. The amenities of life are a necessity; work, trade, learning, and other things are mere incidentals. The notables, civil and religious, require an exceptional amount of formality and deference in their salutations. Their hand or the hems of the garments must be kissed, the bowing and genuflections must be profuse, and their blessings invoked on every conceivable occasion.

All this implies much delay. Several minutes are spent in bowing, gesturing, and repeating the words, *Salaam, alai-Kum*, "Peace be upon you," and the reply, *Wa-alai-Kum as-salâm*, "On you be peace," that is, "of God." So Elisha saluted the Shunammite—*Shalōm*, "Peace to thee," "peace upon thy husband," "peace upon thy child." And the Shunammite answered by the customary salutation, "*Shalōm*, Peace." [1] Then the woman caught Elisha by his feet—a further customary act in salutation. In Syria the physician is now so saluted at almost every visit to a hospital. "So quickly is this done," says Prof. Post, "that there is no chance to prevent it." "It was peculiarly un-Oriental for Gahazi to endeavor to frustrate the woman's homage to Elisha, and to interfere with her petition. . . . Syrian servants do not like to turn away street beggars even from their masters, lest they defraud them of some possible alms."

100. *The Delays.*—When these formalities in saluting are so punctiliously observed, we can imagine the delays. They may

---

[1] 2 Kings 4 : 26. She did not say, "It is well," as the A. V. incorrectly renders the greetings.

be repeated ten times, and a long exchange of news, a chat in the shade of a tree, a *narghileh* or two, come fairly within the category of a salutation, says Prof. Post. The Arabs, according to Stapfer, still say, *Marhaba*, "May you be enlarged," which may correspond to the New Testament greeting, *chairein*, "hail" or "rejoice," while they have also the counterpart, *eirene soi*, "Peace to you," or *chaire*, "Be joyful." This was the same as the Roman salute in our Lord's day, *salve*, "Be in health" and *vale*, "well or fare (thee) well"; the latter was said at parting. W. M. Thomson asserts that there is such an amount of insincerity, flattery and falsehood in the terms of salutation prescribed by etiquette that our Lord wished his disciples "to dispense with them as far as possible." [1] But the hindrance to their work was also a strong reason for the command. So, too, he forbade them to go from house to house.[2] For when a stranger arrives in an Oriental village, strict etiquette requires all the families, one after another, to invite him to a meal. This would take much time, for formal salutations must be made to every person and upon every occasion. Any business calling for despatch could not be done were one to stop for salutations. Hence, the Scripture charge "not to salute" any by the way.[3]

101. *The Strict Etiquette.*—Modern Moslems have special customs to observe in salutations. Thus, one riding should *first* salute a person on foot; one who passes by should *first* salute persons standing or sitting; a small party those of a large party; a young person should be first to salute the aged. One who enters the house should first salute the people of that house, and do the same when leaving it. But in a crowded city, or on a road where many are passing, it is not necessary to salute many whom one may pass. And yet, some man of rank or a venerable Sheikh usually salutes another who appears to be of rank, of wealth, or of learning, even in a crowded street; a salutation must always be returned. If, however, one should salute another of a different religion by mistake, as a Moslem greeting

[1] See Luke 10 : 4.   [2] Luke 10 : 7.   [3] 2 Kings 4 : 29 ; Luke 10 : 4.

a Christian, the latter need not return it, and the former, on
discovering his mistake, will generally revoke his salutation, or,
if first greeted, will respond, "Peace be on us," meaning on any
of the same faith.

102. *Returning Salutations.*—With polite Orientals it is the
custom for one who gives or returns a salutation to touch his
breast with his right hand when giving the salaam, or he may
touch his lips, his forehead, or his turban. An inferior or a
subject simply goes through the gestures to a man of high rank,
and does not speak his salaam. He may further take the hand
of a superior and kiss it and put it to his forehead. In the
fawning conduct of Absalom this mode of salutation was employed.[1]

103. *Shalōm, "Peace."*—The most common Hebrew phrase
in salutation was *Shalōm*, "Peace," "prosperity." The
stem-word meant "to restore," "make good," or "to complete,"
then "to live in peace." Thus Oriental monarchs began their
decrees by this salutation, as Nebuchadnezzar did, "Peace be
multiplied unto you."[2] And it was the word of dismissal and
benediction at the conclusion of an interview.[3] So Jethro
parted with Moses, and it was part of the blessing of Jehovah
to Aaron.[4] With this (Shalom, "peace") the angel of the Lord
greeted Gideon,[5] and David and Jonathan used this salutation.[6]
With this benediction the prophet Elisha sent Naaman healed to
his own land.[7] Priests were also accustomed to dismiss suppli-
ants with the same blessing.[8]

The Korean village peasants salute the American missionary
with, "Have you come in peace?" And when he departs, the
parting salutation is, "May you go in the peace of God!"[9]

104. *"Grace in Salutation."*—In New Testament times the
Greek and Latin equivalents—*eirene* and *salve*, "peace," were
the words of greeting and parting in speech and in epistle, more
frequently used than any other, except "grace." The thirteen

[1] 2 Sam. 15 : 5; see also Job 31 : 7.
[3] Gen. 26 : 29–31.   [4] Ex. 4 : 18; Num. 6 : 26.
[6] 1 Sam. 20 : 42; 25 : 6, 35; 2 Sam. 15 : 9, 27.
[8] Judg. 18 : 6; 1 Sam. 1 : 17; Jer. 6 : 14; 8 : 11.
[9] "Nearer and Farther East," p. 267.
[2] Dan. 4 : 1; 6 : 25; Esther 9 : 30.
[5] Judg. 6 : 23.
[7] 2 Kings 5 : 19.

Epistles of the Apostle Paul begin with "peace" be multiplied unto you, frequently coupled with grace, love, or mercy also. The two Epistles of Peter open with a like salutation. The angel Gabriel greeted Mary with χαιρε, *Chaire*, "joy," or "hail."[1] So the soldiers mockingly greeted Jesus.[2] It is significant that the Apostle John forbade Christians thus to salute apostates and unbelievers,[3] lest they seem to share in the unbelief. Paul's letters were usually written by an amanuensis, but he added the closing salutations with his own hand.[4]

105. *Symbols and Gestures.*—Lane notes that in Egypt compliments usually followed the *salaam*, such as "God bless thee," "God preserve thee." When one asked "Your health?" the response would be "Praise God," the tone of voice alone indicating whether the person was ill or well. When a friend meets another that has been absent several days, after the *salaam*, he declares, "Thou hast made us desolate by thy absence," and is answered, "May God not make us desolate." If one happens to sneeze, he exclaims, "Praise God," to which others reply, "God have mercy" or "God guide us." If he makes a breach of good manners he makes apology for it by exclaiming, "I beg pardon of God, the great." Some imaginative Orientals explain the gestures of the hand in salutation, especially touching the head, the lips, and the breast, as symbolizing, "with my head I worship, with my lips I honor, with my heart I love thee."

---

[1] Luke 1 : 28.   [2] John 19 : 3.   [3] 2 John 9 : 10.
[4] 1 Cor. 16 : 21, 23; Col. 4 : 18; 2 Thess. 3 : 17.

6

XIII

SOCIAL INTERCOURSE—HOSPITALITY.

106. *Tokens.*—The old Roman dramatist, Plautus, relates a story that graphically illustrates one feature of Oriental hospitality. The old Latins had a token of hospitality, *tessera Hospitales*, consisting of a tile of wood or stone, which they divided into two pieces. Each wrote his name upon a piece, and at parting they exchanged pieces. Hanno inquired of a stranger about an old guest, and was surprised to find that he was addressing the person he asked for. Then to test the identity of the person, he drew out a token of hospitality, saying, "Look carefully at this *tessera.*" And the man replied, "I have the exact counterpart of it in the house." Hanno answered, "I rejoice to meet thee. Thy father was my guest, I divided this token with him." The other responded, "Yea, and thou shalt have home with me; I reverence hospitality."

107. *A Foe-guest.*—The Oriental idea of hospitality is vividly illustrated also by the fact that the host in the East gives the foremost place even to an enemy, so long as that enemy is his guest. Such a guest is perfectly safe from harm while he remains within this charmed circle of Oriental hospitality.

Mr. MacGregor, "Rob Roy," tells how he adroitly outwitted a Sheikh, who had made him prisoner, by using strategem in getting the Arab to eat salt in his presence. Partaking of salt together, even by accident, is regarded among Arabs as a pledge of friendship. Thus, MacGregor had become the Arab's guest, "We had now eaten salt together, and in his own tent, and so the Sheikh was bound by the strongest tie, and he knew it."

108. *Stranger-guest.*—The wandering Bedouins regard every stranger as a guest. Burckhardt relates, "We alighted at an encampment of Bedouins, and entered the Sheikh's tent, though

KILLING THE FATTED CALF.   P. 83

(Copyright by Underwood & Underwood, New York.)

he was absent. The Arabs had a long and fierce dispute among themselves to decide who should have the honor of furnishing us a supper and a breakfast next morning. He who first sees a stranger from afar, and exclaims, There comes my guest, has the right of entertaining him, whatever tent he may alight at." "A lamb was killed for me, which was an act of great hospitality; for these Bedouins are poor, and a lamb was worth a sum that would afford a supply of butter and bread to the family for a whole week."

This throws light on an early and thoroughly Oriental example of hospitality mentioned in Scripture. Abraham "sat in the tent door in the heat of the day; ... and, lo, three men stood over against him: and when he saw them, he ran to meet them from the tent door, and bowed himself to the earth." [1] The sitting in the tent, the running to greet them, the low bowing, the *salaam*, the water for the feet, the rest in the shade of a tree, the bit of refreshments, the baking of bread, the slaying of a calf— are courtesies that every modern traveler has experienced in the East among native tribes whose simple habits of hospitality have not been corrupted by contact with Western civilization.

109. *Lot and Job.*—In like manner, even Lot, though dwelling among the coarse, wicked people of Sodom, would not allow two strangers to abide in the street, but insisted upon entertaining them in the house, and it proved that he had unawares secured two angels for his guests. [2] So Jethro reproved his daughters, when they reported meeting a stranger in a Midian desert. "Where is he? Why is it that ye have left the man? Call him, that he may eat bread"; and that man proved to be Moses. [3]

Job indicates his character by asserting, "The stranger did not lodge in the street: but I opened my doors to the traveller." [4] Still another typical example of ancient Oriental hospitality is that of Gideon, who found a stranger sitting under a terebinth tree at Ophrah, and besought him not to depart until the customary present could be brought. So Gideon made ready a

---

[1] Gen. 18 : 1, 2.   [2] Gen. 19 : 1-3.   [3] Ex. 2 : 20.   [4] Job 31 : 32.

kid and baked cakes of bread, and brought them in a basket and in a pot to entertain the stranger under the oak or terebinth tree. He too was surprised to discover that he had entertained an angel unawares.[1]

110. *Arab Hospitality.*—Modern travelers, as Burckhardt, Morier, Robinson, Harmer, Thomson, Hamlin, Pococke, Irby and Mangles, and many others testify to the continuance of this custom among Bedouins to this day.

But Palmer did not gain a very rose-colored idea of the Kerek-Arabs on this point. A Sheikh of the Beni-Hamideh tribe invited them to feed at his tents. Palmer says, "Arabs are still as fond as ever of exercising the virtue of hospitality. As they practice it, it is a lucrative speculation. The Bedawi Sheikh, knowing that he must not nowadays expect to entertain angels unawares, takes especial care to entertain only such as can pay a round sum for the accommodation or give their host a good dinner in return. The casual and impecunious stranger may, it is true, claim the traditional three days' board and lodging, but he must be content with the scraps 'that fall from the rich man's table,' and prepare to hear very outspoken hints of the inadvisability of his presence." And of his experience among the Arabs in the Mountains of Moab, a pastoral tribe, Palmer adds: "On arriving at an encampment, the traveler enters from behind, and makes for the Sheikh's tent, not dismounting until he reaches the door. This is, in most cases, a necessary precaution." He was provided an extemporized divan, made of carpets and clothing, and served with *leben* and coffee. If you stay the night, a male kid is cooked, and the scraps passed over the curtain into the women's apartment for the women and servants to eat. They talk, laugh, smoke, and quarrel alternately, until sleep overtakes them. He adds, "On leaving the encampment, the visitor is expected to make a present to the Sheikh of a good round sum of money. The Sheikh, however, protests violently, declaring that he cannot think of receiving money from a guest, and insists on restoring it. On one or two

AT THE CITY GATE, JERUSALEM.
BUILDING ON THE LEFT IS TOWER OF DAVID.
(Vester & Co.)

occasions, we took our entertainers at their word, and received back the money; but the good man always rode after us before we had got far, and expressed his willingness not only to accept the gift, but his decided disapprobation of the smallness of it." [1]

This throws light on the act of Gehazi and the readiness of Naaman to hand him the present, previously refused by the prophet.[2] When Palmer asked for a drink of water, it could not be found in the Arab encampment in the desert, but milk was brought to him instead of water. Thus Sisera asked Jael for a drink of water, "And she opened a bottle of milk, and gave him drink." [3]

111. *Presents, Not Pay.*—J. L. Stephens, in his travels, speaks also of the hospitality of the Arabs. "I had read beautiful descriptions of its manifestation," and had the notion that "the Bedouin would be offended by an offer to reward his hospitality." Not wishing to make a blunder in so delicate a question, he adds, "I applied to my guide Toualeb for information. His answer was explicit." "I could give or not give as I pleased but that if I did not, the hospitable host (Sheikh) would wish his lamb alive again!" Stephens made a gift and adds: "from the exceeding satisfaction with which that estimable person received it, I am very sure I did better in taking Toualeb's knowledge for my guide than by acting upon what I had read in books." Again, among the Bedouins of the Arabian desert, he speaks of "the great friendship they had conceived for him," quaintly adding, "the friendship was not for what I was, but for what I had." "They welcomed me as they would a bag of gold." [4] Many other travelers have observed similar dark colors in Oriental hospitality, not the simple, unselfish entertainment that springs from a profound sense of the brotherhood of the human race.

112. *Hospitality Rewarded.*—Many even of the Scripture instances might be open to such suspicion also, for did they not realize a reward? Even when the courtesy is based upon

[1] *Desert of Exodus*, pp. 403–406.   [2] 2 Kings 5 : 20–27.
[3] Judg. 4 : 19.   [4] *Travels in Egypt and Arabia*, Petra, II, 30.

love, the sacred writers hint at the probability of recompense. Thus, "Let brotherly love continue" is followed by, "Be not forgetful to entertain strangers; *for* thereby some have entertained angels unawares."[1] Abraham, Lot, and Gideon were not alone in receiving strangers, who turned out to be angels.[2] Laban took in a stranger, and found a servant and a son-in-law.[3] Rahab received two strange men, and her life was saved as her reward.[4] The widow of Zarephath shared her last morsel in time of famine with a stranger, and she and her son were kept from starving to death thereby.[5] The woman of Shunem entertained a chance stranger, who turned out also to be a prophet, and she had a rich recompense.[6] These did it not for the reward, but they received a recompense.

In view of instances like these, the Apostle Paul urged the grace on Roman Christians, "given to hospitality."[7] " Given " represents a strong Greek term; strictly "pursuing" the grace, as though it were in danger of escaping from them. In old times the prophet seems also to have made it a test of godly character.[8] In New Testament times the recompense came unexpectedly. Zaccheus entertained the despised Galilean Teacher, and salvation came to his house.[9] Publius, a barbarian of Malta, entertained a strange prisoner for "three days courteously," and had his father restored to health by his guest, the prisoner Paul.[10]

113. *Hospitality Unrewarded.*—On the other hand, there are noble instances of Oriental hospitality among the rude and uncultured Bedouins of the far East, who would scorn the offer of a reward therefor. Thus, Tavernier says, "On the road to Bagdad, we met with a comely old man, who came up to me, and taking my horse by the bridle, said, "Friend, come, wash thy feet, and eat bread at my house. Thou art a stranger, since I have met thee on the road, never refuse me the favor I desire of thee." He feasted us in the best manner he could, " giving us barley for our horses, killed a lamb and some hens."

[1] Heb. 13 : 1, 2.   [2] Gen. 18 : 2, 19–19 : 1, 5; Judg. 5.
[3] Gen. 29–31.   [4] Josh. 6 : 22, 23.   [5] 1 Kings 17 : 8–24.   [6] 2 Kings 4 : 8–37.
[7] Rom. 12 : 13.   [8] 1 Kings 17 : 13.   [9] Luke 19 : 6, 9.   [10] Acts 28 : 7, 8.

The traveler was impressed with this invitation, so like many examples in Scripture. Another young Oriental riding with two servants greeted the same traveler, and wanted to carry him to a friend's house for entertainment, "but, seeing we were resolved to keep our way," adds Tavernier, "he would give me his pipe, notwithstanding all the excuses I could make, and though I told him I never took tobacco, I was constrained to accept it." [1]

114. *Public Guest-room.*—The American explorer, Robinson, also out of numerous instances during his researches in Palestine relates: "In every village there is a public room, . . . *Menzil* or *Medâfeh*—guest-room. The guest lodges in the *Menzil*, and his food is supplied by the families to whose circle it belongs. The guest gives nothing as a remuneration when he leaves. To offer money would be taken as an insult, and to receive it would be a great disgrace." Robinson adds, "Such is universally the manner of entertainment in the villages," prevailing about Hebron and other parts of Syria two generations ago, before the natives had come so fully in contact with representatives of Western civilization. [2]

115. *Pay Resented.*—Dr. Hilprecht had an illustration of this primitive hospitality in the Lebanon region. After entertainment over night he arranged to have his muleteer hand the host —a Sheikh—a silver coin. This was indignantly refused. The excited Sheikh, flinging the coin upon the ground, exclaimed, "Am I a dog? Do they dare to give the Sheikh of Zeta money in return for hospitality?" No apologies of Dr. Hilprecht for the mistake of his servant could remove the insult in the mind of the host, and the guests hastened departure, for their own safety, from the offended Arab. [3]

Thus, these illustrate the Old Testament precepts, and throw light on the basis of hospitality as practiced by Orientals; "If a stranger sojourn with thee in your land, ye shall not vex him." "The stranger . . . shall be unto you as one born

---

[1] *Travels*, p. 111.   [2] See *Researches*, II, 19.
[3] Trumbull, *Studies in Oriental Life*, p. 90.

among you, and thou shalt love him as thyself." "For the Lord . . . loveth the stranger, in giving him food and raiment. Love ye therefore the stranger."[1]

116. *Questions.*—In further illustration of Scripture incidents, telling of questions asked, Dr. Merrill speaks of the curiosity of the desert people, the Bedouin. "Wherever you meet an Arab," says Merrill, "you will find him, as a rule, full of questions." His first inquiry will be, "Where is your face?" a Semitic idiom for "Where are you bound?" If you meet him on the road he will wish you to stop until he has asked where you come from, why you came from that place, where you are going, why you are going there, of what nation you are, and other questions about your gun and horse, until you are thoroughly tired, and spur on your horse to escape his volley of interrogations."[2]

Pharaoh asked Jacob, "How old art thou?" and his sons were asked, "What is your occupation?"[3] Dr. Merrill also commends Bedouin generosity: "As a rule, they are really very liberal, according to their means, in presents they make to friends. But they are too human not to expect some reward. Where large gifts are offered to a foreigner, it is expected that he will immediately, or at some future time, make a generous gift in return."

117. *Treatment of Guests.*—The acts of hospitality vary widely among different tribes and peoples of the East, yet have some broad features in common. Thus, after the salutations, gestures of joy, or greeting with kisses, common among Arabs in Egypt, Arabia, Syria, and eastward, the guest is invited into the dwelling, and water offered to wash his feet. Even where sandals are not worn by the guest this is done. Robinson in 1838 had his host at Ramleh propose that a servant wash his feet, and adds, "This took me by surprise, for I was not aware that the custom still existed here." The Nubian slave poured water upon his feet over a shallow copper basin, rubbing the feet with her hands and wiping them with a napkin, affording

[1] Lev. 19 : 34; Deut. 10 : 17-19.   [2] *East of Jordan*, p. 499.   [3] Gen. 47 : 3, 8.

him Scriptural illustration of the custom.[1] Jowett earlier in the last century had a like experience when entertained in Mt. Lebanon. "Before supper, the master of the house directed his servant to bring in a large brass pan, full of warm water, in which for the first time, he illustrated the ancient custom of washing the feet of strangers."[2] Henry Martyn had a like treatment in his journeys in the East as did also the author of a "Mission to the Jews," and Dr. H. Malcolm in Burmah was thus reminded of John 13 : 10.

118. *Anointing Guests.*—Another act of hospitality was anointing the guest with perfume or oil. Tavernier states that he made Arabs presents of olive oil. Soon as an Arab received it, he lifted his turban, anointed his head, face, and beard, and then lifting his eyes to heaven, devoutly exclaimed, "Thank God!" Burder tells of an Oriental traveler, the guest of a rich man in India, where the master of the house poured over the traveler's hands and arms a delightful odoriferous perfume, put a golden cup in his hand, and filled it with wine to overflowing, reminding him of the Psalmist's words, "Thou anointest my head with oil, my cup runneth over."[3] Bruce in his travels was entertained by an Eastern dignitary and adds, "Our coffee being done, I rose to take my leave, and was presently wet to the skin by deluges of orange-flower water." And Niebuhr, the traveler, narrates a similar experience at a merchant's house in Rosetta, the servant throwing the perfumed water over his face and clothes.

119. *Bible Instances.*—A common *order* of entertaining a guest is set forth in the narrative of Jesus dining with a Pharisee. "I entered into thine house, thou gavest me no water for my feet: but she hath washed my feet with tears, and wiped them with the hairs of her head. Thou gavest me no kiss: but this woman since the time I came in hath not ceased to kiss my feet. My head with oil thou didst not anoint: but this woman hath anointed my feet with ointment."[4] And this was the occasion when our Lord said, her sins were forgiven her. She

[1] *Researches*, II, 229.   [2] *In Syria*, p. 69.   [3] Ps. 23.   [4] Luke 7 : 44–46.

had a reward; again the promise was fulfilled, "He that receiveth a prophet in the name of a prophet shall receive a prophet's reward." [1]   Rawlinson describes a costly ointment prepared by the rude Parthians composed of cinnamon, spikenard, myrrh, cassia, gum-styrax, saffron, cardamom, wine, honey, and sixteen other ingredients, and that they adopted it from the old Persians who also had an ointment of palm-wine, saffron, and the fat of lions, with *Lelianthus*, which was believed to increase the beauty of the complexion.[2]

120. *Proverbs on Hospitality.*—So it became a proverb, "Ointment and perfume rejoice the heart." [3]   And the preacher reckoned among the comforts of this life, ointment for the head. [4]

It was a custom in ancient Egypt, to treat guests by sprinkling precious ointment or oil on their heads, as we know from representations of the act pictured on their monuments. It was part of the ceremony in crowning a king,[5] and at the installation of the high priest,[6] as well as a part of courtesy and hospitality to vistors.   Anointing the face (with the oil of gladness) was a sign of joy, and the neglect of it a sign of mourning.[7]

121. *Lodges.*—There is another significant expression of the Oriental idea of hospitality.   It is found in the Eastern caravansary, khan, or inn, and in the "guest room" called the "*Menzil*" or "*Medâfeh*."   There are three or four grades of these public guest rooms or lodges.   An Eastern inn is entirely different from a hotel in our country.   Usually it is without furniture, landlord or food, for man or beast.   The traveler is provided with shelter only.   He must carry his own bedding, provisions, and cooking utensils.   The caravansary is a large building in the city, and sometimes a place for shelter for travelers in the desert.   The khan is a similar building in a village or town, while the *Menzil* is a dwelling, or more often a room, set aside for

---

[1] Matt. 10 : 41.
[2] *Ancient Monarchies*, III, 212. Compare Ex. 30 : 23–25; 2 Kings 20 : 13; Ps. 133 : 2; Eccl. 7 : 1 with John 12 : 3, 5; Mark 14 : 3, 5; Matt. 26 : 7–9 and Sol. Song 1 : 3; 4 : 10; Is. 57 : 9; Rev. 18 : 13.
[3] Prov. 27 : 9.   [4] Eccl. 9 : 8; compare Ps. 92 : 10.   [5] 2 Kings 11 : 12.
[6] Ps. 133 : 2; Lev. 6 : 20.   [7] Ps. 104 : 15; Heb. 1 : 9; 2 Sam. 14 : 2; Dan. 10 : 3.

guests and travelers. The better class of caravansaries are striking objects to the traveler, looking not unlike some great palace, or fortress, or castle. An inn with a keeper is alluded to in the parable of the good Samaritan.[1]

122. *Khan, Inn.*—Buckingham, in his Arabian travels years ago, says, "Some of the finest buildings in Damascus are the khans or caravansaries, appropriated to the reception of goods brought in caravans from various quarters . . . one consisted of a spacious court, the entrance to which, from the street, was by a superb gateway with pointed arch, vaulted, and highly ornamented with sculpture. The court was paved throughout with broad flat stones, smoothly polished, and admirably joined together; and in the center of this stood a large fountain, sending forth cooling and agreeable streams; the whole being crowned with a cluster of lofty domes. The masonry of this pile was formed of alternate layers of black and white stone . . . and the ornaments were profusely rich."

Another traveler, about a century ago, was conducted to an empty room in a khan. He adds, "The khan was of large dimensions, covering apparently an acre of ground, with high buildings all around. The ground floor was occupied with horses and carriages of all kinds. The second floor was devoted to passing travelers, and the third to those who were to stay above six months. The second floor had a wide promenade all around, and on it were gathered groups from many different countries."

123. *Menzil.*—In the *Menzil*, food is usually supplied by the families to whose circle it belongs, as before stated. At a *Menzil*, if the guest is a dignitary, or person of position, a sheep, or a goat, a lamb or a kid may be killed and served. If the guest is a common traveler or a muleteer, he is fed with rice, or whatever may be the ordinary food of the people themselves.

Dr. H. C. Fish describes an ordinary khan or inn, where his party lunched, between Ramleh and Jerusalem. "The building was in a state of utter dilapidation. It stood by the road

[1] Luke 10 : 25–37.

side, is built of stone, and covers quite an area. It has a ground floor, and a second flat, reached by stairs on the outside. On the upper floor," he adds, "travelers who have the means, take their quarters, paying a pittance for the use of the furniture there, which consists of a few rickety chairs and tables, and two or three verminous cots, dignified with the name of beds. [Chairs, tables, etc., are not used and not seen among Orientals, though they were not unknown in ancient Egypt.] The poor traveler stays down stairs, in fact most khans (in Palestine) have but one story. The ground is the floor, except in the little arched recesses let into the sides of the walls, a foot or two above ground, which are perhaps cemented. In these small recesses (without doors to them, and some five or ten feet square) the travelers sleep, their animals being close by. It is common to see 'mangers' made of pebbles and mortar, in the shape of a box or kneading trough, fastened against the wall, or lying around loose." The "crib" of the Old Testament, and the "manger" of the New, were doubtless like these mangers.[1]

124. *Fed by Strangers.*—Of the hospitality provided in the common khan, and *Menzil*, Fellows gives us this picture: "I was beginning to make my meal upon the food we had with us, when in came nine people, each bearing a dish. A large tray was rested on the rim of a corn-sieve placed on the ground, in the center of which was placed a tureen of soup, with pieces of bread around it. The stranger, my servant, and a person who seemed to be the head man of the village, sat around the tray, dipping their wooden spoons or fingers into each dish as it was placed in succession before them. Of the nine dishes, I observed three were soups. I asked why this was, and who was to pay for the repast. I was informed it was the custom of the people, strictly enjoined by their religion, that, as soon as a stranger appears, each peasant should bring his dish, he himself remaining to partake of it after the stranger—a sort of

1 Job. 39 : 9; Proverbs 14 : 4; "the ass his master's crib," Isaiah 1 : 3; Luke 2 : 7, 12, 16.

picnic, of which the stranger partakes without contributing. The hospitality extends to everthing he requires; his horse is fed, and wood is brought for his fire, each inhabitant feeling honored by offering something. This custom accounts for the frequent recurrence of the same dish, as no one knows what his neighbor will contribute. Toward a Turkish guest this practice is perfectly disinterested, but from a European they may have possibly been led to expect some kind of return, although to offer payment would be an insult. All the native contributors afterward sat down and ate in another part of the room."

125. *Not Eat Alone.*—Oriental etiquette invites others to partake of food. So Job protests that he had not "eaten my morsel myself alone." [1]   Shaw, in his travels, gives an instance in point while in Arabia: "No sooner was our food prepared, whether it was potted flesh boiled with rice, a lentil soup or unleavened cakes, served up with oil or honey, than one of the Arabs, having placed himself on the highest spot of ground in the neighborhood, calls out thrice, with a loud voice, to the sons of the faithful, to come and partake of it; though none of them were in view, nor perhaps within a hundred miles of us."

126. *Token of Friendship.*—Then, too, we must bear in mind that hospitality meant far more to the Oriental than brief entertainment. It was a token of friendship, of protection, and a pledge to defend the guest from any harm, even at the sacrifice of his life. This pledge seems to rest upon the idea of the brotherhood of man, in part, but more fully upon the ancient Oriental conviction that all men are "guests of God," dwelling in a vast sky covered tent, where God is the host. William Ewing, resident among the dwellers of Lebanon, and familiar with those of the Hauran, found this idea in the minds of the people in those lonely places. To them the traveler is "the guest of God," and if they neglect to care for him out of what God has given them, it shall not be well for them.

[1] Job. 31 : 17.

XIV.

EATING AND MEALS.

127. *Vegetarians.*—The Orientals are largely vegetarians, rather than flesh eaters. Their foods are chiefly fruits, vegetables, grains, and other cereals. Rice is the most common article of diet in the far East. There are some who hold that primitive man was a vegetarian, supporting their claim on passages in Genesis.[1] It was common to eat the green kernels of grain without cooking or baking. This custom has prevailed for thousands of years. Thus, Robinson on the road from Hebron to Carmel (in 1838), when the wheat was ripening, says, "We had here a beautiful illustration of Scripture. Our Arabs were an hungered, and going into the fields, they plucked the ears of corn (grain) and did eat, rubbing them in their hands. On being questioned they said this was an old custom, and no one would speak against it; they were supposed to be hungry, and it was allowed. We saw this afterward in repeated instances."[2]

128. *Eating Raw Grain.*—This practice is as old as the ancient Israelites. "When thou comest into the standing corn of thy neighbour, then thou mayest pluck the ears with thine hand";[3] but they were required to bring an offering at the same time. "Ye shall eat neither bread, nor parched corn, nor green ears, until the selfsame day that ye have brought an offering unto your God."[4] The disciples with our Lord were "going on the sabbath day through the grainfields; and his disciples began, as they went, to pluck the ears."[5] Green kernels of grain have been used as food for many centuries in the Orient.[6] Sometimes the grain was parched or roasted and

---

[1] Gen. 2 : 16 and 3 : 2, 6.   [2] *Researches*, vol. I, 492, 493.   [3] Deut. 23 : 25.
[4] Lev. 23 : 14.   [5] Mark 2 : 23.   [6] See 2 Kings 4 : 42.

CHURNING IN GOATSKIN, BEEROTH. P. 96

(Copyright by Underwood & Underwood, New York.)

eaten. Thus Boaz treated Ruth to parched grain,[1] and Abigail sent David similar food.[2]

Lane saw a similar practice in Egypt, where he found the diet of the common people was almost the same as that of the Israelites, three thousand years before. Of modern Egyptians he says, "Their food chiefly consists of bread made of millet, (or barley), milk, new cheese, eggs, small salted fish, cucumbers, and melons and gourds of a great variety of kinds, onions, and leeks, beans, chick-peas, lupins, the fruit of the black egg-plant, lentils, and dates. Most of the vegetables they eat in a crude (raw) state."[3] This closely resembles the list of foods, for which the Israelites in the desert longed. "We remember the fish, which we did eat in Egypt freely, the cucumbers, and the melons, and the leeks, and the onions, and the garlick."[4]

129. *Milk.*—Milk is also an extensive article of diet among Orientals, and has been so from the earliest historic times. Andrew A. Bonar notes the use of milk among Orientals: "Before leaving the poor villagers, we partook of the first fruits of the land in the shape of fine ripe apricots, and drank a little of a kind of sour milk, which is very cooling and pleasant when well prepared." It was this *leben* or sour milk that Jael offered to Sisera; "She brought him butter [thick milk] in a lordly dish."[5] The original word is of the same stem as that now used by Arabs to describe a form of milk. It is said that it is made by putting milk into an earthen jar, and letting it stand for a day. The taste is not unlike that of butter-milk; the Arabs say, "It makes a sick man well." Robinson was also treated to a similar diet in camp: "A large bowl of *leben* (sour milk) was already prepared for our breakfast; but as we were neither hungry nor thirsty, we left it to our attendants, by whom it was greedily devoured." Although butter made from churning cream is not unknown to Orientals, probably the "butter" often mentioned in the Old Testament is this *leben*, for in another passage, the drink offered to Sisera is called "milk."[6] So, also, "butter

[1] Ruth 2 : 14. [2] 1 Sam. 25 : 18. [3] *Modern Egyptians*, I., 242.
[4] Num. 11 : 5. [5] Judg. 5 : 25. [6] Judg. 4 : 19.

of kine, and milk of sheep" may designate a similar preparation.[1]

130. *Butter.*—Buckingham tells of the way he saw Arab
tribes make butter. "The milk is placed in a goat's skin, which
is filled as full as possible, and then tied to the mouth; after which
it is rolled or shaken on the ground, by a woman who sits
before it, this operation continuing for several hours on each
skin, till butter is formed from the milk, when the bag or skin
is untied, and the two parts separated from each other."
Burckhardt tells how the Bedouins, who are extremely fond of
butter, make it from the milk of goats or sheep. They put the
milk into a large pan, over a slow fire, adding a little sour milk.
The milk separates and is then put into the goat's skin, which is
tied to one of the tent poles and for one or two hours constantly
moved backward and forward. The mass coagulates, has the
water squeezed out, and the so-called "butter" is put into
another skin. Sometimes they place that over the fire again,
throw in a handful of dried wheat, boil and skim and drain
through a bag of camels' hair. The thick substance is then dried
in the sun, or used as *semen*, a kind of hard butter. There are
many allusions in Scripture to this kind of "butter," thus,
"The churning of milk bringeth forth butter."[2] As a picture
of prosperity, the prophet declares that a man for "the abundance of milk that they shall give, he shall eat butter," and in the
glory of the New Kingdom it is said, "Butter and honey shall
he eat."[3] This product of milk is also sometimes called
"cheese." Telling of the afflictions which tested him, Job
said, "Hast thou not . . . curdled me like cheese?"[4] And
David was sent by his father to carry "ten cheeses" to the
captain of the army where his brothers were soldiers.[5]

131. *Bread.*—It will give us some idea of the large place
peculiar forms of food, and the taking of it, held in Oriental
life, to know that "eat" or "eating" occurs upward of eight
hundred times in the Scriptures, and that "bread" occurs

---

[1] Deut. 32 : 14; Job 20 : 17 and 29 : 6.   [2] Proverbs 30 : 33.   [3] Isaiah 7 : 15, 22.
[4] Job. 10 : 10.   [5] 1 Sam. 17 : 18; see 2 Sam. 17 : 29.

about four hundred times, and "meat" (meaning food in general) about two hundred times, and "corn," referring to all kinds of small grain, about a hundred times.

Bread is the staple diet in an Oriental meal. Prof. Post found that "with the bread a man laps up his soup, or grasps and enfolds his meat, or dips up his honey. In the loaf of bread are wrapped the olives and cheese, and morsels of figs or dates or other food." "It constitutes half of a dinner, and nearly all of breakfast and lunch" in the East. The grain or substance from which bread can be made usually indicates the class to which the family belongs. Wheat is used only by the better class of peasants. A family that has attained to the wheat-bread level is well up in the scale of comfort. Bread from barley or millet is used by the poorer class. Barley loaves or bread is often noted in Scripture; thus "a cake of barley bread tumbled into the host of Midian" as in the frightened dream of a soldier.[1] The lad had "five barley loaves," which Jesus used to feed the 5000 men in the desert.[2]

132. *Flour Unbolted.*—The crushed grain or flour is unbolted, the coarser bran is sifted out by a coarse hair-cloth sieve, made by gypsies. The grain is ground in a mortar, or in a stone hand-mill; mixed into dough, rolled out into circular thin loaves, like cakes, and baked on a hot stone, or in a clay oven. The loaves are about six inches in diameter, and from one-third to one-half an inch thick. Sometimes a few seeds are sprinkled over the loaf. The "fitches" mentioned in Isaiah 28 : 27, a species of black cummin, is a coarse seed resembling our fennel. When first baked the loaf, or cake, puffs up, and becomes a flattened spheroid filled with air. The top and bottom crusts are crisp and quite thin. The loaves collapse when cold. This flat, thin loaf, rough of surface, would resemble a flat stone. Hence the allusions of our Lord, to giving a stone for bread. "If his son shall ask him for a loaf, will give him a stone?"[3]

133. *Kamaj.*—Another form of bread is called *markook.*

[1] Judg. 7 : 13.   [2] John 6 : 9.
[3] Matt. 7 : 9; see also Matt. 4 : 3; Luke 4 : 3; 11 : 11.

This is made like the former loaf, which is called *kamaj*, but is larger, fifteen to eighteen inches in diameter, and about half the thickness. This is baked in a hollow barrel-like domestic oven, called *tannoor*. The oven is built of stone and plastered inside with clay; has a hole at the bottom for the draught, and is open at the top for putting in and taking out the bread. When the loaf or dough is wet it sticks to the sides of the oven, but when it begins to dry and brown it loosens, and sometimes falls into the fire. The women acquire great skill in twirling the loaves off the side of the oven and out of its mouth just as they are nicely done, rarely burning their hands and arms. Again, the bread may be baked upon a convex iron plate, under which a fire is kindled, producing a dry and inferior sort of bread.

134. *Nutrition.*—As illustrating the importance of bread as an article of diet, Burckhardt declares that his native helpers walked five hours a day, and were sustained on a piece of dry, black bread, about one and a half pounds' weight, which was their only food for the twenty-four hours of each day.[1] Our Lord declared that man should not live by bread alone, as it seems many Orientals think to do.[2] On coarse bread loaves, resembling stones, Prof. Palmer humorously says of the bread he saw daily doled out to the monks of St. Catherine's on Mt. Sinai; they were of decidedly stony character. "One of these loaves I brought back with me; an eminent geologist pronounced it a piece of metamorphic rock, containing fragments of quartz embedded in amorphous paste." Palmer adds, "No decently brought up ostrich could swallow one without endangering his digestion for the term of his natural life" (p. 61). This well illustrates the coarseness of the crushed grain, and that gravel sometimes remains mixed with it when carelessly fanned or winnowed. Compare Luke 11: 11 with Matt. 3: 12, the latter showing how thoroughly the coming Messiah would use the "fan" to clean his grain.

135. *Grain Pits.*—Joseph's order for his meal was, "set on

[1] See Robinson, *Researches*, II, 118.   [2] Matt. 4 : 4; Deut. 8 : 3; Luke 4 : 4.

bread," as when his brethren cast him into a pit, "they sat
down to eat bread." And Moses was invited to "eat bread,"
for in each case that was the chief food at the meal.[1] Raised
bread is now made by "leaven" or a form of yeast, as it was
in olden times. And unleavened cakes and bread made with
simple flour and water or oil are still widely used and relished
by the nomadic tribes of the East, and in the desert where
Moses and the Israelites ate their "unleavened cakes."[2]

136. *Cooking.*—The Orientals are fond of dishes boiled,
roasted, or fried, but baked dishes are not popular with the
peasants of Palestine now.

The natives consider the lentil a nourishing food, made into
soup, as we use dried peas. In Palestine also the squash, cabbage, cauliflower, lettuce, beet, parsnip, bean, pea, onion, garlick,
leek, radish, mallow, and egg-plant are common articles of
diet. Prof. Grant says of the egg-plant, there are so many
ways of preparing it; "Should a woman say to her husband
during the egg-plant season, 'I know not what to provide for
dinner,' he has a sufficient cause for divorcing her."[3]

137. *"Mashee."*—There is also a great variety of preparations of food, called by the natives *mashshy* (or *mashee*), meaning "stuffed." A dish of this kind is made of cabbage, the
leaves being rolled, and each leaf stuffed with finely chopped
mutton, suet, and grain; either rice or barley, with a little
celery and spice. The leaf is then rolled like a cigar, and a
number of them laid in a kettle for boiling. Grape leaves are
also used in a similar manner. Another dish is made of young
marrows, like cucumbers, stuffed and fried in hot butter in a
pan. But the principal stuffed dish is made with egg-plant,
served with *leben* sauce or with lemon juice. Caraway, anise,
thyme, and mint are used in seasoning, as well as salt. The
favorite form of cooking is to fry in fat or *semen*, olive oil, or an
oil made from simsim seeds. The carob pod (Luke 15:16)
is eaten raw, or if green may be cooked with milk. It is said

[1] Gen. 37 : 25; 43 : 31; Ex. 2 : 20; 1 Sam. 28 : 22.
[2] Ex. 12 : 39; Lev. 2 : 4; 7 : 12; 8 : 26; Num. 6 : 19; Josh. 5 : 11.
[3] *Peasantry*, p. 83.

to have a flavor similar to that of sweetened chocolate. Locusts are in great variety, and in Palestine they are not an uncommon article of diet; they are eaten fried or roasted. Prof. Grant tells of the tenacity to life of these insects. "A man in great haste caught a locust, and holding it by the legs, roasted it over a fire, not waiting long before he put it in his mouth, but fearing it would burn him, he delayed shutting his teeth on it, and when the grasp of his fingers loosed, away went the locust," which gave rise to the proverb, "Better at escaping than a locust."

138. *Locusts.*—The diet of John the Baptist was locusts and wild honey.[1] Fruits were also freely used, and are abundant in variety and quantity in Oriental lands. Grapes, figs, apricots, and pomegranates are common fruits. These fruits are dried and used freely during the winter season. Grapes are mashed and pressed. From them is made *dibs,* a thick pasty substance or sometimes thin like our thick molasses. Honey is also prepared and kept in similar form.

139. *Wine.*—The Moslems in the East do not, as a rule, drink wine. It is forbidden them by their religion, but some of them break over. Intoxication is gaining ground, even among the Moslems, where they have come in contact with Western civilization. Rev. Charles A. S. Dwight speaks of drinking as greatly on the increase in the seaboard towns of the Levant. "A vile concoction, the basis of which is methylic alcohol, is consumed in large quantities under the name of *raku.*" A recent resident in Palestine tells of a Moslem girl whose brother had fallen under the habit, and she aimed forcibly to picture his abject dissipation by saying: "Why, my brother drinks like a Christian." On the other hand, a Moslem governor not long ago invited an Englishman to dine, with the apology that his religion would not allow him to offer wine. When informed that his guest was an abstainer, the governor exclaimed with surprise "And he is a Chistian!" Prof. Post says of Syria, that "half the population, the Moslems, are

[1] Matt. 3 : 4; Mark 1 : 6.

ORIENTALS FEASTING, BEEROTH.   P. 102

(Copyright by Underwood & Underwood, New York.)

VILLAGE OVEN.   P. 98

(Vester & Co.)

total abstainers on principle; of the Christian population, more than half are abstainers in practice. Wine is seldom seen on the table, although very cheap, and of excellent quality. Arack and brandy, with the addition of anise oil, is used by few of the people."

140. *Diet and Meals.*—Oriental meals are usually quite simple, not as frequent, and not served at as exact hours as with us. They vary also in character and in the variety of food served in different lands of the East.

Coffee, or some substitute, comes early in the morning. The first meal is not usually taken until the middle of the forenoon. It is often nothing more than bread and coffee, or bread and onions, with a bit of fish in the season.[1] In ancient times the Orientals had a meal near noon. Thus, Abraham prepared a mid-day meal for three angels, and Joseph made ready a meal at noon for his brothers.[2] The reapers of Boaz ate about mid-day also.[3] The chief meal is at evening. Thus, the Passover was eaten at evening,[4] or between two evenings, being the Paschal lamb with bitter herbs. But flesh food now is a luxury in most Oriental lands, and is used by the peasants and common people in Syria only on special occasions.

141. *Wash Before Eating.*—Before eating Orientals take a pitcher or ewer of water and a clean basin.[5] One pours water on his hands, held over the basin, to wash them. Orientals would think it untidy and disgraceful to pour water into the basin, and wash in the same water that has been fouled by the dirt already washed from the hands, as Europeans do. The basin often has a concave cover, perforated with holes, so that the dirty water from the hands runs through out of sight. The same water never touches the hands a second time.

142. *Why Wash.*—It is needful to wash the hands before and after a meal, for knives, forks, and spoons are unknown

[1] John 21 : 4–13.   [2] Gen. 18 : 1; 43 : 16, 25.   [3] Ruth 2 : 14.
[4] Ex. 12 : 6.   [5] 2 Kings 3 : 11.

to native Orientals. Their fingers are freely used for serving, separating, and conveying food to the mouth. So it is said, "all the Jews except they wash their hands oft [literally 'washing with the fist,' showing how they washed their hands] they eat not."[1] Hence, the Pharisee "marveled" that Jesus "had not first washed before dinner" [or breakfast].[2]

143. *Dining Furniture.*—Chairs, sofas, and high tables are not found in native Oriental dwellings. The country people eat out of one large common dish, placed in the middle of the room, or upon a raised platform at the side. The dish is put either on the floor or on a low round table, about one foot high and five or six feet in diameter. The men squat around this low table on the floor, or on mats, or rugs, curling their feet under them. It is not polite for them to show their feet. In Moslem lands the women never eat with the men.

144. *Place of Honor.*—The place of honor at the table is at the right hand of the father or master of the household.[3] Should a stranger appear, or pass, he would be invited to eat. An Oriental household aims to be always prepared for an unexpected guest. It was always a disgrace not to be prepared. Hence the urgency of the man who waked his neighbor to borrow three loaves for a guest.[4] Usually grace is said before and after the meal. Thus, the prophet Samuel declared to Jesse, "We will not sit down till he [David, the youngest son] come."[5] If a seer or prophet was present, the people waited for him to bless the food. So the maidens told Saul, who was inquiring for the seer, that they knew he was in the city, "for the people will not eat until he come, because he doth bless the sacrifice."[6] Lane found that in Egypt each person bares his right arm to the elbow by tucking up the hanging end of his sleeve. Before he begins to eat, "each one says after the master of the house, 'in the name of God' or 'praise Allah,' 'God be praised.'"

145. *Chief Dish.*—The common dish from which all eat

---

[1] Mark 7 : 3; Matt. 15 : 2.   [2] Luke 11 : 38.
[3] See Matt. 20 : 23; 25 : 34; Acts 2 : 33; Heb. 1 : 3.
[4] Luke 11 : 5–8.   [5] 1 Sam. 16 : 11.   [6] 1 Sam. 9 : 13.

is in the center; bread in round thin cakes or loaves will be laid on the knee of each person. With torn bits of bread, formed into a spoon, each dips into the dish filled with barley, lentil, or other soup, thickened with cracked grain or flour, in which may be floating balls of rice, bits of chicken, or mutton, or, more often, some kind of fruit, deftly carries food to the mouth without losing a drop, and devours spoon and all each time. Bits of meat are torn off with the fingers. The bread takes the place of spoons, and with it they scoop up sauces, soups, gravies, and any partially liquid dish with ease if not always with grace. The fingers are used for forks and knives also.

146. *The Guest.*—The mouthfuls are usually large, the food thickly garnished with rich sauces, and plentifully dripping with fat. If an unexpected guest comes in, the master of the household sweeps his long fingers into the common dish, to fish out some dainty morsel, and, putting his hand on the guest's shoulder, begs him to open his mouth wide, and take this morsel for his sake, or to "praise God." He begs him not to leave his tent or dwelling hungry, and this he may repeat many times over. Sometimes it may be, a covenant of friendship is proposed to be formed with the chance stranger. Then the master selects an enormous morsel, and while the stranger is wrestling with this, another chunk is quickly fished out, and thrust into the open mouth after the first. But it is no breach of delicate etiquette to hold one's hand over the mouth, and the other over the stomach, and with suspicious contortions, to suck in one's breath, and to smack the tongue, or to make sundry gurgling sounds, indicating a serious struggle to retain the food.[1] Irby and Mangles tell of an Arab Sheikh, who had a chance rare treat of roasted partridges brought him, and insisted, "as a mark of distinction, on throwing a leg and a wing to each of us."

147. *Desserts.*—The desserts, if any, at the ordinary meal

---

[1] See Trumbull, *Oriental Life*, 92; Wad El-Ward, *Palestine*, 53; Irby and Mangles, *Travels*, 263.

consist of fruit, fresh, dried, or crushed, or of *leben* and honey, or fig paste.

After the meal, tidy men and Moslems wash the mouth, teeth, and mustache, using soap freely, as is rather necessary. The Moslems turn over what is left of the contents of the common dish and any scraps of the meal for their women to eat. Coffee is universally served. The men smoke pipes, the *narghileh*, and chat together at the conclusion of the meal. There is little conversation ordinarily during the meal. Business, social chat, and all important matters come after the feast, and over the coffee, or more commonly, over the *narghileh* (pipe).

The Morsel and Sop.—A Sheikh of a wild desert-tribe once made a feast for Dr. Cyrus Hamlin. The Sheikh, with long bony fingers, swept into the common great dish before them for a delicious morsel. Finding it, he motioned to his guest to open his mouth, and dropped the morsel into it. Then he asked, "Do you know what I have done?" Dr. Hamlin replied, "Yes, indeed, you have given me the daintiest bit in that dish." The Sheikh with chagrin said: "You are wide of the sign. By that morsel we are brothers. I am now pledged to defend you to the last drop of blood in my veins, while you are in my territory."

Apply this to interpret the sop to Judas.[1] Judas was a guest of his Master. But he had forfeited his friendship by conspiracy. Jesus would give Judas a pledge of love. So the choice morsel was selected from the common dish and given to Judas, a sign that the Lord would forgive and call him back from his base betrayal. How this lifts the incident, otherwise trivial, into the highest spiritual significance! Pointing out the traitor to John was merely incidental, not the main purpose of giving the morsel to Judas, as it is commonly, but erroneously understood. This brings the incident into harmony with the most ancient and significant of Oriental customs.

[1] John 13 : 26.

SMOKING NARGHILEH.   P. 104

BUSINESS AND SOCIAL CONFERENCE AFTER ORIENTAL FEAST.

(*Copyright by Underwood & Underwood, New York.*)

XV.

DRESS AND ORNAMENTS.

148. *Costume Healthful.*—To any person of wide observation the native Oriental costume will be thought more graceful, if not more artistic and modest, than most of our European and American styles of dress. If any one questions this statement, he will be convinced should he see an Oriental peasant decked out in the highest fashion of Western dress-making. Tourists may smile at the simplicity of dress of the native man or woman of the East, because it is new and to him unfamiliar, but there is little doubt of the costume being more healthful, as well as more simple, than ours. Nor need we think them untidy or lacking in comfort because they dispense with some articles of dress which we deem essential. The climate often calls for a different costume for comfort. Thus, they count stockings an unsanitary snare. The native women seldom wear shoes in the dwelling or village lest they be laughed at, while women with us would not go without them for fear of ridicule. Men wear large roomy shoes or sandals. On rough roads the women wear the same kind of shoe as the men, especially in Syria.

149. *Turban and Aba.*—The most conspicuous article of dress among the Orientals is the turban, called by various names. This cap or covering for the head comes handy for several purposes to the native Oriental. He not only uses it for a head dress, but for a barley measure to measure grain, and for a nose bag when feeding his donkey. The most important article of dress is the cloak, sometimes called the *aba*. This is a large mantle or garment completely covering the wearer. He uses it for this purpose in the day time, as a rug when he sits down, as a mat for his visitors at home, which is a high honor, and as a blanket under which he sleeps at night.

For this reason, when a man gave his coat as a pledge, it must be returned to him at sundown, because this cloak or coat is his bedding.[1]

150. *Kuftan.*—The Jewish rabbis have a tradition growing out of this command: "On the Sabbath day, if you use or call a coat a bed, it remains a bed all that day, and a man must not carry it." For it would break their interpretation of the law of the Sabbath.[2] It was either this coat, chiton-kuftan, outer garment, or possibly the tunic (under garment), for which the Roman soldiers cast lots.[3] The coat is now sometimes made without a seam, a mixture of wool and camels' hair. The so-called "tunic" is a long cloth skirt reaching from the shoulders nearly to the ankles, like a bath robe in modern times.[4] Sometimes the natives go upon the street with the tunic, and a short jacket over it, having a sash or shawl as a girdle around the loins.

151. *The Girdle.*—The girdle is not only a picturesque article of dress with the Orientals, but it may also indicate the position and office of the wearer. It is sometimes used to signify power and strength.[5] The laborer and the poorer classes use rawhide or rope for a girdle; the better classes use some woolen or camels' hair sashes, woven of different widths. The more richly dressed persons have a girdle of silk in bright colors; in fact, the Orientals delight in strong colors, not only for the girdle, but for other portions of their dress. The women wear long garments reaching to the feet, and a girdle of silk or wool, usually having all the colors of the rainbow, and with a fringe hanging from the waist nearly to the ankles. Sometimes they have on the breast ornaments of gold, brass, silver, or colored stones or gems, or a breast-plate of silver and gold coins.

152. *String of Coins.*—The head-dress is a cap (when the woman is married), flat on top, covered with silver or gold coins, which indicates her wealth. The loss of one of these

---

[1] Ex. 22 : 26, 27.   [2] Talmud.   [3] John 19 : 23.
[4] Luke 6 : 29.   [5] 2 Sam. 22 : 40; Isaiah 11 : 5; Jer. 13 : 1; Eph. 6 : 14.

coins would be a calamity, hence the force of the parable of our Lord, "What woman, having ten pieces of silver, if she lose one piece, doth not light a lamp, and sweep the house, and seek diligently until she find it?"[1] The costume of women, in general, is distinguished from that worn by men by the head-dress, veil, ornaments, and the style of wearing other portions of the attire.

153. *Dress in Africa.*—Laborde, in his travels among the Bedouins of Northern Africa, found the two chief garments to be a kind of "coat" and a "mantle." The first was, in fact, an under garment like a shirt with sleeves, and was bound by a leathern girdle such as Elijah and John the Baptist wore.[2] The outer garment, called *aba*, or large mantle, has "one corner made fast to the girdle, and permits the rest to fall in majestic folds from the shoulders." Lane describes the dress of the middle and higher classes of modern Egyptians as quite the same as their ancestors had for centuries. They wear *libas* or full drawers, like very baggy trousers of linen or cotton, fastened by a running string or band around the waist, and reaching below the knees. Next they have a shirt, with full sleeves made of linen, cotton, or silk, of a loose open texture. Over this they wear the *soodeyree* or vest of striped silk or cotton, and then put on the *kuftan*, a long garment reaching to the ankles, with flowing long sleeves, so that the hands may be concealed in them. Sometimes a loose robe or outer mantle, called *joobeh*, may be worn, an outside rich robe or some loose flowing robe of cloth like the *kuftan*, but more ample. This robe is for state occasions or some great ceremony. The head-dress or turban is of many kinds, colors, and sizes. But a *shereef* only (follower of the prophet) may wear a green turban or bright green attire. The shoes are pointed, turning up at the toes, and of thick leather. Often two pairs of shoes are worn, one within the other, but no stockings. The *murkoob*, or outer shoes, are taken off on entering a mosque or walking upon rugs, but the *medz* or inner

[1] Luke 15 : 8.   [2] Kings 1 : 8; Matt. 3 : 4.

shoe is not removed. A pipe goes with the Egyptian wherever he goes, except, perhaps, to his place of worship. The turban of the peasant may be a white, red, or yellow shawl several yards long, deftly wound into a huge cap or head-gear.

154. *Dress in Syria.*—Prof. Post tells us that religious personages in Asia, such as the great lights of Islam, wear long, loose, flowing robes, often lined with fur reaching to the feet, reminding us of what our Lord said to his disciples; "Beware of the scribes which love to go in long clothing." [1] "It is not uncommon in Syria to wear over the whole dress a loose, long, bag-like garment, sometimes also called *aba*, and with a hole for the neck and arms, to protect from dust and mud." Sometimes also "two coats," tunics, or mantles were worn as a mark of elegance—a habit forbidden the disciples.[2] Again, if a person has only a tunic or under garment on, he is often said to be "naked," as in our Lord's day.[3] Thus, it is said of Peter that he girt his fisher's coat about him, for he was naked.[4] So it is said of Saul he "lay down naked all that day," because he had stripped off his clothes, that is, he had thrown off his outer garment.[5] And Isaiah is described as "walking naked and barefoot" when he had put sackcloth from off him, that sackcloth being worn over the coat or under garment.[6]

155. *In Walking.*—The flowing robes interfered with walking, so if one is said to gird up his loins, he is preparing for a walk or for work. Peasants take off shoes also when rainy.

An "old garment" of an Oriental is described by a keen observer "as a series of holes with the borders worn out." [7]

The hopelessness of mending such a garment with new cloth is a forcible illustration of our Lord's parable.[8]

156. *Signet.*—As the Orientals are fond of bright colors in dress, so they are also fond of ornaments, both men and women. Thus, Tamar asked Judah to give her "Thy signet, and thy bracelets, and thy staff." [9] The signet ring identified the owner, and attested any letter or writing which he might make.

[1] Mark 12 : 38.   [2] Mark 6 : 9.   [3] Mark 14 : 51; Matt. 25 : 36.
[4] John 21 : 7.   [5] 1 Sam. 19 : 24.   [6] Isaiah 20 : 2.
[7] S. S. World, 1882.   [8] Mark 2 : 21; Matt. 9 : 16; Luke 5 : 6.   [9] Gen. 38 : 18.

Thus, Pharaoh gave his signet ring to Joseph as a sign of authority.[1] Ahasuerus gave his ring unto Haman.[2] The carefulness with which this signet ring was guarded is well illustrated by the declaration of Jehovah, "Though . . . the king of Judah were the signet upon my right hand, yet would I pluck thee thence."[3] This signet ring was the valid mark of authority and confidence. "Almost every person who can afford it has a seal ring, even though he be a servant," says Lane of modern Egyptians. Dr. Perkins found the same ornament worn in Persia, and it was common not only to Egyptians and Asiatics, but with Greeks and Romans, as it is with Turks to this day.

157. *Nose Rings.*—Earrings and nose rings are also special delights to Orientals. Harmer tells us "In almost all the East the women wear rings in their noses, in the left nostril, which is bored low down in the middle. These rings are of gold, and have commonly two pearls and one ruby between, placed in the ring. I never saw a girl or young woman, in Arabia or Persia, who did not wear a ring after this manner in her nostril." Layard describes an Arab lady with a prodigious gold ring, set with jewels of such ample dimensions that it covered her mouth, and had to be removed when the lady ate.[4] Bruce describes a similar nose ring upon a lady, and adds, "I think she must have breathed with great difficulty."

158. *Earrings.*—Earrings were of like extraordinary size. Thus Layard says of a woman of the East, "Hanging from each ear, and reaching to her waist, was an enormous ring of gold, terminating in a tablet of the same material, carved and ornamented with four turquoises." Bruce describes the Queen of Nubia with earrings reaching to her shoulders.

159. *Chains and Mirrors.*—Gold chains are still worn with necklaces, bracelets, armlets, anklets, and metal mirrors, as they were three thousand years ago.[5] Thus, Pharaoh put a gold chain around Joseph's neck, and Daniel was clothed in

---

[1] Gen. 41 : 42.
[2] Esther 3 : 10.
[3] Jer. 22 : 24.
[4] *Nineveh*, I, 101.
[5] Gen. 41 : 42; Dan. 5 : 29; See Song of Sol. 1 : 10.

a similar chain of gold by Belshazzar. And Jehovah, describing his love and his blessings upon Jerusalem, declared, "I deck thee also with ornaments, and I put bracelets upon thy hands, and a chain on thy neck. And I put a ring upon thy nose, and earrings in thine ears, and a beautiful crown upon thy head."[1] Layard speaks of "loud jingling made by the loose silver rings on the wrists and ankles," which illustrated the prophet's statement about the daughters of Zion "walking and mincing as they go, and making a tinkling with their feet."[2] Dr. Arthur J. Brown tells of the intense curiosity of Korean women over Mrs. Brown's American dress. They thronged about her, feeling of her shoes and dress, trying on her hat, wanting to undo her hair, trying to take off her wedding ring, and rubbed her cheek to see whether her complexion would come off, all the while excitedly jabbering and laughing at so strange an object.[3]

160. *Korean Dress.*—The Korean's dress is so distinctive, as well as Oriental, that you cannot mistake him among any number of other nationalities. If his hat is white, he is betrothed; if he has a thin white cloth over his nose and mouth, he is in mourning; if his hair is in a top knot, he is married. Usually his garments are white, his hat with a small round crown, a broad brim of black thread or horse-hair, is tied under his chin.[4]

Of the Siamese in the far East it is said, "he is sleek and well-fed, and wears more gold and silver ornaments than any other native of Asia. Naked children playing in the street are decked with silver anklets, wristlets, and necklaces."[5]

---

[1] Ezek. 16 : 11, 12.   [2] Isaiah 3 : 16–23.
[3] See "The Nearer and Farther East," p. 266.   [4] Ibid., p. 264.
[5] Ibid., p. 167.

XVI.

DISEASES AND MEDICINE.

161. *Evil Spirits.*—To heal the sick among Orientals is a part of the work of the priest, the dervish, or the holy man in the mind of most of the natives. This comes from the belief that a large number of the disorders of the body are a punishment for, or a consequence of, sins committed by the sufferer or his relatives. In a large number of cases these disorders are attributed to the influence of evil spirits. Hence, a pious man is, in their view, the proper person to treat disease. For the most part, Oriental methods of dealing with physical disorders are what we would call the methods of the charlatan. The *hakim,* or medicine man, like the dervish, uses charms, amulets, incantations, as well as herbs, for effecting a cure. Of the diseases common now in Syria, Prof. Grant names fevers, digestive troubles, influenzas, rheumatism, and diseases of the eye.

162. *Leprosy.*—Thomson found leprosy common in Jerusalem and in different parts of Syria, and declares that it still cleaves to Damascus, the city of Naaman. On the other hand, Mr. Haddad, himself a native of Damascus, says the people of Damascus have never known natives of their city to be afflicted with leprosy. There is a "hospital" for lepers in Damascus, which tradition says was founded by Naaman, the Syrian. Another in Jerusalem, founded by a German woman, is managed by Moravians. It is a great house, with separate rooms, and meals are served to the lepers separately, or two or three of a family together.

163. *Dr. Post on Leprosy.*—Prof. Post, out of a lifetime of medical practice in Syria, and after special study of leprosy, tells me he is confident that the leprosy of the East, now known as *Elephantiasis Arabum,* is not the leprosy of Leviticus and other Scriptures. He holds that the so-called *Aleppo button* or, as the

Arabs call it, "*year boil*" is often followed by tetter or *lepra vulgaris*, "a spreading scabby eruption following much the course described in Lev. 13 : 18–23." He asserts that none of the well-known signs and appearances of the greater leprosy are described in Lev. 13 and 14. In his opinion the spreading of the chronic form of *lepra vulgaris* "is a more visible and disgusting disease than *elephantiasis* (modern leprosy), is very intractible, incurable by ordinary medical means, loathsome to the beholder, and suitable as a legal and ceremonial illustration of moral uncleanliness." Thus, he adds, "the description of the healing of Naaman looks more like the cleaning off of an eruption than the remaking of carious bone and re-creation of lost members." So, too, "Gehazi went out as white as snow" is an exact description of a man with *lepra*, and not at all accurate of a victim of *elephantiasis*. Miriam also became as " white as snow." [1] This *lepra* is not an uncommon disease in Syria now.

164. *Leprosy in Palestine.*—P. J. Baldensperger, in the Palestine Quarterly, 1900, takes the same view as Prof. Post, "The leprosy now found in Palestine is not the disease so often mentioned in the Bible. The modern leprosy is different, and is only contagious if the matter from a leper be brought into the blood or into the wound of another."

Mr. Haddad found a young man in a pitiful condition, a case of epilepsy probably. "His eyes bloodshot and glaring; fiercely biting his tongue, frothing at the mouth, bleeding at the nose, and tossing about unconsciously. He tried to restore him by bathing his face in cooling water and giving him inhalations of ammonia. One of the crowd, looking on, said, 'Your trouble is in vain. Many physicians have tried to cure him and have failed. He is possessed of an evil spirit.'" [2] Cripples are also numerous throughout Syria and the East. They are still seen at the entrances to mosques and churches, often five or six lame persons begging for bread.

---

[1] 2 Kings 5 : 10, 14, 27; Num. 12 : 10.
[2] Compare Matt. 4 : 24; 8 : 6; 17 : 15; Mark 9 : 18; Luke 9 : 39.

165. *Demon Possession.*—The Christian sects do not, as a rule, now believe in demoniacal possessions, but some people in Syria still believe that demons enter men, and they try to drive them out by prayers, readings from sacred books, beating the possessed one with shoes, and other ways. Dr. Nevius found a similar belief widely prevalent throughout China, and, after a long experience and careful examination of a great number of cases, he reluctantly was forced to the conviction that there were well-established cases of such possessions now among the Chinese similar to those noted in our Lord's day in Syria.

166. *Barber-doctors.*—Physicians and medical science were known in Egypt five thousand years ago, but Lane found that modern Egyptian medical and surgical practitioners were mostly barbers, miserably ignorant of the science which they professed and unskilful in practice. In fact, it is widely true now that among the lower classes of Orientals everybody attempts to give medical advice and to prescribe for the sick. Van Lennep says that the description of Herodotus is an excellent sketch of the state of things at the present day in all parts of the land, except that the sick man remains at home.[1]

167. *Shepherd-doctors and Dogs.*—Out of his experience as a native, Mr. Haddad declares that shepherds, being in a habit of bandaging the broken legs of their sheep and goats, are asked to bandage the bones of people, for native physicians are not to be found in Syria, except those recently trained in Beirut College and similar mission schools. "The so-called Egyptian eye disease is prevalent in Syria, due to the sandy dust in hot weather, and to the eating of green fruits, especially green figs, without being careful to clean their hands and eyes, and the carrying of foul matter by flies, thus transferring the germs of disease from inflamed eyes to sound ones." He further notes that the poor who are afflicted with sores, expose them purposely to the dogs to be licked, trusting their saliva will help to cure them.

168. *Feeding Lepers.*—Lepers may still be seen frequently

[1] See Herodotus, Book I, chapter 197.

8

near the town of Nablūs (ancient Shechem).   Mr. Haddad found many of them by the road, who cried to him and his companions from a distance. They have no home. If they had relatives they could not live with them. They sleep in caves or in cabins erected by themselves or by charity, and in the ruins of old buildings. Food is given to them by the people, who leave it near by for them to come and get after the givers have gone away.

A malignant form of malarial fever attacks with fatal results nomadic Arab tribes, who come into the marshes and low ground in the Jordan valley.

169. *The Insane.*—The number of demented persons does not seem to be large in Syria; a few dangerous maniacs are sometimes chained in the houses of their friends. Some pretend to healing powers, generally Moslems, who wander around in coarse robes, almost naked, with a tin box for alms, and a spear, perhaps to protect themselves against dogs and wild beasts. "Their persons are never washed and their hair is long, matted, and filled with vermin. In fanatical outbreaks these dervishes take a leading and mischievous part."

170. *Oil and Honey Remedies.*—The Orientals regard honey as a remedy of great efficacy for many diseases of the stomach, the nerves, and even for healing broken bones.

The great remedy among Orientals is oil. It is not only used to restore weary limbs after a fight or violent exercise, and to set apart persons to sacred offices, but it is regarded as almost indispensable to keep one in health. Olive oil is esteemed the foremost of necessities. Orientals generally, and Moslems in particular, consider the olive a sacred tree, one of the trees of paradise, and that its oil is good for healing. It is mentioned 175 times in the Scriptures. The use of oil for the sick is commended: "Is any sick among you? let him call for the elders of the church; and let them pray over him, anointing him with oil in the name of the Lord."[1] When Jesus sent forth the twelve, it is said, "they cast out many demons, and

[1] James 5 : 14.

anointed with oil many that were sick, and healed them."[1]
The good Samaritan is represented in caring for the man who
fell among robbers, as binding up his wounds, "pouring in oil
and wine."[2] "The oil of the East," says Post, "is almost
wholly extracted from the olive." "There are, however, oils
used for food and medicine and arts, extracted from the ses-
ame, castor-bean, flax, and other plants. No animal oils seem
to have been used in Bible lands or times."

171. *Medicine-man.*—The *hakim*, or medicine-man, can
safely travel anywhere in the East. When he appears in a
village "the people gather together where he stops," says Mr.
Haddad, "some from idle curiosity, but many who are sick
for advice, and to be cured. The crowd follow him from house
to house, and from one village to another, not giving him time
to eat."

The reader will be struck with the close similarity of the
Oriental "hakim" to a description of the American Indian
medicine-man by Longfellow in Hiawatha:

> "Wandered eastward, wandered westward,
>   Teaching men the use of simples
>   And the antidotes for poisons,
>   And the cure of all diseases.
>   Thus was first made known to mortals
>   All the mystery of Medamin,
>   All the sacred art of healing."

172. *Sick Everywhere.*—Most of the diseases known in the
East now are the same as those of long ago. All travelers
in the Orient tell of the helpless cripples, the half-naked
wretched creatures, covered with sores, in misery lying at other
people's gates. Ophthalmia and fevers are widely prevalent.
Every traveler in Eastern lands has observed its serious and
widespread ravages. Thus, Mr. Baldensperger says of
Ramleh and Lydda, there was not a single family free from
eye-disease of one kind or another. "Out of a hundred boys
in the mission school, ninety-five had sore eyes or were wholly

[1] Mark 6 : 13.   [2] Luke 10 : 34.

or partially blind." Trumbull declares, "At Cairo the blind, or the sick, or the crippled sat at every street corner and on every square, and were laid at every mosque door, and were crying out for help or alms before every bazaar."

The "healing art" has been sadly lost in Egypt and even Assyria. The ancient oculists which Cambyses brought from Egypt, the dentists, the special medical experts of Pharaoh's time in diseases of the head, the digestive and the vital organs, have passed away, their art lost, and they have no successors there in modern times. Their sensible rules as to diet and the prevention of disease have also been lost.[1]

Dr. D. O. Allen affirms[2] that medical men among the Hindus practiced inoculation for small-pox long before it was known in Europe. They had long lists of remedies, mineral, vegetable, and chemical preparations, which were given, but often mixed with superstitious notions regarded as essential for their efficacy. The profession of medicine was and is confined to the same families for successive generations, the father handing down to his sons his knowledge, skill, books, and reputation. They were never skilled in surgery because of their imperfect knowledge of anatomy.

[1] See Kenrick, I, 290; Wilkinson, II, 355-358; Lane, I, 277; A. T. Clay, *Light On Old Testament*, 216.
[2] India, Ancient and Modern, p. 457.

XVII.

MOURNING AND BURIALS.

173. *Hysterical Display.*—Mourning in the East, like other customs, varies in different Oriental lands. Sometimes the mourners are hired, but they do not take the place of mourning by the relatives. Sometimes, also, the mourning begins before the person is actually dead. There are often formal exercises, with as much pomp and display as the condition of the sick or dying person will permit. The bereaved beat the breast, tear the hair, throw dust over their persons, fall in hysterical or cataleptic paroxysms, and in India the widow throws herself on the funeral pyre. To the Oriental the quiet, deep sorrow of the West seems cold and unfeeling.

174. *A Syrian Case.*—When death comes the wailing and violent emotions of the impulsive nations of the East are alarming and terrible to Western beholders. Prof. Post describes such a scene witnessed in his medical practice as an average example of the extravagant grief of Asiatics. "The patient had fallen into an old stone quarry, a depth of sixty feet, and suffered an injury of the spine. For a week the lower portions of the body had been paralyzed, and he had suffered in his whole body from the shock of the fatal injury. . . . As I sat watching, the wife, observing the anxiety of my countenance, fell on her knees at her husband's feet, and began to weep and beat her breast. In a few minutes the eyes became fixed, the breathing shallower, and the pulse was gone. The sister then burst into the room like a maniac, shrieking with anguish, and threw herself down by her brother's side, as he lay on his bed on the floor, seized his hand, and implored him to give her one look. Immediately, while he yet breathed, the crowd of women surged into the room and filled it with their loud wailings, tossing their arms in the most extravagant gesticulations.

The men pressed back the wife and sister, and endeavored to check the shrieks, until at least the sick man should have expired. Presently they too yielded to the infection and joined in the tumult. No voice of remonstrance or sympathy could be heard, and no strength of will or power of persuasion could restrain the wild mass which now filled the room and clogged the approaches to the house. The chief mourners tore their hair, rent their garments, beat their breasts, threw themselves wildly on the ground, invoked the dead, implored the bystanders, did everything but pray to God for patience and comfort. Little children added their songs and screams to the clamor, and I was glad to retire from the harrowing scene, and to reflect on the blessing of a calm trust in God and patient resignation to his utmost will. These wailings last for hours, and but for the speedy burial of the dead, would end most disastrously to the living. As it is, the chief mourners are often made ill by the violence of their grief."

Dr. F. J. Bliss, the explorer of Lachish, tells of a mourning delegation at the *mahal*, or mourning house, for a great man. As they approach, no matter how gaily they may have been chatting, they rush forward, handkerchiefs to face, sobbing, weeping, with demonstrations of great grief, going through these for perhaps the tenth time in the day.

175. *Death Shriek.*—Thus the late Dr. Amelia B. Edwards, the Egyptologist, describes her first experience in hearing this death shriek. "All at once we heard a sound like the far off wavering sound of many owls. It shrilled, swelled, wavered, dropped, and then died away, like the moaning of the wind at sea. We held our breath and listened. We never heard anything so wild and plaintive." Such a custom is alluded to by the prophet in bemoaning the desolations of Samaria, "For this will I lament and wail, I will go stripped and naked; I will make a wailing like the jackals, and a lamentation like the ostriches."[1] Another old prophet tells of the mourning over the desolations of Israel: "Wailing shall be in all the broad ways; and they shall say in all

[1] Micah 1 : 8, R. V.

the streets, Alas! alas! and they shall call the husband unto mourning, and such as are *skillful* in lamentation to wailing."[1] The mourning of women is also repeatedly mentioned, both in the Old Testament and in the New. Thus, the prophet breaks out, "Call for the mourning women, that they may come; and send for the cunning women, that they may come: and let them make haste, and take up a wailing for us, that our eyes may run down with tears, and our eyelids gush out with waters."[2]

176. *Lamentations.*—The calamity of being denied a proper burial finds a pathetic lament in the prophet's exclamation, "They shall not lament for him, saying, Ah, my brother! or, Ah, sister! they shall not lament for him, saying, Ah, lord! or Ah, his glory! He shall be buried with the burial of an ass, drawn and cast forth beyond the gates of Jerusalem."[3] But the most pathetic dirge of lament is that of David over his son, "The king . . . went up to the chamber over the gate, and wept: and as he went, thus he said, O my son Absalom! my son, my son Absalom! would God I had died for thee, O Absalom, my son, my son!"[4]

177. *Cries and Dirges.*—Sir J. Chardin speaks of the ungoverned and excessive grief of Eastern peoples, which he heard at Ispaham, when the mistress of the house died. "The moment she expired, all the family, to the number of twenty-five or thirty people, set up such a furious cry that I was quite startled." This happened in the middle of the night, and Chardin imagined that his own servants were actually murdered. "The suddenness of the outcry is terrifying, together with a shrillness and loudness which one cannot easily imagine." And Lane speaks of the same custom in Egypt, "Even before the spirit has departed, the women of the family raise the cries of lamentation, call *welweleh* or *wilwal;* uttering the most piercing shrieks and calling upon the name of the deceased. In Syria the custom also prevails at some remote villages, and the women singers chant the same song at funerals as the men singers often sing at marriage feasts. The dirge or death song

<hr>

[1] Amos 5 : 16.　　[2] Jer. 9 : 17, 18.　　[3] Jer. 22 : 18, 19.　　[4] 2 Sam. 18 : 33.

is mentioned by Lane as common in Egypt. The chant is in Arabic; this is a translation of the beginning of the chant:

> "The glory of him who createth every form,
>   And reduceth his servants by death,
> Who bringeth his creatures to nought with mankind,
>   They all shall lie in the graves,
> The absolute glory of the Lord of the East,
>   The absolute glory of the Lord of the West,
> The absolute glory of the creator of the two lights,
>   The sun and also the moon,
> His absolute glory; how bountiful is he!
>   His absolute glory; how gracious is he!
> His absolute glory; how great is he."

In Egypt this dirge is sung by a procession of boys who precede the body. Behind the body come female mourners, with hair disheveled, but concealed by the head veil, who are crying and shrieking, often aided by hired mourners, who likewise celebrate the praises of the deceased.

178. *Endangers Life.*—Even to this day in that region mourners are so violent in their emotions that often serious injury comes to the health and persons of the mourners. One physician says that the women especially beat their breasts in such a way as to develop tumors and bring on serious disease. They wail until they are so hoarse that they cannot speak, they fall fainting to the ground, and refuse to eat or sleep. The neighborhood of the house where the dead is resounds with the frantic cries of mourners, and professional mourners are hired to add their artificial wailings to the agony of real sorrow. No wonder the apostle reminds the Thessalonians that such sorrow is not born of Christian hope.[1]

179. *Burial.*—Burial usually takes place soon after death. Prof. Post says, "It seldom occurs more than ten hours after death, almost never on the succeeding day. The rapidity of decomposition, the excessive violence of grief, the reluctance of Orientals to allow the dead to remain long in the houses of the living explain what seems to us indecent haste." Notice

1 Thess. 4 : 13.

the case of Ananias and Sapphira.[1] So, too, the quickness with which the bodies of Nadab and Abihu were carried out of camp is in strict accordance with present Oriental custom.[2] The dead are often in their graves within two or three hours after death. Thus the dead son of the widow of Nain was carried outside the walls of the city, where Jesus and his disciples met the procession going to burial.[3] Tombs and cemeteries within the walls of a city were, and still are, repugnant to Oriental ideas.

180. *Wrapping the Body.*—Dr. Tristram, from his observations in Western Asia, says: "Interments always take place, at latest, on the evening of day of death, and frequently at night. There are, and can be, no elaborate preparations. The corpse is dressed in such clothes as were worn in life, and stretched on a bier, with a cloth thrown over it."[4]

A native of Syria states, "It is still the custom to wrap the dead. The face is covered with a napkin, the hands and feet are bound and swathed in cloths, usually of linen. This binding is sometimes by a napkin and sometimes by the corners of a sheet. The body is then placed on a bier, which has a pole at each corner, by means of which it is carried on the shoulders to the tomb." Christians use coffins, but this is quite a modern custom there. Moslems do not use them.

Prof. Grant adds,"Death, among the peasantry, is an occasion for long mourning. The body is wrapped and placed in the ground, and protected from the falling earth as well as may be by the use of stones. On the top of the grave the heaviest stones obtainable are packed, to make it difficult for hyenas to secure the body. It is customary to watch the grave many nights to keep these creatures away."[5]

181. *Spices in Burial.*—It is still common to place with the wrappings of the body spices and preparations to retard decomposition. Thus, the friends at Bethany wrapped the body of their brother Lazarus, and he came forth bound

[1] Acts 5 : 5, 6, 10.　　[2] Lev. 10 : 4.　　[3] Luke 7 : 12.
[4] Eastern Customs, p. 94.　　[5] Compare Job 21 : 32.

or wrapped in these linen clothes, with a napkin bound about
his head.[1]   Nicodemus also brought "a mixture of myrrh and
aloes, about an hundred pound weight," so they took the body
"of Jesus, and wound it in linen clothes with the spices, as the
manner of the Jews is to bury."   And Mary Magdalene and
two other women brought spices for the same purpose.[2]   This
is a very old custom, for Asa, the king, was laid "in the bed
which was filled with sweet odours and divers kinds of spices
prepared by the apothecaries' art."[3]   The widow's son at
Nain was carried out on a bier, not in a coffin.[4]

182. *Embalming.*—In Egypt, however, embalming the body
of the dead was a common custom for many centuries.   Long
before Jacob or Abraham visited it, the priests, or a special
class of persons, were trained in this art, as we know from the
embalmed bodies of the Pharaohs which have been recovered
in our time from those ancient tombs.   It was further the custom for the nearest relative to close the eyes of the dying.
Thus, it is said, "Joseph shall put his hand upon thine
(Jacob's) eyes."[5]   This clearly refers to that custom.   Joseph
closed the eyes of his father Jacob at death.   When Jacob died
"Joseph commanded his servants the physicians to embalm his
father."[6]   And Joseph when he died was also embalmed and
"put in a coffin (Sarcophagus) in Egypt."   The process of
embalming is too long to be cited here, but a description of it
may be found in Herodotus 2, 86, and in Wilkinson-Birch's
Ancient Egyptians, vol. iii, pp. 470–491.

Modern Egyptians do not thus prepare the body for burial;
according to Lane; they thoroughly wash the whole body,
sprinkle it with a mixture of pounded camphor and rose-water,
bind the ankles together, and place the hands upon the breast.
If a poor man, the body is wrapped in a piece or two of cotton
cloth; if of wealth, it is generally first wrapped in muslin, then
in cotton cloth of thicker texture, and lastly in a piece of striped
silk and cotton intermixed, or in a *kuftan* of similar material,

---

[1] John 11 : 44.   [2] John 19 : 39, 40; Mark 16 : 1; Luke 24 : 1.
[3] Chron. 16 : 14.   [4] Luke 7 : 14.   [5] Gen. 46 : 4.   [6] Gen. 50 : 2.

and over this is wrapped a Cashmere shawl. The body of a man of middle rank is clothed also with a *yelek*. The colors most approved are white and green, but any color is used excepting blue or what approaches to blue.[1]

183. *Rending the Garment.*—In some countries the first sign of grief is the rending of the garment of the living mourners. Dr. Tristram further says, "In preparing for burial the women whose special duty it was, would provide a cerecloth, and before wrapping the body in it, sprinkle spices in the folds, as in the case of our Lord's burial, to check decomposition in some slight degree." They then "dressed the deceased in his best outer garments, and laid him on a bier, a simple flat board, borne on two or three staves, by which the bearers carried it to the tomb." It must be remembered that the dress of the East was loose, so that by unfastening the girdle, the garments could be wrapped around the body, like a winding-sheet, so as to cover it from head to foot.

184. *At the Tomb.*—The burial places of Moslem, Jewish, and Christian peoples of the East are now quite distinct; in ancient times they were alike, in that each had their own family tombs, either a natural cave, prepared with stone shelves to receive the body, or hewn out of rock in the hill side, each tomb or sepulchre having many niches or *loculi*, in each one of which a body could be placed. No Jew could sell his burying place, and in China it was and is held to be a capital offense to disturb a tomb, no matter how ancient it might be.

185. *Weeping at Tomb.*—In Syria, as elsewhere also, there is a stated time for mourning at the tomb. The friends go to the tomb without ornaments, often with their hair disheveled, some of them with blackened faces, either with soot or with mud, some also with their oldest and poorest clothing, sitting in a circle, or together near the tomb, often breaking out also into a weird dirge-like song. In some parts of Syria it is the custom to visit the tomb thus on the third, seventh, and fortieth days, and one year after the burial. When the tomb was a cave or

[1] Lane, Modern Egyptians, vol. ii, pp. 288, 289.

dug out from some rock, the entrance was often closed by a
large round stone set up on its edge, and rolled in a groove in
front of the mouth of the tomb, so as to close it.   This stone
could also be secured by a strap and sealed.   In that case it
would be known if the stone had been disturbed.   Thus,
Pilate directed that the tomb of Joseph, in which the body of our
Lord was laid, should be closed and sealed, and made as secure
as the officials were able to make it.   "So they went, and made
the sepulchre sure, sealing the stone, the guard being with
them." [1]

186. *Tear Bottles.*—Another Oriental custom is the use of
tear bottles, to gather and preserve the tears of the mourners.
This custom prevailed in recent times in portions of Persia
and in parts of Polynesia.   Thus, Morier notes that in Persia,
"In some of their mournful assemblies, a priest goes about to
each person, at the height of his grief, with a piece of cotton in
his hand, with which he carefully collects the falling tears, and
then squeezes them into a bottle, preserving them with great
caution. . . . Some persons believe that when all medicines have
failed, a drop of tears, so collected, put into the mouth of the
dying, has been known to revive him."   The tears are also
used as a charm to ward off evil.   This practice was once more
widely common than at present.   For tear bottles are found in
many of the ancient tombs in Egypt and elsewhere throughout
the East.   This custom appears to be alluded to by the Psalmist, "Put thou my tears into thy bottle." [2]

187. *Yearly Mourning.*—The violent demonstration of grief
in the East goes so far as sometimes to lead to lacerations of
the body and a shedding of blood.   Thus a modern traveler
describes a celebration taking place annually in Persia to commemorate the death of the grandson of the prophet Mohammed:
"I have seen the most violent of them, as they vociferated *Ya
Hossein!* walk about the streets almost naked, with only their
loins covered, and their bodies streaming with blood by the
voluntary cuts they have given to themselves, either as acts of

[1] Matt. 27 : 66.   [2] Ps. 56 : 8.

love, anguish, or mortification." A similar custom was found by missionary Ellis in the South Sea Islands.[1] Beating their breasts in cadence to the chanting of one who stood in the center of the circle, and with whom they now and then joined their voices in chorus, is a universal act in mourning. The breast is made bare for that purpose by unbuttoning the top of the undergarment.

188. *Cutting Forbidden, Wailing.*—Cutting of the flesh for the dead was forbidden by the Mosaic law.[2] Excessive wailing and mourning for the dead seem to be often alluded to in Scripture. Thus, David rent his clothes, and mourned, and wept, and fasted for Saul and for Jonathan.[3] And the Psalmist breaks out, " I am wearied with my groaning; every night make I my bed to swim; I water my couch with my tears," and again, "rivers of water run down mine eyes."[4] And the prophet, seeing the destruction of his people, exclaims, "For these things I weep; mine eye, mine eye runneth down with water," and again, "Mine eye runneth down with rivers of water for the destruction of the daughter of my people."[5] And because he could not find expression for his excessive grief, he again exclaims, "Oh that my head were waters, and mine eyes a fountain of tears, that I might weep day and night for the slain of the daughter of my people."[6] Perhaps the custom of dirge songs may also be alluded to when the ruler's daughter was believed to be dead, "Jesus came into the ruler's house, and saw the flute-players, and the crowd making a tumult."[7] The funeral procession, similar to that described by Lane, where the boy singers went before chanting the dirge, is alluded to in the description of the burial of Jacob.[8]

189. *Good Burial, Comfort.*—Any lack of proper burial is still regarded in the East, as in ancient times, a judgment from God; it was thought the greatest calamity that could come to any person. They are still greatly distressed lest they shall not

---

[1] Morier, Second Journey in Persia, 176, 177.
[2] Lev. 19 : 28; 21 : 5; Deut. 14 : 1.
[3] 2 Sam. 1 : 11, 12.
[4] Ps. 6 : 6; 119 : 136.
[5] Lam. 1 : 16; 3 : 48.
[6] Jer. 9 : 1.
[7] Matt. 9 : 23; Mark 5 : 38.
[8] Gen. 50 : 6–13.

receive a suitable burial, according to their respective customs. Even to this day, so deep-seated is this feeling that the China-man is accustomed to secure a coffin, when still young, and keep it in his house as a sacred treasure against the day of his death. This Oriental sentiment is repeatedly alluded to and used as an illustration to enforce spiritual teaching in the Scriptures. It was one of the severe denunciations of Jezebel, that "the dogs shall eat Jezebel in the portion of Jezreel, and there shall be none to bury her." [1] And the prophet breaks out in denun-ciation, thus, "Thou art cast forth away from thy sepulchre like an abominable branch, clothed with the slain, that are thrust through with the sword, that go down to the stones of the pit; as a dead body trodden under foot. Thou shalt not be joined with them (Kings of nations, who sleep in glory) in burial." [2] On the other hand, it was the constant longing of the patriarchs, kings, and prophets of old that they should find a final rest-ing place with their fathers in the family tomb. This hope gave them comfort and peace, as they drew near to the end of life.

[1] 2 Kings 9 : 10. [2] Isa. 14 : 19, 20.

XVIII.

LAND TENURE.

190. *Tribal Titles.*—In Oriental countries to-day land tenure
is of almost every kind known in the civilized world.   Thus in
Syria there are broadly three kinds:

1. *Ard emiri*—land of the emir, or taxed crown land—belonging to the Sultan or some ruler. This includes nearly all
large fruitful plains, as of Jaffa, Ramleh, Esdraelon—land
which is leased to individuals, or to villagers for the lifetime of
the lessor at nominally a rental of one-tenth of the produce.

2. *Ard wakûf*—glebe land—left to mosques, holy places, and
religious orders. It cannot be sold, but is leased, and is in
charge of a *mutaweh*—bailiff who retains a share (sometimes
the lion's share) of the tithes for himself. Thus, *Effendis* often
"eat up" the people.

3. *Ard mulk*—or freehold land—usually small pieces of
ground near villages, often fig and olive orchards, gardens, and
vineyards. Lands thus held can be sold or exchanged.

There are also other kinds of land, such as *ard bawr*, or fallow
land—chiefly in the hill districts, of a poor quality; and also
ard majhule—dead land, which has not been cultivated for
years, but is sometimes reclaimed and put under cultivation;
it then usually becomes the *mulk* "freehold" of the reclaimer;
and third, *arādi majhule*, which means "unknown land,"
because deserted and left vacant, either by the death of some
owner or by his sudden disappearance, leaving behind the land,
with debts and taxes, in which case it usually reverts to the
government.[1]

191. *Personal Titles.*—In the distant mountains lands are
generally owned by individuals or families, not by the community, as a rule. This ownership reaches only as far as the village

[1] F. A. Klein, Pal. Fund Quar., 1883, p. 41 ff.

lands. Even on some of the plains, lands belonging to the inhabitants before 1872 were not held by deed, but by tradition, which gave a qualified ownership until a stranger came to oust the possessor. On the plains of Sharon and Philistia the villagers were usually co-proprietors of lands, but when the new law of deeds came the poorer classes denied owning any land in order to avoid paying the cost of the deed, and were either deprived of it, or sold their right for a trifle.

Lands belonging to mosques, churches, and welys are extensive; the leases of them being valuable, and the income or rental being used to maintain the expenses of these buildings and institutions. Thus, the Haram of Hebron is one of the richest land owners in Palestine. The lands are expected to give one-fifth of the entire revenue to the support of the Haram.

192. *Buying Land.*—In Syria the fellahin, or peasants, buy and sell lands, giving such lease-hold title as they may possess, but they must contract for their relations to desist from their "right of redemption," a right which constructively still exists, as in the days of the old prophet.[1] The story of Abraham buying Machpelah of the Sheikh Ephron and of the tribe of Heth, is a scene often repeated in the East to-day. The owner, with a conspicuous Oriental show of boundless generosity, would not deign to accept pay for such a trifle as a bit of land and a cave for a stranger to bury his dead! Take it as a present! But the other native Sheikh would, likewise in his turn, stand upon his dignity, as Abraham did, and insist upon paying for the land, giving four hundred shekels of silver by weight, and thus he bought the field, the cave, and all the trees, the people of Heth witnessing to the purchase at the gate of the city.[2] It was needful especially to name the trees, and all the trees, in this Oriental purchase, otherwise there might have been trouble. Prof. Post, of Beirut, bought a piece of land in the Lebanon Mountains, but a venerable oak was not included in the purchase, nor the path thereto. He was compelled to make a new

---

[1] See Jer. 32 : 8.   J. G. Baldensperger, P. F. Q., 1906, p. 192 ff.
[2] Gen. 23.

path to that oak, and agree to keep the path open forever to the public.   In large tracts owned by the government the peasants or farmers become tenants.   They may not be liable to eviction and may sell their privileges, but are not owners in fee simple of the land.   The taxes are farmed out and collected by aid of soldiers, which proves an odious form of tyranny.   "The crops cannot be measured until threshed out and winnowed in heaps on a threshing floor.   The farmers are forced to leave their harvest exposed to birds, insects, rats, and other vermin, and to the depredation of thieves, and the danger [not great] of showers until the government officer chooses to come and measure out the grain.   The officer has the power to quarter his horsemen and other animals without compensation on the poor villagers, who are glad to buy him off and get rid of him by paying two-tenths or more."   There are large portions of land upon the deserts, or more strictly uninhabited regions, upon which wandering tribes of Arabs pasture their flocks and their herds, as in the days of the patriarchs.

193. *Allotted Land.*—The land of Canaan was allotted to Israel by tribes; Jehovah was the primal owner.   No tribe or family could alienate his land, except for a period and in special cases.   It must be retained in the family, and if alienated for a time, it came back on the year of Jubilee.   This throws light on the story of Ahab and Naboth.[1]   The law of inheritance varies in different Oriental nations, but generally the eldest son is the chief heir.

194. *Climate and Soil.*—In physical features Palestine, Syria, and the Sinaitic Peninsula form the geographical meeting point of the three great continents of the East.   The same region has been the pivotal point of national contests, the scene of great decisive battles, the highway for the marching forces of the mighty empires and monarchies of Old Babylonia and Egypt, whose immense military hosts for ages swept over and often desolated these lands in which Biblical history and interest have centered.

[1] 1 Kings 21 : 1-16.

9

The climate of Syria has a wide range, from the torrid heat in the depressed Jordan Valley to the cool, ever snow-capped mountains of Hermon and of the Anti-Lebanon.

The soil of the plains by the sea is a rich brown loam, with sand behind the promontories and capes. The terraced mountain sides yield figs and olives at an altitude from twenty-five hundred to five thousand feet. Cœle-Syria is supposed to be largely the bed of an ancient lake, and is of black loam soil of great fertility.

The water supply of Syria is well suited for storage and for irrigation. It can easily be artificially distributed over large portions of Palestine and Syria. When this is done, Palestine may again become a garden—a land "flowing with milk and honey."

Guarding Well-springs.—Navy Chaplain C. Q. Wright, U. S. Navy, writes me that he once saw mounted men with long guns, stationed under stunted olive trees beside large rocks in Palestine, carefully guarding a well of sweet water, the chief supply for a near-by village. Marauders might capture it, and rob the village of it. This illustrates,[1] "Keep thy heart above all that thou guardest, for out of it are the issues of life."

194a. *Babylonian Code.*—The oldest Code, that of Hammurapi, which was about a thousand years older than Moses, gives the rules which must govern tenant and owner in land culture. These rules illustrate the efforts of rulers to deal justly and equitably between owner and farmer in agriculture, as in a multitude of other social relations that reveal a complex state of society and a high sense of equity and fair dealing. These early laws of Hammurapi and the Mosaic Code are so different that scholars generally agree that the Mosaic laws were not derived from those of Hammurapi, nor from the same source.[2]

[1] Prov. 4 : 23.
[2] See Rice, *Our Sixty-Six Sacred Books;* and Barton, *Archæology and the Bible,* p. 340.

XIX.

ORIENTAL OCCUPATIONS AND PROFESSIONS.

195. *Tent Life and Herds.*—An ideal occupation for life to the Oriental is resting in the door of his tent and contemplating his possessions. He reckons his wealth, not in lands and houses nor in bonds and securities, but in camels, cattle, sheep, and goats. Travelers in Oriental lands still charm us with glowing descriptions of the simple and free life of the picturesque tribes, wandering over desert and plain, in that great continent where the human race wandered when it was yet young. Camps of the Bedouins now dot the plain, with their many tents, spreading over an immense space of ground. Groups of camels may be seen standing lazily, with herds of cattle, and flocks of goats and sheep, and spirited Arabian steeds, seeming to swarm upon the plain, mingling with groups of hooded or turbaned Arabs, who watch and attend them. Often these flocks and herds are scattered far as the eye can reach over the plain, grazing on the fine pasture or foraging upon the scanty herbage—a panorama of Oriental life worth journeying thousands of miles to behold. For this same scene has repeated itself generation after generation in this region for more than four thousand years, and ever since the days of Abraham and the patriarchs of earliest Hebrew history. On these plains are re-enacted over and over again in our time the strife that took place between the herdsmen of Abram and Lot from lack of ample pasture and water for herds and flocks.[1]

196. *Edenic Picture.*—The occupation of the primitive man, as pictured by the sacred writer is, "Jehovah God took the man, and put him into the garden of Eden to dress it and to keep it."[2] Or, literally, it reads, "Jehovah Almighty took the man and caused him to rest in the garden of pleasantness to till it and to

[1] Gen. 13 : 5–12.   [2] Gen. 2 : 15.

preserve it." This implies that without man's care the plants, flowers, and trees of that early age would have degenerated, or would have been less perfect without the training of the hand of man. It also implies that the garden needed a protector to preserve it or keep it. Possibly the animals were not all so peaceful as we are wont to imagine they were, nor so careful to restrain themselves from depredations, even in this Edenic state.

197. *Two Occupations*.—But whatever we may infer from this narrative, the picture here drawn is tinged with strong Oriental color. The naming of the cattle, of the birds of the air, and of the beasts of the field are characteristic of Oriental life of to-day. The sacred account further tells us that when man left the garden and his state of innocence he took up two leading occupations; "Abel was a keeper of sheep," but his elder brother "Cain was a tiller of the ground."[1] These continue to be two of the leading occupations among Orientals to this day. In the professions and in scientific discovery the children of Cain seem to have been leaders, one of them " was the father of such as dwell in tents and have cattle"; another "was the father of all such as handle the harp and pipe"; and still another was the "instructor of every artificer in brass and iron."[2] Cain was the elder son. Abel met with an untimely death, and perhaps years elapsed before Seth and his descendants came to maturity, hence the early development of Cain and his children in the arts, sciences, and professions. The sacred writer seems here to represent the occupation and professions of primitive man, the earliest mentioned in the annals of history.

198. *Oriental Farmers*.—The chief occupation of the *fellahin*, or peasants, of Syria is farming. Sometimes they go into partnership with the wandering tribes. The nomad Arabs raise horses and camels, while the villagers or peasants till the ground and raise sheep, goats, and cattle. Crops of grain-lands are gathered every other year, the ground being left fallow on each alternate year, that it may recover itself. Wheat, barley, and

[1] Gen. 4 : 2.   [2] Gen. 4 : 20-22.

spelt (rye, A. V.) are the most common grains raised in Palestine to-day.   Oats are little known to the peasants of Palestine. The Oriental farmer lives in villages or hamlets, and not sequestered and alone upon his farm.   This is necessary for safety and protection from wandering bands of robbers and lawless brigands.

199. *Grain.*—Besides wheat, barley, and a kind of millet, there is a great variety of other grains and grasses, such as clover, vetches, fitches, lentils, rice; and in later times maize and oats have been introduced into some portions of Northern Syria. All kinds of vegetables, and many kinds of fruits, as oranges, lemons, citrons, pomegranates, plums, grapes, figs, apricots, peaches, nectarines, pears, and quinces, with the blackberry, strawberry, gooseberry, myrtle berry, and mulberry; also olives, dates, and bananas are usually abundant in the East. Of nuts, besides walnuts, filberts, and almonds, the pistachio is common, with a great variety of aromatic plants and sweet-scented flowers, the rose, the lily, and the anemone, violet, poppies, mustard, mallows, caraway, dill, fennel, mint, thyme; and of trees for shade and timber the terebinth, oak, sumach, maple, shittim, plane, pine, cedar, fir, cyprus, juniper, and carob tree.

200. *The Farms.*—In the East farms, as a rule, are not divided by fences or even hedges.   The extent of a farm is marked by a path or a line of stones.   This custom has come down through the ages.   In olden times a curse was pronounced against one "that removeth his neighbour's landmark." [1]   The farmer now sometimes divides his land into three parts: one portion is for pasture, another is sown with grain, and the remaining portion, which is cultivated one year, is left fallow the next year for recuperation.   These portions may be marked off from one another by a path.   These paths across lands were evidently common in our Lord's day.   For in the parable of the sower, he says, "Some seeds fell by the way side, and the birds came and devoured them." [2]

[1] Deut. 27 : 17.   [2] Matt. 13 : 4.

Seed-time and Harvest.

201. *Sowing.*—The season for sowing depends on the time of the "former" or winter rains.[1]

The "latter" rain comes during our April or May, and is needful to perfect the growth of the grain. Thus, while the former rains in November or December are often heavy showers, washing the lands and swelling the streams, and are good for the fruits, the latter rains are necessary for bringing wheat, barley, and spelt to perfection. Hence, both the former and latter rains were symbols of abundant harvests and great prosperity.[2] This refers specially to Syria.

202. *Life Work.*—In some Oriental lands the plowman, or farmer, is a farmer for life. A merchant, a soldier, or a man of a trade might change his employment for a livelihood, but a farmer, once a plowman or tiller of the soil, is a farmer for life. So the Oriental would see great force in the proverb, "No man, having put his hand to the plough, and looking back, is fit for the kingdom of God."[3] That is, as a farmer could not forsake his plow and retain his good reputation, so could not a disciple, having entered upon a Christian life, turn back and find himself fit for the kingdom. The plowing is sometimes done before the grain is sowed, but oftentimes, when the land is not overgrown with weeds, the seed is first sown and then is ploughed in.

203. *The Plow.*—The Oriental plow is a very primitive implement. That used in Oriental lands to-day closely resembles similar ones represented on the old monuments thousands of years ago. It now consists of a flat, wooden share, pointed at the end, without any earth-board. When the point is of broad iron, it is bent up on the sides, and the wooden standard is fixed into the rounded iron like a heavy staff. The top of the staff has a cross piece, by which the farmer holds and guides his rude instrument. A long beam or stick is fastened to the

---

[1] Deut. 11 : 14; Jer. 5 : 24; 14 : 4; Hosea 6 : 3; Joel 2 : 23.
[2] Job. 29 : 23; Prov. 16 : 15; Jer. 3 : 3; Zech. 10 : 1.   [3] Luke 9 : 62.

PLOWING WITH CATTLE AND CAMEL ON SYRIAN PLAIN.

(Copyright by Underwood & Underwood, New York.)

P. 134.

upright, projecting forward, and that is again spliced or pieced at the further end with another stick, that often bends downward and passes between the cattle. At the end of this there is a pin to hold the ring of the yoke from slipping off. The yoke is a rude stick, often not hollowed, to fit the neck of the cattle. It has two straight sticks projecting down on each side, and the yoke is held on the neck by a string at the end of these sticks and underneath the neck of the cattle. A plow for a single ox is lighter than one made for a pair of cattle. The plowman has a long goad or stick, with a spike at one end, shovel shaped at the other. The sharp point is to prod his cattle and the other end is used to clean the rude share of the plow.

There are frequent allusions to the iron share of the plow, which by a little change could be beaten into a sword for defense. Thus, the prophet urges men of war, "Beat your plowshares into swords, and your pruninghooks into spears." [1] Times of peace are predicted by a reverse prophecy when men were exhorted to "Beat their swords into plowshares, and their spears into pruninghooks." [2] Such a rude instrument only scratched the soil. Oxen are generally used now for ploughing, sometimes asses or donkeys, rarely camels or horses. In olden time the law forbid plowing with an ox and an ass yoked together. [3] The sower takes his seed to the field now on the back of the donkey in a large sack and the light plow is also hung on the same animal. He has a leather bag under his arm, which he fills with seed from the sack, and carefully sows it broadcast, as he walks along, and the plow drawn by the oxen turns the soil over the seed. Sometimes the ground may be previously made soft by plowing; sometimes the ground is harrowed without plowing, as in the prophet's time. (See Isaiah 28 : 25.) If the ground is very wet, the grain may be trodden in by the feet of animals. This is alluded to in Isaiah 32 : 20. In Egypt the grain is sometimes scattered on the overflowing waters of the Nile as they are settling, so that the seed sinks into the soft mud when

[1] Joel 3 : 9.   [2] Isa. 2 : 4; Micah 4 : 3.   [3] Deut. 22 : 10.

the water recedes. Barley is sown in Palestine usually some-time in October or November, before the winter rain sets in, and wheat a little later.

204. *Barley Harvest.*—The barley harvest comes earliest, usually about the last of March or April, varying according to the season and the altitude. Thus, in the Jordan Valley, harvest would be nearly a month earlier than upon the table-lands about Jerusalem or upon the higher lands in the north of Syria. While the grain is growing, or less than half grown, it is counted "good luck" among the Arabs and peasants to have a path made through it. The Oriental farmer now, as of olden time, must be careful to have good seed in sowing wheat. If he finds tare seed mixed with his wheat, he must carefully separate the tares or he will have a poor crop. The tare seed is in shape like half of a kernel of barley. It is bitter in taste. If even barley bread is mixed with tares, the person who eats it becomes sick, dizzy, and drowsy, as if he had taken a small quantity of poison. The stalk of the tare closely resembles that of the wheat. Now, when a farmer finds tares springing up in the wheat, he waits until it is five or six inches high, and then women, children, and laborers enter the field to pull out the tares. When told of the parable of the wheat and tares, and asked why they do not leave the wheat undisturbed to harvest, they say, it is easier to remove the tares at this period if they are few, but if the tares were abundant, then it would be no doubt safer to allow the two to grow together until the harvest.[1]

205. *Hunger Limit.*—When the grain is nearly ripe, it is still a custom, as of old, to allow persons passing to break off the heads, rub them in their hands, and eat them to satisfy their personal hunger.[2] But to this day, should a native or a traveler allow his beast to eat any of the grain, he would find himself in trouble at once. The fertility of the soil of Palestine even to-day is shown by abundant testimony of natives and of tourists. Thus, Mr. Haddad says, "I know of some plantations in Galilee where from thirty to three hundred fold is produced when not

[1] Matt. 13 : 27-30. [2] Matt. 12 : 1; Mark 2 : 23; Luke 6 : 1; Deut. 23 : 25.

injured by storms, extreme cold, or drought. A man planted one bushel of barley in a piece of land belonging to me, and the yield was one hundred and forty-four bushels. The richest farms now are in Galilee and Hauran (Bashan-land) east of Galilee." As in the days of our Lord, so now, the sower, scattering his seed, finds that some fall by the wayside in the paths, some on rocky places, where the soil is thin, some among the thorns which grow over the paths or by the side of them, while other seed falls on good ground. The birds, such as larks, come in flocks, to eat the seed on the hard path. The hot sun wilts the young sprouts on the thin rock soil, and the thorns and nettles spring up to-day and choke the farmer's wheat and barley as they did two thousand years ago.

206. *Time of Harvests.*—Barley harvest often comes early, as it did near Bethlehem in the time of.Ruth and Boaz.[1] The wheat harvest comes a few weeks later usually, and is the occasion of great rejoicing if it is abundant. So, if the barley harvest came about the time of the Passover, the wheat harvest would come nearly a month after it. At the present time it may be said generally that the barley harvest in the Jordan Valley is sometimes as early as March or, under Mount Hermon, it may be as late as May. Dr. Tristram speaks of having eaten bread at Jericho in the end of March which was made from barley sown in the previous December.

207. *"A Barley Cake."*—There is an interesting speech common among the Arabs of to-day, who contemptuously call a peasant who tills the soil a "barley cake." This may throw light on the dream of the Midianite, who thought a cake of barley rolled into his camp and overturned a tent.[2] The wheat in Palestine is said to have a somewhat larger head than the wheat which grows in America. There is another variety grown in Egypt, called "mummy wheat," not found in Palestine. Grapes and figs are commonly gathered in August; so common is this that the natives often designate the season of the year by saying, "in grapes" instead of "in August."

[1] Ruth 2 : 17, 23.   [2] Judges 7 : 13, 14.

The mandrake apples also are found usually between the wheat harvest and August. The seeds of these if eaten are said to make persons crazy. The pomegranates are ripe in September, while other fruits mature and gather the largest crop late in October or in winter.

208. *Sowing and Reaping Together.*—So varied is the climate in Palestine and Syria that plowing, sowing, and reaping may be all going on at nearly the same time. You may see a peasant planting one field, while nearby is another ready to enter upon harvesting his crop. Thus, it is true, as it was twenty-five hundred years ago, "the plowman shall overtake the reaper, the treader of grapes him that soweth seed."[1]

Nor was that an imaginary, but a real scene, which our Lord used with his disciples: "Say not ye, there are yet four months, and then cometh the harvest? behold, I say unto you, Lift up your eyes, and look on the fields; for they are white already to harvest." [2] A similar real scene has been looked on by many a modern tourist over the plains near Samaria. Early in April, near Jacob's well, a traveler tells of seeing grain well ripened for harvest, and just southward and also northward of it, plowing and planting were going on.

209. *Two Seasons.*—The reader must not forget that in Oriental lands, of which we are speaking, there are practically but two seasons, and not four, as with us. The two seasons are the rainy or winter season, and the summer or dry season; for from April or May until October it rarely rains in Syria. This is true now as in the days of the prophet Samuel, when the people were alarmed at a thunder storm in wheat harvest.[3]

It is very remarkable now to have a shower of any kind in harvest. The barley harvest is usually about Passover time (our Easter). The wheat harvest is later, followed by the feast of weeks, or of harvest or firstfruits, seven weeks after the Passover, hence the name Pentecost, "fiftieth" day.[4]

210. *Reaping.*—Reaping in Oriental lands is chiefly with

---

[1] Amos. 9 : 13.   [2] John 4 : 35.   [3] 1 Sam. 12 : 17, 18.
[4] Lev. 23 : 15, 16; Ex. 23 : 16; Num. 28 : 26.

the sickle.[1] The Oriental sickle is of three kinds or sizes, much like the sickle in use with us. But vetches are pulled up, put in heaps, and carried away in bundles on donkeys or camels. Maundrell saw this on the way from Aleppo, reminding him of Jehovah's words: "Then will I pluck them up by the roots."[2] Compare also Eccl. 3: 2, with Ezek. 17: 9, and with the Psalmist's words: "Let them be as the grass upon the housetops, which withereth before it groweth up."[3] Allusions to sowing and reaping abound in Scripture; thus, "They that sow in tears shall reap in joy."[4] "They sow the wind, and they shall reap the whirlwind." "Sow to yourselves in righteousness, reap according to kindness."[5] "Sow trouble [or mischief], reap the same."[6] Proverbs impressing nature's inflexible law, that as we sow, so shall we surely reap, are current now in the Orient as they were thousands of years ago: "He that soweth iniquity shall reap calamity."[7] "Whatsoever a man soweth, that shall he also reap."[8]

Reaping barley—the earliest crop—opens a merry season in Palestine. "The entire population of a village turns out into the fields; the men reap and the women glean, the children play about, and the cattle crop the stubble. Everyone is in good spirits. As they work they sing, the men and the women responsively, each a line of the harvest song. At noon they may stop for a bit of bread, dipped into a salad, just as the reapers in Ruth's time ate and dipped the 'morsel into the vinegar.'"[9]

211. *Gleaning.*—The ancient custom of leaving some grain for the poor is quite rare now in Oriental lands, but it is not wholly forgotten. A modern resident in Syria thus describes a harvest scene: "When a village possesses lands in common, the inhabitants go there and build huts, and live there for several months around the threshing-floor. . . . All the women, rich or poor, go to glean behind the reapers. . . . A diligent gleaner

[1] Joel 3 : 13.   [2] 2 Chron. 7 : 20.   [3] Ps. 129 : 6.
[4] Ps. 126 : 5.   [5] Hosea 8 : 7; 10 : 12.   [6] Job. 4 : 8.
[7] Prov. 22 : 8.   [8] Gal. 6 : 7.
[9] Ruth 2 : 14.   (Bliss, S. S. W., 1907, p. 439.)

can gather more wheat than would be her usual pay for a day, especially in a fertile field where many stalks are left." "In the plains of Philistia the gleaners are more numerous than the reapers," says one observer, "and it is difficult to keep them away from the sheaves. A North African is employed to watch, and when they become too impertinent to remonstrate with them; but 'what can one young man do before so many young women?' Besides, there is so much scolding and cursing, and where goes the blessing? A curse, in their view, invites the genie to carry away food, as they neither sow nor reap, yet want to eat." This illustrates Ruth 2 : 5, where Boaz had a servant that was set over the reapers to watch, but he was commanded to allow Ruth to glean "even among the sheaves." [1]

Modern harvesters in the Orient have a like trouble to prevent the gleaners wandering among the sheaves. Every bad act is avoided as much as possible before "the blessing." "The gleanings may enable a widow to have bread enough for the winter, and in case of married women, who have not to harvest for themselves, or for girls, the wheat or barley is sold or changed for chickens, pigeons, or oil. These are the woman's property." [2]

212. *Parched Grain.*—Robinson saw reapers and gleaners working together, and eating parched grain and resting together; the stranger was courteously invited to take her place among them, and the master lying down "at the end of a heap of grain" to protect it against thieves, just as Boaz lay down. For now owners of crops sleep every night on the threshing-floor during grain harvest to guard the heaps of grain. This illustrates the allusions in Scripture to gleaning. [3]

213. *Threshing.*—The Oriental threshing-floor is a circular plat of ground, sometimes a platform, from twenty to fifty feet in diameter. It may be bounded by a coping of rough stones. When possible the top of a flat rock is preferred, because it would be free from mouse holes and ants' nests, and cleaner.

---

[1] Ruth 2 : 6, 15.   [2] Pal. Fund. Quar., 1907, p. 19.
[3] See Lev. 19 : 9, 10; 23 : 22; Deut. 24 : 21; Judges 20 : 45; Jer. 6 : 9; 49 : 9; Micah 7 : 1.

ORIENTAL PLOWBOY.   P. 138

(Vester & Co.)

SHEEP AND SHEPHERD BY STILL WATER.   P. 174

(Copyright by Underwood & Underwood, New York.)

Thus the rock under the present mosque in Jerusalem is on the site of the temple of Solomon, and that was built on the ancient site of the threshing-floor of Araunah.[1] These threshing-floors were sometimes famous landmarks; thus when Joseph went up to bury his father in the land of Canaan, they stopped at the threshing-floor of Atad to mourn.[2] To make a threshing-floor, the loose earth was first scraped away, and the ground made solid by pounding, and then smoothed over to make it sufficiently hard and suitable for the threshing of the grain, so that there should not be waste or loss to the farmer.

214. *Ways of Threshing.*—The Oriental has three ways of threshing grain: (1) With a staff or rod, called *chabat*, as in the days of Gideon.[3] (2) With cattle driven over heaps of straw to tread out the grain. This method is still common in Syria. Thus, Robinson saw the threshing-floors piled high with sheaves of grain, no less than five such floors, where the grain was being trodden out by oxen, cows, and young cattle, arranged five abreast, and driven round in a circle, or rather in all directions over the floor.[4] We know that this way of threshing is very old, from the command, "Thou shalt not muzzle the ox when he treadeth out the grain."[5] And the prophet says, "Ephraim is a heifer . . . that loveth to tread out the grain."[6] (3) The more common way of threshing now in the East is with a drag or threshing instrument. The drag is made of planks, like the old American stone boat used on mountain farms. The planks are bent up in front and have holes in the bottom. Sharp flints or stones are wedged into these circular holes in the bottom, or the drag may have rollers under it with cutting wheels, or spikes, which tear the straw into bits, and loose the kernels of grain. This drag is drawn by a pair of oxen, cows, or mules, a woman or a boy riding on the drag, and driving the animals over the sheaves of grain. "They go round and round the floor until the straw is all cut into

[1] 2 Sam. 24 : 24.   [2] Gen. 50 : 10.   [3] Judges 6 : 1; Isaiah 28 : 27.
[4] Researches, vol. i, p. 550.   [5] Deut. 25 : 4.   [6] Hosea 10 : 11.

bits of an inch or two in length by the sharp edges of the drag, and the kernels of grain are thoroughly separated from the straw. When the sheaves are threshed a fresh layer of sheaves is placed on the threshing-floor, and the threshing repeated."

215. *Treading Grain.*—Threshing with cattle was common in other Eastern countries than Syria in the last century. Thus, a traveler in India tells of seeing the treading out of grain with two sets of oxen, four abreast, the one set following the other in a circle; as they trod out the grain they continued eating. The traveler asked the man why they allowed the oxen to eat. They replied, "It is contrary to our *shastras* to muzzle the ox that treadeth out the corn." Thus, the Mosaic command has its counterpart in the Buddhist sacred books, and Hartley speaks of seeing horses in Greece used to tread out the grain. Lane tells of a threshing instrument "in the form of a chain, which moves upon small iron wheels or thin circular plates, generally eleven, fixed to three axle trees, . . . and drawn in a circle by a pair of cows, or bulls, over the grain." [1] Two travelers in the last century saw men beating out grain with a staff instead of a flail.

216. *Winnowing and Sifting.*—The grain is separated from the straw and chaff by being tossed up in the air, the wind causing the mass to fall into three separate heaps, the grain being the heaviest, fell immediately beneath the four-tined fork, with which it was tossed in the air. The straw was blown a little to one side into a heap, while the dust and lighter chaff was carried away into a flattened winrow beyond the straw. One traveler, who watched this winnowing, says, "The grain was thrown toward that side from which the wind blows, the ground swept, and the winnowing shovel or fork used to fling the mass into the air. One portion of the grain, quite clean, is removed; another portion, still mixed with some chaff, must go through a second winnowing or be sifted with a sieve." This winnowing the grain is alluded to in Psalms, where the wicked are said to be like chaff, which the wind carrieth away.

[1] Lane, II, 164.

The dust which is blown farthest away is worthless, and the farmer burns it, because it cannot be used to feed the cattle nor for any other good purpose. It is seldom that any instrument was used to increase the wind. The fan is, in fact, the shovel or wooden fork with which the unseparated grain and straw is thrown into the air. The allusions to the fan and the winnowing of grain are too abundant in Scripture to need citation. The allusions by the prophet to fanning, as in Jer. 15: 7 and Isaiah 30: 24, and 41: 16 refers to what was the ancient, as well as the modern, custom of winnowing the grain by a shovel or fork.[1] The most significant allusion to this Oriental way of cleaning the grain is the prediction respecting our Lord, " whose fan is in his hand, and he will thoroughly purge his floor."[2] There is another significant passage in Psalms 139: 3, "Thou searchest (or winnowest) out my path and my lying down." The image here is a bold Oriental one of the farmer, who throws his threshed grain many times into the air in the process of winnowing that he may make it thoroughly clean. So God would winnow us to make us thoroughly godly.

217. *Granaries.*—The present unsettled condition of most of the countries of the East causes the farmers and peasants to have the most secluded and secret places for storing their grain. Often it was in a carefully prepared cistern or pit under ground, sometimes within the house. One traveler speaks of finding such a grain pit in the reception room of an Oriental house. Dr. F. J. Bliss, the explorer, found large pits dug in the hard ground, with narrow mouths, in which wandering Arabs store their grain to-day. He adds, "Pits of the same kind, but smaller, containing perhaps the stores of a single family, were recognized in our excavations at Lachish and elsewhere. These were filled up quite solidly when we excavated them, but their circumference of hard earth was distinctly preserved. In one case at Lachish a chamber was found full of charred barley, which had been stored away

---

[1] See also Jer. 51 : 2.   [2] Matt. 3 : 12; Luke 3 : 17.

some three thousand years ago, and then burned before it could ever be used."[1] And Tristram tells of how "wheat is now universally stored in *silos* or underground pits, hollow chambers, about eight feet deep, carefully cemented on the inside, so as to be impervious to damp, and with a circular opening at the mouth about fifteen inches in diameter, just large enough to admit the passage of a man, and which is boarded over, then, if needed for concealment, covered with earth or turf. In such receptacles the corn will remain sound for several years (?). These *silos* abound in all parts of the country, and are probably, in some cases, the identical store-houses used by the Jews, who first constructed them. They are frequently close to an old-wine press, where has been the homestead of some Israelite farmer." Such store-houses are alluded to in Jer. 41: 8, "Slay us not: for we have treasures in the field, of wheat, and of barley, and of oil, and of honey." These store-houses are often under the women's apartments,[2] where a woman hid Jonathan and Ahimaaz in one of these *silos*, covering it over and spreading grain on the top, so that those who were searching for them did not suspect the place of their hiding. The Arabs of to-day have such places for keeping and secreting their grain from the wandering bands of brigands and from the more lawless government spies.

[1] S. S. W., 1907, p. 165. [2] See 2 Sam. 4 : 6; 17 : 18, 19.

ORIENTAL THRESHING FLOOR.　　P. 140

WOMEN WINNOWING.

(Copyright by Underwood & Underwood, New York.)

XX

FRUITS AND VINES.

218. *Kinds of Fruits*.—Fruits abound in Bible and all Oriental lands. Syria now has many kinds of fruit trees and fruit-bearing shrubs. Dr. Post gives a list of about forty principal ones that abound in Palestine alone. Among the best known fruit trees are the olive, fig, orange, apricot, pomegranate, mulberry, cherry, nectarine, plum, and medlar. "Medlar" is a fruit known by a Turkish name, which means, "the next world." Apples and pears are grown near Damascus, but are not indigenous to, and do not thrive well in, Palestine. The pomegranate tree seems like an uncared-for shrub. Large and good apricots grow near Solomon's pools.

219. *Figs*.—Fig trees are cultivated in gardens, usually by women. If the fig garden is away from the village, it may have a hut, to which the family owning the garden removes in the summer months, not only from villages, but from towns like Hebron, Gaza, Ramleh, and Lydda. The women gather the figs, dry them on the red earth in the sun in an enclosed space, to keep away the dogs, chickens, and children by day, and the jackals and foxes by night. The fruit harvest is a happy time for women and girls. They sing, sometimes from morning until night, one girl sings a line and another in the next garden, or across the valley, sings a second line, and so they continue the songs antiphonally all the day. The figs, when dried, are put away for winter, or are sold in the markets, as at Jerusalem and Jaffa. Sometimes "long garlands of dried figs are put on a string, weighing together seven or eight pounds. This method is common in villages like Bethel, Gibeon, Nazareth, and other small places. Es Salt (east of the Jordan) is renowned for figs and raisins."

220. *Early Figs*.—There are several kinds of figs, and

they vary in their time of ripening. The fig and olive orchards are plowed in the spring, when the leaves are starting, and sometimes again when the first crop has been stripped off, and the second crop is sprouting, and again in the autumn after the first rains. Some figs ripen as early as February or March, even as far north as Beirut. They would also be ripe that early in the Jordan Valley, and there might be fruit found as early as March or April (the time of the Passover) beneath Olivet near Jerusalem. Sometimes also the late violet-colored autumn figs hang upon the trees through the winter and until the spring leaves begin to come. Of these figs, the Orientals are said to be particularly fond. This throws light upon the narrative of the barren fig tree.[1] Prof. W. M. Thomson tells of having picked ripe figs in May from trees on the Lebanon, one hundred and fifty miles north of Jerusalem, where the season is nearly a month later than in Palestine. He does not think it improbable that ripe figs might have been found at Easter " in the warm sheltered ravines of Olivet." As the fruit-bud begins to come before the leaves, when there is no fruit on a tree full of leaves, it would properly be counted barren. The fact that Oriental figs mature in Palestine as early as April was formerly sharply questioned. Some years ago I investigated the matter, and found that they did so, by a line of testimony which has not been since successfully questioned. Thus, Prof. Post wrote me from Beirut, "Figs do not *usually* ripen until June or July. . . . In my garden in Beirut, in places well sheltered from the wind, I have two fig trees, on each of which there are now [Jan. 22] young figs. One of them began to bear this late crop in October; and the figs have been ripening, one after another, until now, and the last will probably be ripe about the first of February." He adds, "In the wilderness (Sinai) I collected branches of wild figs March 16, on which were young figs as large as filberts, while as yet, not a leaf had unfolded." Dr. Manning refers

---

[1] Mark 11 : 12–14, and also upon passages like the following: Isaiah 28 : 4; Jer. 24 : 2; Hosea 9 : 10; Nahum 3 : 12; Matt. 21 : 19; Luke 13 : 7.

to another kind of early fig: "In the early spring, when the leaves first appear, an immense number of small figs are produced, which do not ripen, but fall from the branches. This first crude, untimely growth, though of no commercial value, is yet plucked and eaten by the peasantry. A young Syrian gentleman, one of his companions, plucked and ate these figs without stint or scruple." [1] Dr. H. C. Fish testifies: "Two kinds of fig trees abound in Palestine; one maturing its fruit in spring, the other in summer or autumn. By the end of March and in April and May the early kind is found." Dr. Tristram says that about May he saw "ancient fig trees laden with nearly ripe fruit near Amman." Mrs. Finn, twelve years resident in Palestine, states that winter figs were still on the trees in March. Dr. S. Merrill found near Tiberias, on February 20th, "A fig tree which had new shoots on it, and also some old figs, which were still green. It was loaded besides with small figs about the size of walnuts." These are only a few specimens of the testimony I gathered in regard to the time of early figs in Palestine.

Sacred writers often describe great prosperity and safety by the expression "Judah and Israel dwelt safely, every man under his vine and under his fig tree."[2] The prophets often used the tree or the fruit of the tree to teach important religious lessons.[3]

221. *The Olive.*—Among the principal fruits of Syria, Mr. Haddad counts the fig, olive, and vine as the most important. The olive requires a long time to bear fruit; "ten or fifteen years after they are planted or grafted, during which they need continual cultivation. . . . In order to have some return before the olives begin to bear, fig trees are planted with them in the same pit, which produces fruit within two years after planting. When the olive trees begin to bear, the owners root up the fig trees and give attention solely to the olives." [4] Usually the branches of the fig trees bend downward, some-

---

[1] See Rev. 6 : 13.
[2] 1 Kings 4 : 25; 2 Kings 18 : 31; Prov. 27 : 18; Isaiah 36 : 16, and Micah 4 : 4.
[3] See Jer. 24 : 1–8; 29 : 17.   [4] Compare Romans 11 : 17–24 and Jas. 3 : 12.

times touching the ground, so a man standing under a fig tree may be quite concealed. Olives, after figs, ripen about November. Women gather the fruit, singing as they work. The olives are taken to the oil mill by the men. The first olives falling prematurely to the ground are gathered by the women alone, and are crushed on a flat rock with a stone, and then put in water to extract the oil. These produce, it is said, poor oil. The mode of beating or gathering the fruit is primitive, as in ancient times.[1] The songs are often improvised, sometimes romantic adventures, princely honors, in which a lover is imagined as coming forth with a camel and a slave to serve the singer, [but he never does].

222. *Old Olive Trees.*—Olive trees are abundant in every part of the Holy Land now and are characteristic of the country. Extensive olive orchards or yards are on the borders of the Phœnician plain, and by the valleys of the plain of Esdraelon, the vale of Shechem, the plain of Moreh, which is studded with them, on the slopes around Bethlehem and Hebron, and on the fertile regions east of the Jordan, as on the plains of Gilead and Bashan-land, which still yield a large return for slight care and culture. Olive trees are among the best possessions of the towns of Philistia and Sharon. The culture of the olive is increasing around Jerusalem also. The oldest olive trees in the country are believed to be those in the garden of Gethsemane. There are seven or eight of them, the trunks gnarled and wrinkled, and cracked from age and shored up with stones. The guides tell tourists that they date back to the time of Christ. They are surely of great age and size, and about twenty feet in circumference. But Titus cut down all the trees about Jerusalem, and the crusaders found the country destitute of wood. We find no mention of those olive trees before the sixteenth century, A. D. The Turkish government taxes each olive tree yearly, which discourages the planting of new olive orchards. Olive trees bear an amazing quantity of blossoms. The traveler may see the blossoms

[1] See Ex. 27 : 20.

in the slightest breeze, falling in showers like snowflakes, as if there were millions of them on a tree, yet enough remains to load the tree with fruit. The sacred dramatic poem of Job alludes to this, "He . . . shall cast off his flower as the olive tree." [1]

223. *Olive and Peace.*—From time immemorial the olive tree has been closely associated with the history of man. It was a sign of peace, reconciliation, and plenty, for the dove brought back an olive leaf to the ark: "Lo, in her mouth an olive-leaf plucked off." [2] There is a Greek tradition that the first olive branch reached them, carried by a dove, from Phœnicia to the temple of Jupiter in Epirus. While the fig is the first tree named in Scripture, the leaves being used to make garments, [3] the olive is also prominent from the time of the deluge, and because it is mentioned in the first parable recorded in the Old Testament, where Jothan says it was invited to be "king over the trees." The olive replied, "Should I leave my fatness, wherewith by me they honor God and man, and go to wave to and fro over the trees?" [4] The fig tree was also invited to be king, and declined, and so did the vine; at last the bramble was chosen. The olive was one of the special blessings of the land of promise. One of the marks of Jehovah's anger was the lack of oil, and that the olive should cast his fruit. [5] David compares himself to a "green olive tree in the house of God." [6]

224. *Olive Oil.*—The mode of gathering the fruit, and of leaving a gleaning for the stranger and the fatherless, are referred to by the prophets. [7] The oil from the olive is abundant, sometimes from ten to fifteen gallons from a tree in a year. The oil is still used in place of butter; nearly every dish is cooked with it, and bread is dipped in it. It supplied the lamp (for candles were not used there); it makes the soap, and the berry is pickled for the peasant, whose dinner often consists

---

[1] Job. 15 : 33.   [2] Gen. 8 : 11.   [3] Gen. 3 : 7.
[4] Judg. 9 : 9.   [5] Deut. 6 : 11; 8 : 7, 8; 28 : 40.
[6] Ps. 52 : 8; see Jer. 11 : 16; Hosea 14 : 6; Deut. 33 : 24.
[7] Isaiah 17 : 6; Deut. 24 : 20.

of a handful of olives, wrapped in a thin barley cake. The oil is used also as a medicine for wounds and bruises, for rubbing the body after a bath, for dressing the hair, and for the mixing of offerings in sacrifice, as of old, and for the consecration of priests.[1]   The olive grows wild in the Orient, and must be grafted, or it produces only small, worthless fruit. (Compare Romans 11: 17–24, where the apostle calls the Gentiles the "wild olive . . . grafted in" contrary to nature upon the good olive.)

225. *Proverbs on Olives and Figs.*—The peasants of Palestine have many curious proverbs coming down, no doubt, from ancient times, relating to the olive, the fig, and the vine. Thus they call the vine a *sitt,* "a delicate town-lady, who needs a great deal of care and attention." The fig is a *fellaha,* "a strong country-woman, who flourishes without care." But the olive is a bold *bedawiyeh,* " enduring hardship; a strong and useful Arab wife."

226. *Oil Press.*—As the olives ripen, the trees are beaten with sticks carefully, so as not to destroy the young leaves and shoots. The olive-berries are collected and spread on the roofs, or somewhere in heaps, often to ferment slightly, then they are taken to the oil press, and crushed under a heavy millstone, and packed in little straw baskets, and finally pressed. The oil (the Arabs call it *zayt*) is caught in a cemented cistern, from which it is drawn out into leather bottles, or earthenware jars, for use or for sale. It is used, as already stated, for cooking, but in most of the Oriental countries of Western Asia it is not now used in lamps, having been superseded by petroleum.

227. *Use of Oil, etc.*—Olive oil and figs are still common in medical practice. Figs are used for poultices now, as in the prophet's time: "Take a cake of figs, and lay it for a plaster upon the boil, and he shall recover." [2]   The olive and its oil are still a large part of the wealth of poor people, as in the days

[1] Hab. 3 : 17, 18; Matt. 6 : 17; Luke 10 : 34; Ps. 23 : 5; Lev. 2 : 1; 1 Kings 6 : 23, 31, 33.
[2] Isaiah 38 : 21; see Matt. 6 : 17; Luke 10 : 34.

of Elisha, who multiplied the widow's oil to enable her to pay her debt and save her children from being sold as bondsmen.[1] The failure of these fruits, both olive and fig, is threatened as a judgment from Jehovah.[2] The putting forth of the first buds of the fig, which comes before the leaves, was counted a sign of summer, and is so still.[3]

228. *Grapes.*—The grape-vine, like the olive, the fig, and the date-palm, is indigenous to Syria. One variety, the fox grape, grows wild now on the uplands of Jordan. Southern Palestine yields an abundance of grapes, perhaps almost as great a quantity as in patriarchal times.[4] The grape-vines are planted about ten feet apart. Some allow the branches to spread on the ground, and some raise them on a trellis. They may be arranged to climb around the porches or upon old fruitless trees, like a terebinth or an oak. The soil and climate of Syria are very suitable for grapes, and some peasants depend largely for their living on the vineyard, taking pains in cultivating them. The grape grows in a great many varieties, as to shape, size, color, thickness of skin, size of seeds, or seedless, and is marked by different degrees of sweetness, hardness, and flavor. Some are best for drying and for raisins; others for making molasses, wine, or vinegar.

The young leaves are tender, and are used as a green vegetable; the sour, green grape is used in place of the lemon. There is nothing wasted of the vine or the fruit. When the green leaves become hard and coarse, and unfit for cooking, they are fed to the sheep and goats to fatten them. The branches are trimmed, and the wood is used to make charcoal, or for fire-wood; so every bit of the vine and of the grape is made useful by the Oriental.

229. *Pruning.*—In the spring, before the young sprouts come, the peasant lops off all superfluous branches, "leaving only the trunk and a few principal branches, which he places on the ground, all turned the same way, so that he can plow

---

[1] 2 Kings 4 : 1–8.   [2] Ps. 105 : 33; Jer. 5 : 17; 8 : 13; Hosea 2 : 12; Joel 1 : 7, 12.
[3] Matt. 24 : 32.   [4] Gen. 49 : 11, 12.

between them. . . . Every feeble, sickly branch and trunk is
cut away so that all the sap goes to the new sprouts. Fresh
cuttings put into the ground are allowed to grow unpruned
for a year or two." The branch which is closest to the trunk
or root bears the most fruit.[1] Even to this day, the peasant
hopes to have an abundant harvest until "the summer is ended."
Thus, the prophet puts himself in the place of the people
and exclaims, "The harvest is past, the summer (or ingather-
ing of summer fruits) is ended, and we are not saved."[2]

230. *Vineyards.*—Vineyards in Palestine are usually surrounded by a wall of stone or a hedge. "In a large vineyard,"
says Mr. Haddad, "a wine-vat is dug or cut in a rock, consisting of a basin in the upper part of it, and a heavy pressing
stone. Below, in the rock, a pool is cut to receive the juice of
the pressed grapes. The juice is made into wine or boiled
into a thick molasses, called *dibs*. A tower is built for the
watchman, who dwells in it, with the workmen that gather
the fruit. The best kinds of grapes in Northern Lebanon
are put in bags, some bunches weigh eighteen to twenty pounds.
There is one kind, in the vicinity of Hebron and in the valley
of Eshcol, a bunch of which sometimes weighs about twenty-
four pounds." He adds, "They carry it on a pole between
two persons, as did the spies of Moses."[3]

Large vineyards are now rented; the owner renting one to
one or two families, and requiring the peasant to give him half
of the product, or more, according to agreement. He sends
his servant to take his share in fruit and to sell it to merchants, as he also takes his share of raisins, or wine, or whatever may be the product of the vineyard. This illustrates the
parable of our Lord in regard to the wicked husbandmen.[4]

231. *Towers and Watchmen.*—Rev. J. E. Hanauer of Damascus tells me that the region of Eshcol is now (1909)
quite surrounded with vineyards, which are enclosed with
stone walls, bordered along the top with thorns, to keep out

[1] John 15 : 4-6.   [2] Jer. 8 : 20.   [3] Num. 13 : 23.
[4] Matt. 21 : 19, 28, 33-40; Mark 12 : 1-9; Luke 20 : 9-18.

SUMMER BOOTHS, SYRIA. P. 153
(*Copyright by Underwood & Underwood, New York.*)

ORIENTAL FAMILY MOVING. P. 153
(*Copyright by Underwood & Underwood, New York.*)

the foxes, jackals, and other creatures that spoil the grapes, and have inside rough stone towers, or kitchens, for the keepers of the vineyards.[1] "The towers usually contain one small chamber, about eight or ten feet in diameter, where the owner of the vineyard, or the keeper and his family, have household goods, a handmill, cooking utensils, and reside there during the summer. From this lower chamber, a rude staircase, sometimes built within the wall, or winding outside it, reaches to the flat roof, where the watchman can see the vineyard, and sound an alarm in case of danger. The watchman may have a booth of boughs and branches of trees as a shelter from the sun's rays." In the winter the vineyards are deserted, illustrating the prophet's description: "The daughter of Zion is left as a booth in a vineyard, as a lodge in a garden of cucumbers."[2] "Hundreds of these vineyard-towers may be seen all over the country. Connected with these towers are old rock hewn wine-presses, often with underwood growing out of them.[3] These wine-presses are of various sizes, generally consisting of a quadrangular excavation, eight feet square, and ten inches deep, for the reception of the grapes to be trodden, and from which the 'must' or grape juice runs through a rock channel into a pit or vat, about 2 x 4 feet and three feet deep at the lower level. In some ancient wine-presses there is a third and smaller pit at a yet lower level, probably to hold a jar into which the grape juice which had collected overflowed, after having allowed the grape seeds and husks to settle."

232. *Dried Grapes.*—"Dried grapes or raisins are, like fresh grapes during the season, a staple article of food. The best raisins are grown near Es Salt (Ramoth Gilead), east of the Jordan. They are the famous 'saltana' [wrongly called 'sultana'] raisins of commerce. The vines there are planted in rows, sometimes raised from the ground on supports, carefully pruned in autumn or spring, that they may bring forth more fruit.[4] When the leaves and grape clusters are formed,

---

[1] Hosea 2 : 6; Cant. 2 : 15; 8 : 11.   [2] Isaiah 1 : 8.
[3] Isaiah 5 : 2; Matt. 21 : 33; Mark 12 : 1.   [4] John 15 : 2.

they are carefully fumigated with sulphur as a protection against pernicious fungi and insects. As symbols of the country the vine or its clusters are frequently found sculptured on monuments."

233. "*Dibs*."—Natives tell us that *dibs* (a syrup) is obtained by boiling the juice of the grapes until it becomes as thick as molasses. The Moslems are said to be fond of *dibs*, eating it with bread, and drinking it, thinned with water, and using it largely in confectionery. The Hebrew name *debash* (honey) is believed by Dr. Tristram to be identical with this syrup, or *dibs*, and not bee's honey. Jacob sent this down as a present to the governor of Egypt.[1] And the men of Tyre exported it to the land of Israel.[2]

The juice of the grape is still pressed out by the simple process of treading. Several travelers have described this process, the treading usually being done by men, who encourage each other, after the Oriental fashion of singing and shouting, as in olden time.[3]

Several kinds of vines and wines are mentioned in Scripture, since there are about eight Hebrew and four Greek words that signify wine. All these kinds may be made from grapes, but some of them are also made from pomegranates and other fruits. Sometimes *dibs* is made so that it can be used as a drink, and sometimes it is eaten like butter. Thus, Dr. W. M. Thomson tells of a Bedouin Sheikh, who dipped a bit of bread in grape molasses (*dibs*) and gave it to him to eat, saying, "Now we are brothers; there is bread and salt between us." The Arab also gave a bit of the bread to all Dr. Thomson's companions, and to the muleteers, and to all about the tent, who tasted of it. This was the ceremony which sealed a covenant of friendship. It gave the missionary and his company permission to travel wherever they pleased in the Sheikh's territory, he being pledged to aid and befriend them, "even to the loss of his own life." The Arabs term this *khûwy*, or the covenant of brother-

[1] Gen. 43 : 11.   [2] Ezek. 27 : 17.
[3] See Gen. 49 : 11; Isaiah 16 : 9, 10; 63 : 2, 3; Jer. 25 : 30; 48 : 33.

hood. This covenant can never be forgotten or renounced. The Rev. F. Moghabghab, a Syrian, tells of three forms of covenants among Oriental shepherds: 1. Of drinking water, coffee, or wine together. 2. Of salt or eating together. 3. Of blood, the most sacred of all, sealed by "cutting" and killing sheep.

234. *How Kept—"Bottles."*—Wine, water, milk, and other liquids are kept in jars or other receptacles, but when carried on a journey these liquids are put into water skins or "bottles." The jars in Egypt are usually of two kinds, one with a narrow, and another with a wide, mouth. Lane says they are made of a grayish porous earth, which cools the water by evaporation. The interior of the jar is often blackened with the smoke of some wood, and then perfumed with an Arabic gum, like mastic.[1] The leather or skin bottles are of several different sizes and kinds. They are usually made from the skin of the goat, rarely, if ever, from that of the sheep, because the sheep skin is not strong enough. Sometimes they are made from the skin of the camel, or an ox skin, which is prepared by tanning. The goat's skin is used whole, being drawn off the body of the animal after cutting off its head and feet; the openings thus made being sewed up, and the joinings well smeared with grease. These bottles become dried by the smoke in the tents or houses of Arabs, and are liable to crack and become worthless when old. Fermenting wine put into old bottles not being strong enough to hold the wine during fermentation, suggested the comparison of our Lord: "No man putteth new wine into old wineskins; else the wine will burst the skins, and the wine perisheth, and the skins: but they put new wine into fresh wine-skins."[2] The large bottles, Bruce says, are besmeared on the outside all over with grease lest the water or the liquid should ooze through. Pliny Fisk used goats' skins to carry water when the skins were new. He says it gave the water a reddish color and an exceedingly loathsome taste. Harmer tells of carrying liquid in smoked leather bottles, which when rent "were

---

[1] See Ps. 119 : 83.   [2] Matt. 9 : 17; Mark 2 : 22; Luke 5 : 37, 38.

mended by putting in a new piece, or by gathering up the piece, or by inserting a flat bit of wood." Burckhardt saw Arabs keeping water for their horses in large bags made of tanned camel skin. These were sewn up on the four sides, so as to leave two openings; two such bags are a heavy load for a camel. Sometimes the wine or water is carried in a cruse, enclosed in a wicker basket, similar to that which David must have taken from beneath Saul's bolster.[1]

235. *Apricots, etc.*—Apples are named six times in Scripture, but they have not been identified with any modern fruit of the Orient. The pear and quince now grow in Syria, and likewise the apricot. The latter is abundant, and may be the apple of the Bible.[2] The citron of the Orient is a species of orange, growing on a tree, as in Moses' day.[3] It is a native of Media. The leaf is larger than that of the orange, and the fruit is larger than the lemon, of oblong shape, and the blossoms are pale purple in color.

236. *Carob Tree.*—The locust, or carob tree, with its fruit, the husks,[4] still abounds in Syria, from Hebron north, and is a conspicuous object. It is the *kharub* of the Arabs. The husks are now found in the markets of Oriental towns, and used to feed cattle, horses, and pigs. They are said to be of a sweetish, agreeable taste when chewed before they are ripe, similar to the tamarind pods of the West Indies.

237. *Mulberry.*—The Mulberry (black and white variety) still abounds in Syria and other Oriental lands. It is probably the *becaim* or mulberry.[5] But it must not be confounded with the fig-mulberry, or sycamine tree, to which our Lord referred in his teaching on faith.[6] The black and white mulberry are now cultivated in Syria, their leaves being fed to silk-worms. The sycamine is still found in Palestine, as in the time of our Lord and of the Maccabees. In ancient times the juice (red like blood) was used to frighten or excite elephants.[7]

238. *The Palm.*—The date-palm is found in Nubia and

---

[1] 1 Sam. 26 : 12.
[2] Cant. 2 : 5; 7 : 8; 8 : 5; Prov. 25 : 11, Joel 1 : 12.
[3] Lev. 23 : 40, margin.
[4] Luke 15 : 16.
[5] 2 Sam. 5 : 23, 24; 1 Chron. 14 : 14.
[6] Luke 17 : 6.
[7] 1 Mac. 6 : 34.

Abyssinia, and in other Oriental lands, though it is not so common in Syria now as in patriarchal times. The date-palm has long leaves, twelve feet sometimes, apparently called "branches" in Scripture.[1] The trunk does not so increase in thickness as in height, so that a tree twenty feet high may be as thick as one that is eighty to one hundred feet high. The date-palm is found in Western India, in the valleys of the Euphrates and Tigris Rivers, and in Arabia and Egypt. There were seventy palm trees and ten wells of water at Elim to cheer Moses and his company.[2] Palm trees must have abounded near Jericho, for it was called, "The city of palm trees."[3] The palms have disappeared, and the thorn and other wild trees have come in their places, though Dr. Tristram observed one wild palm tree there with a clump of young trees about it, nearly a generation ago. So, too, there must have been date-palms about Jerusalem, for Bethany signifies, "House of dates," and the multitude welcomed Jesus on his entry into the holy city with branches of palm trees.[4] A few palms are still seen in the gardens of Jenin, Nablūs, Beisan, and near Nazareth. It is counted a famous, stately tree still, as in the days of the Psalmist: "The righteous shall flourish like the palm tree: he shall grow like a cedar in Lebanon."[5] For this reason the grace and beauty of the palm are frequently used to picture some scene or illustrate some truth in the Bible.[6]

239. *Pomegranate.*—The pomegranate is a fruit-bearing shrub of the myrtle family, and is cultivated in all the warmer climates of the Orient. The fruit of the wild plant is bitter and astringent; when cultivated it is highly prized now, as it was of old.[7] The juice makes a cool and pleasant drink, and is sometimes made into a light wine.[8] The pomegranate was also the model for ornamentation in various ancient buildings.[9]

240. *Sycamore.*—The sycamore is a species of fig tree allied

[1] Lev. 23 : 40; Neh. 8 : 15.   [2] Ex. 15 : 27; comp. Num. 33 : 9.
[3] Deut. 34 : 3; Judg. 1 : 16; 3 : 13; 2 Chron. 28 : 15.
[4] John 12 : 13.   [5] Ps. 92 : 12.
[6] Gen. 38 : 6; Song of Sol. 7 : 7; Jer. 10 : 5.
[7] Num. 13 : 23; 20 : 5; Deut. 8 : 8; 1 Sam. 14 : 2; Cant. 4 : 13.
[8] Comp. Cant. 8 : 2.   [9] See Ex. 28 : 33, 34; 39 : 24-26; 1 Kings 7 : 18

to the famous Banyan-tree of India, and quite unlike the
sycamore or plane tree of our Western world. It grows to a
large size, often fifty feet in circumference, and is evergreen.
It is common in Egypt, and was used for making mummy cases,
sound now after being entombed for thousands of years. It
was formerly more abundant than now in Palestine, for Solomon
made "Cedars . . . to be as the sycamore . . . for abundance." [1] Its forking branches make it an easy tree to climb
and hence it was chosen by Zaccheus, who climbed into one,
when he wanted to get a good view of our Lord as he passed.[2]
The fruit is sometimes poor, insipid, and inferior to the true fig
tree, as the prophet declared in his day, "the other basket had
very bad figs, which could not be eaten, they were so bad." [3]
Another prophet (Amos) counted himself as a "dresser,"
literally, "a [scraper] of sycamore trees." [4] The leaves have a
spicy or aromatic fragrance.

240a. *Oaks or Terebinths.*—There are three species of this
tree, variously rendered "oak," "elm," or "teil," in English
versions. But correctly they are the *terebinth*. One kind bears
large acorns, which the peasants often eat as fruit. This tree is
early noted in the Bible as marking the place, near Mamre or
Hebron, beside or beneath which Abram pitched his tent.[5]
A tree still standing at that spot is very old. Its four branches
had a spread of about two hundred and seventy-five feet; it
stands about two miles west of the present city of Hebron.
Josephus mentions it and records a tradition that it was as old
as the world! The terebinth is usually believed to live for a
thousand years, and new shoots spring from its roots that may
live another thousand years. The Hebrew word is wrongly
rendered "elm" in Hos. 4 : 13.

[1] 1 Kings 10 : 27; 2 Chron. 1 : 15; 9 : 27.   [2] Luke 19 : 4.
[3] Jer. 24 : 2.   [4] Amos 7 : 14.
[5] Gen. 13 : 18 (R. V.).

WATER CARRIERS.　　　P. 155

(Vester & Co)

GOATSKIN WATER BOTTLES.　　　P. 155

(Pal. Exp. Fund)

XXI.

SHEPHERDS AND FLOCKS.

THE shepherd is now, as he ever has been, the picturesque and prominent figure in Oriental life. No subject has inspired such enthusiasm, or given greater attractiveness to the sketches of painter's pencil and artist's brush than the shepherd and his sheep; and no songs are sweeter in literature than those which the poet sings of the ideal shepherd life in the Orient. There are no stories of the imagination, there are no historical narratives that so universally interest young and old as the adventures and experiences in Oriental shepherd life. They have carried with them more lessons, brought deeper impressions, and inspired nobler results than almost any other form of literature or art.

241. *Shepherd Life.*—The shepherd is secluded from society, living in the fields and sparse woodlands with his flock, wearing simple garments, eating plain food, satisfied with bare necessities, and none of the comforts of social life. In the summer he dwells upon the hillsides or mountain slopes with his flocks, where he has pure air, sweet water, basking in the sunshine of pasture or in the shade of green foliage and bright flowers. He may be a specimen of natural simplicity; he is an example of simple virtue; his kindness is proverbial, usually he is truthful, temperate in his language, and kept from many of the evils of civilized society. He is skilled with the sling or the gun, is said to be able to hit a hair, if he can see it, is gentle with his flocks, keen to find fertile and safe pastures, and to protect them from the heat of summer and the cold of winter. He is equally bold in defending them from the wild beast or the robber. The modern shepherd is aided by a courageous, powerful, and well-trained dog. He has a wonderful memory, which retains the name of every sheep. The flocks sometimes contain several hundred, and

yet each one has a name and the shepherd knows it, and calls every sheep by its proper name. He is sharp to discover a missing one, and searches until he finds it or finds out what has become of it, whether it has fallen into the river or been seized by a wild beast. The hurt sheep or lamb he hunts out, dresses its wounds or binds its broken bones with skill and success. He thus becomes a surgeon, not only for sheep and goats, but also sometimes for people. He is a reverent student of the stars.

242. *A Poet.*—His provisions are in a skin bag, slung on his shoulders, chiefly bread and salt. His cooking utensils are a copper bucket and a bowl. His weapons are a long staff or club, a sling, a knife under his girdle, and, in modern times, a pistol and a long flint-lock musket. His memory is a wonderful book. Out of it he recites poetry made by other shepherds or himself, poems which the great poets have sometimes worked over and molded into beautiful forms; some of the most brilliant passages of their poems having been borrowed from the plainer, but forcible, thoughts of these shepherds. He eats his quiet meal, thanks God, and if his flock is safe from wild beasts or brigands, he takes out his pipe, or flute, and plays some weird tune or sings some of his expressive and beautiful verses.

243. *His Loving Care.*—Mr. Haddad tells of watching shepherds with flocks upon the slopes of Mount Hermon: "Each shepherd watched his flock closely to see how they fared. When he found a new-born lamb he put it in the folds of his *aba*, or great coat, since it would be too feeble to follow the mother. When his bosom was full, he put lambs on his shoulders, holding them by the feet, or in a bag or basket on the back of a donkey, until the little ones were able to follow the mothers.

"He trains his sheep to come at his call, to go in order, in twos or fours, in squares and circles; one from the outer circle in a flock of a thousand will come when its name is called." It is the voice of the shepherd that the sheep recognizes.

A stranger once declared to a Syrian shepherd that the sheep knew *the dress* and not the voice of their master. The shepherd said it was the voice they knew. To prove this, he exchanged dresses with the stranger, who went among the sheep in the shepherd's dress, calling the sheep in imitation of the shepherd's voice, and tried to lead them. They knew not his voice, but when the shepherd called them, though he was disguised, the sheep ran at once at his call.[1] The reader must not forget that an Oriental shepherd never drives his sheep, but always goes before them, and leads them, and they follow him. Even when some unruly sheep does not heed his call, but starts to stray away, the shepherd puts a stone in his sling, and deftly lands it just in front of the straying sheep as a warning, which usually brings the wandering one back to the flock.

244. *Syrian Sheep.*—Sheep are usually kept on the plains, hills, and mountains. Each flock is by itself, under the care of a shepherd. The Syrians think that sheep in the Orient are superior to those found in America, being, as they claim, much prettier, having more intelligent and nicer faces. The Syrian sheep is counted meek, gentle, and obedient, going peaceably and quietly, seldom quarreling with each other. The milk is very rich, and some Orientals prefer the butter made of it to that made from the milk of the cow. The flesh is sweet and delicious, and Orientals prefer it to beef or goat's flesh.

The shepherd must take the responsibility of his flock, finding it good and fertile pasture, and when one pasture is eaten bare, take his flock to another, sometimes over dangerous rocky cliffs, but always by the safest and easiest path.

245. *Stray Sheep.*—Sometimes a sheep or goat gets venturesome and wild, and runs away to the woods or the caves. The shepherd does not get angry at the sheep because it did not hear his voice when he called it back, nor will he let it perish. He leaves his flock in the hands of an assistant, or

[1] John 10 : 5.

11

to the care of his dog, and himself goes after the stray lamb or sheep, through the woods and the rocky mountains, in the heat of summer or the cold of winter, to bring that stray lamb back to the fold. Why does he take this trouble? Even if he were the owner, its value is not much; the loss would not be great, hardly worth exposing himself to the fatigue and danger, or worth leaving the rest of his flock; but the shepherd's reputation is at stake. These shepherds, gathered together, mention what has happened during the day. For days, months, and years afterward it would be mentioned as a disgrace to any shepherd who permitted a stray lamb or sheep to perish without going in search of it. Or, if he has exposed himself to great danger to save the lamb, that will be mentioned to his great credit. Others will praise him as a brave shepherd. They would say Ibrihim went after his sheep and saved it from the mouth of a lion or a bear. If he had not done this he would be branded as a coward. Other sheep of his flock would lose confidence in him, even though he were their leader. This explains the parable of our Lord: "If any man have a hundred sheep, and one of them be gone astray, doth he not leave the ninety and nine, and go unto the mountains, and seek that which goeth astray? And if so be that he find it, verily I say unto you, he rejoiceth over it more than over the ninety and nine which have not gone astray."[1]

246. "*Rod and Staff*."—The Oriental shepherd always carries a staff or crook, and usually a rod or club for defense. The *nabūt*, or club, is a heavy wooden stick, large and thick at one end, and studded with spikes or flint stones to make it a more deadly weapon. Sometimes he uses this with a dexterous swing, or he flings it at an enemy, as the Australian bushmen use a *boomerang*. It is smaller at the handle end, and often has a string put through a hole, so that it can be carried, swung on the shepherd's wrist, or over his shoulder. The shepherds about Bethlehem are still equipped with these two sticks, the longer one with a crook to lift out the sheep, or lambs from a

[1] Matt. 18 : 12, 13.

hole or crevice of rock, and to hold up at the entrance of the fold as the sheep pass in or out, and are counted by the shepherd. Anciently this was called "passing under the rod."[1]

247. *Sheepfolds.*—The Oriental sheepfolds differ widely in their structure and character. Often now, even as in primitive times, the fold is in a large and convenient cave, in the hill or mountain side. On the open plains, or in the valleys, the sheepfold is an enclosure of low walls of rough stones, on the top of which are thorn branches placed to prevent the flock from jumping over, and to keep wild beasts and robbers from getting in. The entrance is by a gate, or door, from which the sheep enter and go out. This door is barred by the master when one flock occupies a fold. In one corner of this enclosure there is a shelter, either a building or a corner roofed over to protect the flock from storms. Oftentimes several shepherds and flocks occupy the same fold to protect themselves from robbers more securely. Then, one shepherd watches part of the night with a dog, and the other shepherds rest and sleep, taking turns in watching. Or, they may employ a "*bowwab*," or porter, to care for the flocks and to guard the gate. The porter will open the gate for one of the shepherds only. Thus, it is said, "He that entereth in by the door is the shepherd of the sheep. To him the porter openeth."[2] In the morning each shepherd calls for his flock, and they hear, and follow him. There may be a thousand or ten thousand sheep mixed together, yet every shepherd can quickly separate his flock from all the rest by calling to them. As the flock enters the fold at night, the shepherd stands at the door and counts his sheep one by one as they pass under his staff, or he may do this when they come out to be led forth to the pasture in the morning. It is an interesting sight to watch the shepherds "telling" their respective flocks, and to see how the sheep will untangle themselves from the mass and come forth, those only coming which belong to the flock of the shepherd who is making the call.

Mr. Hanauer says such sheep-cotes, or folds, are found all

[1] Ezek. 20 : 37; Lev. 27 : 32.　　　[2] John 10 : 2, 3.

over Syria, "many have been used for thousands of years, as is evident from the enormous accumulation of sheep's manure, sometimes several feet deep, on their floors. . . . In the summer when the pasture close to the towns and villages is exhausted, the sheep are led further afield, at some distance from their village, and are folded in caves which generally have a small enclosure built of large stones in front of the entrance, and serving as a bivouacking place for the shepherds, . . . who 'were abiding in the field, keeping watch over their flocks by night.'[1] The folds in towns or hamlets consist of regular buildings, comprising a row of vaults or chambers occupying one side of a courtyard, protected by a stone wall, in which is one door only, locked at night, the key being held by the porter."

248. *Flocks.*—Sheep abound in numbers and variety in Oriental lands. The Arab tribes of the Adwān and the Beni Sakk'r tribes have great flocks on the east of the Jordan. Thus, Dr. Tristram speaks of riding mile after mile "through flocks, countless as the sand, while winding up the gently sloping valley. In the open spaces among the temples at Rabbah were flocks of sheep and goats at night, whose bleating was almost deafening." Thomson tells of the great flocks which were driven over from the valleys of the Euphrates to the seaboard in 1853, and of the vast numbers of these flocks when they set out from the distant deserts. "The northern plains literally swarm with sheep."

249. *"Broad-tailed" Sheep.*—From time immemorial the sheep has been known as a domesticated animal. There are species of Oriental wild sheep, but they are not apparently of the same family as the domestic sheep. In Syria now there are two kinds of sheep, one with short fine wool and short small legs. But the common Syrian sheep is tall, with a larger frame, and a long Roman nose. This breed also is marked by a remarkable development of the rump, or tail, from which they are sometimes called "broad-tailed sheep." These were noticed in early times by Herodotus and Aristarchus, who greatly

exaggerated this characteristic of the sheep. Their accounts were magnified, and were presented in some Bible dictionaries of our day. These erroneous descriptions were pointed out years ago by Doctors Van Lennep and Thomson. The broad-tailed sheep were early known in Arabia, where Herodotus heard of them. Harris, a traveler of a century ago, and Russell, in the history of Aleppo, drew a picture of these sheep out of their imaginations, whose tails were of so prodigious size as to require to be supported by thin boards, under which were toy wheels, to help the animal in carrying them. Of course this story is fanciful. The fat is really a growth of the rump, as stated in the Bible, rather than of the tail proper. Neither one of these ancient authors or their copyists claim to have ever seen such a sheep as he describes. The broad-tailed sheep, when fully covered with wool, has a comely form, for the wool covers the cushion of fat, and is long, so that this peculiarity would not be noticed. It is only when the sheep has been just shorn that this enlargement of the rump, or tail, is to be seen. Then it appears rather as a large cushion, ending in a somewhat broadened tail, but not long, and rarely falling below the knee of the hind leg. The statement of the broad tails of Arabian sheep, three cubits, if not more long, must be credited to Oriental imagination.

250. *Fattening Sheep.*—" The people have a curious way of fattening the sheep," says Prof. Post, "in order to make the tail grow to an enormous size, that they may try out the fat, and use it in cooking as we use butter or lard. Syria and Palestine are full of mulberry trees, the leaves of which are used in the spring-time to feed the silk-worms. As soon as the cocoons are spun, each family buys a lamb, and commences to fatten it on mulberry leaves. But the sheep would not of itself eat enough to make it as fat as its owner wishes, so three times a day the mistress of the house sits down beside the sheep and commences to feed it from a bushel basket of mulberry leaves, which she and her children have just stripped from the trees. She crumples a handful of these tender leaves in her

hands, and crowds them into the sheep's mouth, and then actually wags the creature's jaws until the morsel is chewed and swallowed. She then follows one handful by another until the basket is empty. In vain does the poor brute roll the green ball around with its tongue, and try to push it and her fingers out of its mouth. With her palm under its jaws, and the thumb and fingers curled around in the corner of its mouth, in the place where there are no teeth, she works the jaws and pushes back the morsel between the grinders, until the sheep fairly pants with fatigue, and only gets rest when the appointed meal is over. In the early part of the summer the mistress of the house takes him daily to the fountain for a bath, that his appetite and power of digestion may be revived. But as the months roll on, the sheep walks more and more clumsily, and finally, he lies down, so heavy with his fat tail and bloated body, that he never rises again. Still she brings the water and pours it over his fleece as before, and continues to feed him until the mulberry leaves are gone. Then comes the great day for the household when the sheep is killed; the meat cut into small pieces and boiled down in the fat, and the whole stored away in earthen jars for the winter, the only animal food, except eggs and milk, which many of the people have during that season."

251. *Shepherd Dog*.—The Oriental sheep is capable of training, some of them becoming special favorites of the shepherd, always near him, and for them he has a name not only, but choice bits of what he gathers to give to them from time to time. On the other hand, the great body of the flock in Oriental lands, as elsewhere, are mere worldlings, running from bush to bush, tumbling into trouble or getting lost, and giving the shepherd no end of anxiety and labor to keep them within safe bounds. These sheep are often brought back by the dogs, which the shepherd sends after them. Thomson regards these shepherd dogs of Syria as lazy, half-starved, ill-conditioned, furious barking, mean curs, and not at all the noble animal known to us, like the St. Bernard dog. And Tristram says that

the sheep dog is the pariah dog of the town, an outlaw and scavenger, but attached to a personal owner or shepherd.

The sheep are also cared for by helpers, who aid the shepherds. These are not properly hirelings, for they share in the flock, receiving one-tenth of the increase as their portion. The sheep respond to a peculiar call in Arabic like "hoo hoo," "ha ha," or "taa taa." They hear this call at all times of the day and respond to it, and they also are quieted if they hear it at night. One who visited a shepherd at his sheepfold in the early night watch, heard him calling out "hoo hoo," "taa taa." This he said, he did so that if the sheep heard the prowling wolves, they would be quieted by hearing the shepherd's voice, and knowing that he was by them to protect them from the wolves.

252. *The Wool and Skin.*—The sheep is one of the most useful animals to the Oriental; its wool clothes him, its milk feeds him, its skin protects him from the cold, and provides him with a cloak or *aba* in which he can traverse the wilderness or the mountains, and which he can fold about him as he lies down at night, thus providing him both his bed and his covering, and the flesh is the most palatable of Oriental dishes for food. From earliest time a sheep or a lamb, without blemish from the flock, was the holiest offering man could make in sacrificial worship.

253. *Black Sheep and Goats.*—"Most Syrian sheep are white, but some are mottled and others entirely black," says Mr. Hanauer. The black sheep are from Northern Syria and the highlands farther north. The sheep and the goats, though led out by the same shepherd, belonging to the same flock, and feeding in the same pasture side by side, do not mix; they enter the fold together, but once within, they keep separate.

The goats are bold, venturesome, very playful, and often give the shepherd trouble by clambering to dangerous places where he cannot follow; and break into crops of corn where sheep blindly follow. They are also headstrong and very lusty.

The goats most common in Palestine are the *Capra mam-*

bricas, remarkable for their long pendant ears,[1] stout recurved horns, and long, black silky hair. The goats used
for milking purposes at Damascus are of a different breed,
somewhat larger than the goats of Palestine, of a tawny and
gray color, and the contour of the head is very peculiar, with a
prominent elevation of the nasal bone, long pendant ears, and
very short horns.

254. *Goats.*—The goat thrives on the mountains, or in the
hilly countries, where there is little pasture, except shrubs and
brushwood. On the lowlands and wherever there is grass, the
sheep thrive better, and are better adapted to the region than
the goat. The great tablelands and plateaus of Arabia and
about the Lebanon and Mt. Hermon abound with flocks of
goats. In fact, the goat has in large measure prevented the
spreading of the forests, having extirpated many species of
trees once covering the hills and low mountains of Syria and
Arabia.

On the border between the plains and plateaus, sheep and
goats are often seen together. In a measure, they mingle with
the sheep, but when folded together at night, the goats may always be seen in separate groups. Even around wells they often
are by themselves as by instinct keeping apart from the sheep.
When a chance stranger comes to an Arab camp, a kid of the
goats is the usual dish at his entertainment.

255. *Flocks of Goats.*—Dr. Tristram reports seeing hundreds
of goats at a village under Mt. Hermon gathered for the night
in the open market place. "It was no easy matter," he says,
"to thread our way among them, the goats had no idea of moving for belated intruders. Every street and open space is filled
with the goats, and women, boys, and girls are everywhere milking in small pewter pots." The goat not only gives its milk and
flesh for the Oriental, but its skin supplies him with bottles for
conveying water, wine, milk, and oil. Stone jars are employed
for storing liquids in pits or cellars, and keeping a supply of
water within the houses. But goat-skins are the common

---

[1] Amos 3 : 12.

ORIENTAL AND DONKEY.   P. 168

GOAT HERDER IN DISTANCE.

(Copyright by Underwood & Underwood, New York.)

SHEPHERD AND FLOCK, MOAB.   P. 167

(Copyright by Underwood & Underwood, New York.)

"bottles" used for conveyance of liquids from one place to another. The skin of the goat is tanned with the hair on; such tanneries where bottles are made are found near ·Hebron. The hair on the bottles preserves them from injury and friction in traveling.

There are various kinds of goats in Palestine, the Syrian goats being usually of two marked kinds, one with short ears, sometimes nearly erect, as in the wild goats of the north, and the other with long ears pendant, sometimes reaching lower than the animal's nose. The goat has recurved horns. It is large and usually black, with long hair. The hair is longer and more silky and the build of the animal more compact than in Western countries. In some Oriental lands, the mohair goat is raised for the sake of its long silky hair. But it is not so well adapted to the rough bushy and thorny districts as the common goat. The wild goat of Arabia and Syria is somewhat similar to those of the Alps and Pyrenees and are called *Beden* by the Arabs. The wild goat is shy and wary, keeping to the mountains, its color resembling that of the foliage and rocky regions which is its habitat, making it difficult to be seen, so that tourists rarely discover them. The goats were once abundant by the Dead Sea near Engedi (Ain Jidy), which means "fountain of the kid."

Mr. Haddad counts the flesh of the goats not very palatable. The milk is delicious and furnishes a very rich cheese. Some Orientals have a superstition that when they go out of the house in the morning, if they meet a lamb or a sheep, it promises good fortune. If they first meet a goat, it will be a day of trouble and disappointment. So, too, when a flock of sheep passes an Arab's path he is pleased because he thinks it a good omen, but if he passes a goat it is a bad omen.

256. *Wild Goat.*—The goat is wild in disposition and quarrelsome. He is mischievous and destructive to orchards and fruits. He is quick and active, climbing up the rocks and over steep places. The common people say goats are "Jinnies," meaning they are possessed with evil spirits, they are so mischievous and wicked. They do not multipy as rapidly as sheep.

They fight over their food, and wander into forbidden fields, and are destructive of grain, as well as fruit.

The Hebrews, like the modern Arabs, had several terms for the goat. He was called Ya'ēl, meaning climber, and Sa'eer, "hairy goat." Goats were an important part of the wealth of the old patriarchs, and were used for food and for sacrifice. Abram offered a she-goat; Jacob sent presents to Esau of two hundred she-goats and twenty he-goats,[1] and Nabal had three thousand sheep and one thousand goats.[2] Laban had a large possession of goats.[3]

257. *Separating Flocks.*—Tristram describes a scene which illustrates our Lord's comparison. "The shepherd was picking his way down a precipitous ridge, toward a well-known cavern, followed by his flocks and herds. The sun was setting, and the sheep quietly following the shepherd along the beaten and more easy paths, while the goats gambolled and skipped from rock to rock a little higher up on the mountain side, still keeping in line with the sheep, but delighting to exhibit their prowess. When the cave was reached, they scrambled down by the most impossible routes, often leaping in over the backs of their more sedate companions." In the final separation of the righteous and the wicked it is said, "He shall separate them one from another, as a shepherd divideth his sheep from the goats: And he shall set the sheep on his right hand, but the goats on the left."[4] The elder brother in the parable of the prodigal son complains, "Thou never gavest me a kid, that I might make merry with my friends,"[5] illustrating how common it was to have a kid for an entertainment, or a feast, even in the days of our Lord. And much earlier, Rebekah tells her son Jacob, "Fetch me from thence (the flock) two good kids of the goats; and I will make them savoury meat for thy father, such as he loveth."[6] When the angel appeared to Gideon, he "made ready a kid,"[7] and Manoah likewise said unto the angel, "Let us detain thee, until we shall have made

---

[1] Gen. 32 : 14.   [2] I Sam. 25 : 2.   [3] Gen. 30 : 33.   [4] Matt. 25 : 32, 33.
[5] Luke 15 : 29.   [6] Gen. 27 : 9.   [7] Judg. 6 : 19.

ready a kid for thee."[1] The old proverb for prosperity is, "thou shalt have goats' milk enough for thy food, for the food of thy household, and for the maintenance for thy maidens."[2] And again, "The goats are the price of the field."[3]

Sheep, goats, flocks, and shepherds are mentioned or alluded to over five hundred (523) times in the Bible, and herds over fifty times. The prophet condemns the shepherds in his day, because they "fed themselves and fed not my flock."[4] The shepherd was an "abomination unto the Egyptians" in the time of Joseph.[5]

In the care of his people, Jehovah is compared to an Oriental shepherd. The greatest poem in Hebrew or any other litera-ture is the Shepherd Psalm. It has been translated into more languages, read by more people, treasured in more memories and in more hearts throughout the world than any other poem known in the literature of the world. So the Psalmist calls Jehovah his shepherd, "The Lord is my shepherd."[6] "Give ear, O shepherd of Israel, thou that leadest Joseph like a flock."[7] Jehovah is said to "feed his flock like a shepherd: he shall gather the lambs with his arm, and carry them in his bosom."[8] He "made his own people to go forth like sheep."[9] The people are called "Sheep of thy pasture."[10] Jesus calls himself "The good Shepherd,"[11] and the Lord Jesus is spoken of as "That great Shepherd of the sheep."[12] And "the Shepherd and Bishop of your souls."[13]

258. *Wealth in Flocks and Herds.*—The wealth of the Oriental in ancient times consisted largely in flocks and herds as at this day. Abram "had sheep, and oxen, and camels," and "was very rich in cattle, in silver, and in gold."[14] Lot was also rich in "flocks, and herds, and tents."[15] Isaac was the envy of the Philistines, because he had such immense flocks, herds, and "store of servants."[16] Before his affliction, Job is said to

---

[1] Judg. 13 : 15.
[2] Prov. 27 : 27.
[3] Prov. 27 : 26.
[4] Ezek. 34 : 8. Compare Zech. 10 : 3; 11 : 3, 5, 8.
[5] Gen. 46 : 34.
[6] Ps. 23 : 1.
[7] Ps. 80 : 1.
[8] Isaiah 40 : 11.
[9] Ps. 78 : 52.
[10] Ps. 79 : 13.
[11] John 20 : 14.
[12] Heb. 13 : 20.
[13] 1 Peter 2 : 25; see 1 Peter 5 : 4.
[14] Gen. 12 : 16; 13 : 2; 24 : 35.
[15] Gen. 13 : 5.
[16] Gen. 26 : 14.

have had seven thousand sheep, three thousand camels, five
hundred yoke of oxen, and five hundred asses; and after his
trial his possessions in flocks and herds, sheep, camels, and oxen
were doubled.[1]   The country east of the Jordan had rich pasture in olden times, sustaining great flocks, perhaps greater than
in modern times.   Mesha, King of Moab, gave to Israel's
king as tribute a hundred thousand lambs, and a hundred
thousand rams in wool or in fleece.[2]   An Arab Sheikh of the
Beni Sakk'r tribe boasted to Dr. Tristram in modern times that
he pastured thirty thousand in his flock on the same plains of
Moab. The Hagarenes also, to the east of Moab and Ammon,
claimed to have lost two hundred and fifty thousand sheep,
fifty thousand camels, and two thousand asses in a war with the
Reubenites.[3] Israel's great king, Solomon, is said to have
offered in sacrifice at the dedication of the temple one hundred
and twenty thousand sheep and twenty-two thousand oxen.[4]
And later King Asa offered seven thousand sheep at one time.[5]
King Hezekiah provided for a great passover feast, following a
rededication of the temple, seven thousand sheep, one thousand
oxen, besides ten thousand sheep furnished by the princes of
Israel for the same occasion.[6] The wandering Arabs brought
tribute to the king of Judah seven thousand seven hundred
rams and seven thousand seven hundred he-goats.[7] Nor are
the sacred writers alone in telling of the wealth of the ancients in
flocks. Homer and Hesiod sing of the great wealth in flocks
and herds which great men possessed. In traveling among the
Arab tribes in 1846 Wilson saw flocks with more than fifty
thousand goats and upward of twenty thousand camels.

259. *Shearing.*—Sheep shearing now, and in olden time,
was an occasion of joy and merry-making. After his wife's
death, Judah being comforted, went up to his sheep shearing.[8]
Nabal, the churl, was having a rollicking time at sheep shearing when David called upon him, and interrupted his revels
and he was too drunk to treat the coming king civilly. Had

[1] Job. 1 : 3; 42 : 12.   [2] 2 Kings 3 : 4.   [3] 1 Chron. 5 : 21.
[4] 2 Chron. 7 : 5.   [5] 2 Chron. 15 : 11.   [6] 2 Chron. 30 : 24.
[7] 2 Chron. 17 : 11.   [8] Gen. 38 : 12.

it not been for his more discreet wife, it would have fared hard
with Nabel.[1] When his brother Amnon, was "merry with
wine" at a sheep shearing, Absalom plotted to have him assas-
sinated.[2] The wool of the sheep was used for clothing, the
first fleece being devoted to the priest in olden times.[3] The
curtains of the tabernacle in the wilderness were made of
dyed goats' wool, blue, purple, and scarlet.[4] So common was it
to have fine clothes made of lambs' wool that it became a
proverb, "Lambs are for thy clothing."[5] In Lemuel's song
of the model housewife, she is commended because, "She
seeketh wool, and flax, and worketh willingly with her hands."[6]

260. *Trumpets.*—The male sheep have recurved horns, and
these were used for trumpets by the soldiers marching about
the city of Jericho.[7]

The horns were also hollowed out and used to carry oil by
the prophets and the priests, as in the days of Samuel.[8] Even
the trumpets used by the priests, which were made of silver,
may also have imitated the shape of the ram's horn.[9] For
the seven trumpets used by the priests at the siege of Jericho
were of rams' horns.[10] Similar trumpets were used by Gideon's
Band in the capture of the Midianite host.[11] And the Hebrew
term for trumpet, which was used to call the people together
at Sinai, is *Yobel*, which signifies a ram's horn.

261. *Shepherd's Peril.*—The danger of the shepherd's life is
further illustrated by the story of David, when he went to the
Philistine army, and proposed to meet the champion giant
Goliath. "Thy servant was keeping his father's sheep; and
when there came a lion, or a bear, and took a lamb out of the
flock, I went out after him, and smote him, and delivered it out
of his mouth; and when he arose against me, I caught him
by his beard, and smote him, and slew him. Thy servant
smote both the lion and the bear."[12] This danger is implied
by the prophet who refers to the lop-eared goats and sheep.

[1] 1 Sam. 25. [2] 2 Sam. 13 : 23, 28. [3] Deut. 18 : 4.
[4] Ex. 26 : 7; 36 : 14. [5] Prov. 27 : 26. [6] Prov. 31 : 13.
[7] Josh. 6 : 4. [8] 1 Sam. 16 : 1. [9] Num. 10 : 2-10.
[10] Josh. 6 : 4, 8, 13. [11] Judg. 7 : 8, 20. [12] 1 Sam. 17 : 34-36.

Thus, "As the shepherd rescueth out of the mouth of the lion two legs, or a piece of an ear, so shall the children of Israel be rescued that sit in Samaria in the corner of a couch, and on the silken cushions of a bed." [1]

262. *Watering Flocks.*—The watering of the flocks in modern times is often done by women, although, as in olden time, men are required to do the heavier work or to defend the flock. Thus, it is said that Jacob first met his future wife, Rachel, at the well: "He looked, and, behold, a well in the field, and, lo, three flocks of sheep lying there by it; for out of that well they watered the flocks: and the stone upon the well's mouth was great. And thither were all the flocks gathered; and they rolled the stone from the well's mouth, and watered the sheep, and put the stone again upon the well's mouth in its place. . . . And he said, Lo, it is yet high day, neither is it time that the cattle should be gathered together: water ye the sheep, and go and feed them. And they said, We cannot, until all the flocks be gathered together, and they roll the stone from the well's mouth; then we water the sheep. While he was yet speaking with them, Rachel came with her father's sheep; for she kept them. . . . Jacob went near, and rolled the stone from the well's mouth, and watered the flock of Laban his mother's brother. And Jacob kissed Rachel, and lifted up his voice, and wept. And Jacob told Rachel that he was her father's brother." [2]

A similar scene may be witnessed among Syrian and Arab shepherds to-day at any spring or well on the plains. Thus, a traveler of half a century ago says, "We came upon a well and a watering trough, where several shepherds had gathered their flocks together to drink. The quietness of the valley, contrasted with the rumors of danger from the Bedouins, reminding us of the passage in Judges, 'Far from the noise of archers, in the places of drawing water.'" [3] At another place the same travelers came to a fine flowing well. "The water was cold and pleasant. Some Syrian shepherds had gathered their flocks around the well. There were many

[1] Amos 3 : 12.   [2] Gen. 29 : 2–12.   [3] Judg. 5 : 11.

hundreds of goats; some drinking out of the troughs, some reclining till the noon-day heat should be past." This, too, reminded the travelers of how the Lord promises to refresh weary souls, and how Jehovah makes his people to rest.

The sheep and the lambs are symbols of meekness, patience, gentleness, and quiet endurance in suffering. Throughout the Old Testament, as in the New, Jesus Christ the Redeemer of mankind is set forth as the sacrifice, the lamb slain from the foundation of the world, brought to the slaughter, suffering with submission, the one offering for sin. The multitude of sacrifices mentioned throughout the Old Testament signified and pointed to this one great sacrifice, when Christ should bear the sin of the world, and should offer a redemption for all the race, a redemption from all condemnation.

In recent times Oriental shepherds often work in couples: one leads the flock, he is the chief shepherd; the other follows the flock, to guard against stragglers getting separated and lost from the flock. This seems to be a modern custom, not prevailing in ancient or primitive Oriental shepherd life. See page 161.

XXII.

CATTLE AND CAMELS.

To the Oriental of to-day the mule is a beast of burden. The patient ox plows his field, the horse speeds him over the hills and valleys, and the camel is still, as of old, the "ship of the desert." Domesticated cattle and camels, exclusive of sheep and goats, are named or alluded to about nine hundred times in Scripture.

263. *The Ox-herds.*—In modern times, chief among the domestic cattle is the ox. All the cattle of Palestine are generally small in size, with short horns, shaggy short legs, usually black, or red, or brown in color, rarely piebald, or with white spots. They are not abundant in the Sinaitic Peninsula, but are found on the plains of Sharon, Akka, Philistia, and about Dothan, as well as abundant east of the Jordan in Gilead, Moab, and Bashan-land. They are less common in Central Palestine. The Hebrew term for cattle, *Miqueh*, signifies primarily "possessions." So much of the wealth of early Hebrews consisted of herds and flocks that the same term was used to designate "possessions" and "cattle." A herd is often made up by the cattle of a number of villagers in the same town, who employ a herdsman to care for them in the pastures near by or some distance away. It is a rough life that the herdsmen have, defending their charge against robbers, wolves, and against wandering away. Van Lennep describes such a herd owned by villagers going out to the pasture: "There are the oxen, the bulls, the cows, and the calves of various ages; the she-asses and their colts, with perhaps some superannuated *paterfamilias* of a jackass, no longer able to work, and favored with his board; there is the huge and ponderous buffalo, accompanied by its calf, whose clumsy gambols excite the admiration of the whole drove." He often watched the herd return

at night; "It is the merriest hour of the day; for all the little children then rush out to meet the drove, for a gambol and a chase home, each after his own pet lamb, calf, or colt. Horses and camels are rarely herded promiscuously with other animals, but fed by themselves."

264. *Wealth In.*—Cattle are often branded upon their haunches or shoulders now, as we know they were thousands of years ago, from representations on Egyptian monuments. The buffalo is believed to have come from Eastern Asia, either India or Hindustan. The horned cattle of Eastern Asia are large bodied, but short legged, and have a hump upon the foreshoulders, and are believed to be of a different species from those of Western Asia.

Oxen and bullocks were perhaps a larger proportion of the wealth of Oriental peoples in olden times than now. The apostle asks: "Doth God take care for oxen?" "Thou shalt not muzzle the ox when he treadeth out the corn."[1] The Mosaic law also provided that on the Sabbath "Thine ox and thine ass may rest."[2] The prophet Elisha "was plowing with twelve yoke of oxen before him, and he with the twelfth," when Elijah met him and called him to the prophetical work.[3] The purchase of oxen was made an excuse for not responding to a social invitation: "I have bought five yoke of oxen, and I go to prove them."[4] The cows and the calves were trained to the yoke in early times. Thus, when the lords of the Philistines wanted to send back the ark, they said; "Make a new cart, and take two milch kine, on which there hath come no yoke, and tie the kine to the cart, and bring their calves home from them: and take the ark of the Lord and lay it upon the cart."[5] And the prophet calls Ephraim "An heifer that is taught, and loveth to tread out the corn."[6]

265. *In Sacrifice.*—While bullocks were offered in sacrifice, and the flesh was eaten by the priests when not offered as a burnt offering, it was not so common to use the flesh with ordi-

[1] 1 Cor. 9 : 9; Deut. 25 : 4. [2] Ex. 23 : 12. [3] 1 Kings 19 : 19.
[4] Luke 14 : 19. [5] 1 Sam. 6 : 7, 8. [6] Hosea 10 : 11.

12

nary meals as it is with us. It is rare now that beef is eaten by the Oriental. When he eats flesh the Oriental prefers mutton. The frequency with which domestic animals were used in sacrifice is illustrated in the time of Saul, who excused himself from the charge of the prophet, saying, "The people spared the best of the sheep and of the oxen, to sacrifice unto the Lord thy God."[1] Generally a young bullock, or a heifer, or a lamb was offered in sacrifice.

266. *Stall Fed.*—I have already noticed the number that were sacrificed at the dedication of the temple and on other festal occasions by the kings of Israel. It is clear, too, that in our Lord's time cattle were a common possession of the people, "Doth not each one of you on the sabbath loose his ox or his ass from the stall, and lead him away to watering?"[2] And the prophet Malachi describes the prosperity of Israel to come by saying, "Ye shall . . . grow up as calves of the stall."[3] Stall-fed cattle are often referred to even earlier: "Better is a dinner of herbs where love is, than a stalled ox and hatred therewith."[4] The princes of old are called so luxurious that "The calves out of the midst of the stall" they could only eat.[5]

267. *Mule and Ass.*—The mule is no longer the royal and highly esteemed animal that he once was counted to be by the Oriental. He has been degraded now to a beast of burden, aided by the donkey, and is usually in modern times classed with that ignoble beast. But in former times a certain variety of the mule and the ass were regarded as superior and noble beasts, upon which only princes and kings rode. Persons of wealth and of quality also made a journey upon these animals. Thus, it is said of Abram that he saddled his ass to go to Mt. Moriah.[6] When called by the king, Balaam proceeded on a similar animal from Chaldea to Moab.[7] A prophet also came from Judah to Bethel in this manner.[8] Thirty sons of a noble judge rode on these colts, indicating their wealth and dignity.[4] And seventy others of the family of a judge rode on like animals as a

[1] 1 Sam. 15 : 15.   [2] Luke 13 : 15.   [3] Malachi 4 : 2.
[4] Prov. 15 : 17; See 1 Kings 4 : 23.   [5] Amos 6 : 4.   [6] Gen. 22 : 3.
[7] Num. 22 : 21.   [8] 1 Kings 13 : 23.   [9] Judg. 10 : 4.

mark of their wealth and rank.[1] In like manner did the prince
Ahithophel and Mephibosheth ride on a like royal beast.[2]
Noble women were also accustomed to ride in this manner, as
Zipporah and Achsah, the daughter of Caleb.[3] Abigail, who
became the wife of David, first met him riding on her royal
beast. The noble Shunnamite woman set off to find Elisha in
a similar manner.[4] White asses were a peculiar mark of great
dignity and high rank. Deborah describes the judges as "Ye
that ride on white asses."[5] Finally, the prophet declared
of the Messiah, "Behold, thy King cometh unto thee: he is just,
and having salvation; lowly, and riding upon an ass, and upon a
colt the foal of an ass."[6] And this prophecy was fulfilled at the
time of the triumphal entry into Jerusalem.[7]

268. *The Horse.*—The horse is not peculiar to Oriental
lands. Though from time immemorial it has been known, it
is probably more widely used now throughout Western Asia and
some other Oriental lands than it was three thousand years ago.
The finest and most celebrated race of horses is the Arabian.
Persians, Kurds, and Circassians are also famous horsemen, and
are noted for their fine horses, each being prized for some peculiar qualities. Thus, the Kurd has long been famous as a bold,
dashing, and skilful rider, and his horse equally famous for
its strength, endurance, and quick response to his master's
will. The Circassian horse is usually smaller than others,
but very alert and hardy in mountaineer work. Women of
the Orient now usually ride astride, and seldom sideways, as
with us.

269. *Wheeled Carriages.*—Chariots and wheeled carriages
drawn by horses are rarely seen in Western Asia or in Africa.
A few of foreign manufacture have been introduced there during the last generation, but long ago they were more common.
The barbarian from the East and the South swept over these
lands of Western Asia, destroying temple and palace, chariot

---

[1] Judg. 12 : 14.
[2] 2 Sam. 17 : 23; 19 : 26.
[3] Ex. 4 : 20; Judg. 1 : 14.
[4] 1 Sam. 25 : 20; 2 Kings 4 : 24.
[5] Judg. 5 : 10. See p. 183.
[6] Zech. 9 : 9.
[7] Matt. 21 : 5. See Mark 11 : 4; Luke 19 : 30; Isaiah 62 : 11. Compare John 12 : 15.

and chariot-roads, and displacing the comforts of civilization
by the rude and raw conditions of a barbarian life. Native
two-wheeled clumsy carts were found in India by the British,
and are still seen in rural sections.

270. *War Horse.*—The horse is mentioned about a hundred
and forty times in Scripture. In the days of the sacred writers,
as now, the horse was chiefly celebrated for his power in war,
and as a terror in predatory excursions by brigands and lawless bands of the wild desert tribes rather than as useful in
harness. The earliest mention of chariots and horses in the
Bible relates, however, to a mission of mercy and peace.[1]
While the horse appears as a widely useful animal in Egypt as
early as the time of Jacob and Joseph, yet from the comparatively late appearance of figures of the horse in Egyptian sculpture, some infer that it was not known in Egypt before the period
of the Hyksos kings. When the Hebrews escaped from Egyptian bondage they were pursued by six hundred chosen chariots
and by all the chariot horses and horsemen, or cavalry, of
Egypt.[2] The Canaanites had "chariots of iron" when Joshua
attempted to conquer them.[3] During the reign of the first
Hebrew king (Saul) the Philistines warred against him with
thirty thousand chariots and six thousand cavalry, that is,
mounted horsemen.[4] And the Syrians hired thirty-two thousand chariots and cavalry from Mesopotamia to war against
David.[5] The Hebrews did not at first use chariots or war
horses in their warfare. The Deuteronomic law required of
the king, "He shall not multiply horses to himself."[6] So when
David captured one thousand chariots and seven hundred
horsemen (or cavalry) from the king of Zobah of Mesopotamia,
he disabled the horses, reserving only a hundred for as many
chariots.[7] But Solomon, who fell into idolatry by alliance with
Egypt, gathered fourteen hundred chariots and twelve thousand cavalry as a military body guard.[8] Later, Israel was

---

[1] Gen. 41 : 43.   Compare Gen. 45 : 19–21; 46 : 29; 50 : 9.   [2] Ex. 14 : 7, 9.
[3] Josh. 17 : 16; Judg. 1 : 19.   Compare Judg. 4 : 3, 13.   [4] 1 Sam. 13 : 5.
[5] 1 Chron. 19 : 6, 7.   [6] Deut. 17 : 16.
[7] 2 Sam. 8 : 4.   [8] 1 Kings 4 : 26; 10 : 26, 28, 29.

stripped of these means of defense, having only fifty horses and ten chariots at the siege of Samaria.[1]

The prophets pronounced woes upon those who put their trust in horses, "Woe to them that go down to Egypt for help, and rely on horses, and trust in chariots because they are many, and in horsemen because they are very strong, but they look not unto the Holy One of Israel."[2]   Again, in foretelling the destruction that should come to the people of Israel, the prophet said of the fury and power of the Chaldeans: "Their horses also are swifter than leopards, and are more fierce than the evening wolves," and of their horsemen he said, "They fly as an eagle that hasteth to devour."[3]   And in predicting the fall of Nineveh, the prophet gives this sublime but awful picture: "Woe to the bloody city! it is all full of lies and rapine. . . . The noise of the whip, and the noise of the rattling of wheels, and prancing horses, and bounding chariots, the horsemen mounting (or 'charging'), and the flashing sword, and the glittering spear, and a multitude of slain, and the great heap of corpses, and there is no end of the bodies."[4]   But when prosperity and blessings were to come from Israel, it was the camel, and not the horse of Midian that would bring these great gifts.[5] Does this imply that the camel was more common in Arabia than the horse at that period? The horses in Egypt seem to have come from the plains of Mesopotamia in early times. The monuments depict horses of a noble breed famed in early times in Syria. A horse not unlike the modern Arabian steed in his build is sculptured at Persepolis, with a string and bells upon his neck. This may illustrate the prophet's prediction, "In that day shall there be upon the bells of the horses, Holy unto Jehovah." There is no more lofty and magnificent description of the war horse than that given in the dramatic book of the Old Testament.[6]

---

[1] 2 Kings 13 : 7.   [2] Isaiah 31 : 1.   Compare Ezek. 17 : 15.
[3] Hab. 1 : 8.   [4] Nahum 3 : 1-3.
[5] Isaiah 60 : 6.   [6] Job 39 : 19-25.

"Hast thou given the horse his might?
Hast thou clothed his neck with the quivering mane?
Hast thou made him to leap as a locust?
The glory of his snorting is terrible.
He paweth in the valley, and rejoiceth in his strength;
He goeth out to meet the armed men. . . .
He swalloweth the ground with fierceness and rage; . . .
And he smelleth the battle afar off,
The thunder of the captains, and the shouting." [1]

271. *The Camel—The " Ship of the Desert."*—From time immemorial the camel has been the characteristic companion of
the Oriental. Wherever you see the one you expect to see the
other. In every scene in all history they are the peculiar
type of Oriental lands, especially of Western Asia and of
Africa. The elephant may be equally conspicuous in India,
but his range is more limited, leaving the camel the undisputed and characteristic animal of the larger part of the Orient.
The camel can scarcely be called a beautiful or a picturesque
animal. Modern travelers who have had experience in riding
upon it would generally approve of Mr. Russell's (war cor-
respondent to the London Times) description: "An abomin-
ably ugly necessary animal." The average life of the camel
is reputed to be from forty to fifty years. In summer it is
shorn of its hair, chiefly under the neck and the legs, and the
hair is used for making sackcloth and garments for men.
There are two kinds of camels: the one-humped or dromedary, and the two-humped or bactrian. The bactrian camel
is seldom seen in Western Asia, but is common in Persia,
China, Tartary, and Central Asia. The dromedary often
designates a finer breed of the ordinary camel. In early times
the camel was one of the chief sources of wealth of the patriarchs. Thus, Jacob gave Esau thirty milch camels with their
colts.[2] Job was said to have three thousand, and later, six
thousand camels. The Egyptians lost their camels, among
other beasts, in one of the ten plagues.[3] The prophet Isaiah

---

[1] Compare also Ps. 147 : 10; Prov. 21 : 31; Jer. 4 : 13.
[2] Gen. 32 : 15.   [3] Ex. 9 : 3.

describes the universal triumph of Christ's kingdom by depicting wild sons of the desert coming with their camels.[1] Outside of its milk and the use made of its hair in clothing, the principal usefulness of the camel to the Oriental is in traveling. (See section on Traveling.)

Asses in Harvest.—Since the foregoing was published Mr. Hanauer calls attention to a graphic picture of harvest work by aid of asses, which he witnessed. In a mountain village high up in the Anti-Libanus he saw, from his verandah, "young men" cutting grain, and loading the sheaves upon asses, the great bundles piled so high and spreading over the animal so that the head only of the ass projected from under the mass of grain. Compare also the story of the Shunammite, who asked that an ass be sent from the harvest field for her to ride.[2] Sometimes asses probably were used to draw small carts. See Amos 2 : 13, margin.

271a. *Pachyderms.*—Thick-skinned animals are found in many Oriental lands. Among them were the elephant, which was not in Palestine nor Syria, though it must have been known to the Israelites. Solomon made a throne of ivory, which shows that ivory was abundant in his kingdom.

The hippopotamus is poetically, but quite graphically, described in the dramatic book of Job, where English versions call it the "behemoth."

What animal is intended by the Hebrew term rendered "unicorn" in the common English Version, and "wild ox" in the Revised Version, is not clear. If the Hebrew designated a one-horned animal, as the Greek Septuagint does, the description fits the one-horned rhinoceros, and many learned interpreters think this is the animal the sacred writers meant. Job, Psalms, Deuteronomy, and Numbers all mention it.

[1] Isaiah 60 : 6. [2] 2 Kings 4 : 22.

XXIII.

FISHING AND HUNTING.

272. *Syrian Monopoly.*—Among Orientals fishing is rarely a pastime; it is the means of livelihood. In some Oriental countries now fisheries are a monopoly, farmed out by the government for a fixed sum or tax. Thus, the center of the fish trade in Galilee is at Safed. The right and privileges of fishing at Et Tabigah and in that part of the Lake of Galilee is annually rented by a party in Safed, and another party in Damascus rents a similar right to fish in the lake near the plain Et Butaiha. The fishermen reside at Tiberias and other places along the lake, and are paid a percentage on the fish caught. These fish are sent daily on mules to the markets in Safed and elsewhere for sale.[1]

Naturalists note with special interest that the fish common in the Jordan and in the waters of Galilee, are very similar to those found in the Nile and in the lakes and canals of Egypt. Fish abound in the Jabbok and about the pools of Heshbon, as in olden times.[2] Fish of the Lebanon streams and those about Damascus are allied to those now found in the streams of Asia Minor, rather than to those in the Nile. Oriental fishermen now, as from time immemorial, take fish in nets, either the cast-net or the drag, or drawnet. Sometimes hook and line are used, but obviously not as generally as in olden time.

273. *Fish Nets.*—Prof. Post furnishes a description of the nets used in the Eastern Mediterranean; similar nets are also used on the sea of Galilee. The cast-net is circular and weighted with pellets of lead upon the outer edge. The net is about ten feet in diameter, having a line attached to the center. He describes its use thus: "When the net is cast,

[1] S. S. W., 1908, p. 94.   [2] Song of Sol. 7 : 4.

it spreads out to its greatest extent; the fishermen hauls the net toward him by a cord at the center, until he can grasp it with one hand, and then pulls it out of the water, gathering up the folds with the other hand, not allowing the meshes to become entangled with the bits of lead, and coils the net around the other hand, wringing out the water. Thus, the leads are all left hanging from the free border of the net, folded together, but not entangled. The fisherman now wades into the water, often waist-deep, and watches for some sign of a shoal of fish. When he sees a ripple on the surface of the water he seizes the border of the net at any convenient point with the right hand, and by a dexterous twirl throws the net free from the left hand, causing it at the same time to rotate on its center in such a way that the whole net is spread flat to its utmost extent, and falls in the water with a splash, just over the shoal of fish. The leads cause the border of the net at once to sink to the bottom and imprison any fish that may not have escaped during the cast, and the net disappears under the surface of the water. He has taken care to retain his hold on the central cord, with which he slowly draws up the center of the net in the manner before described, and captures any fish that may have been included within the circle of the leads. This mode of fishing is exceedingly picturesque."

274. *Drawnet.*—The drag or drawnet is a strip of netting, often hundreds of feet in length, and from six to eight feet in breadth, like our seine. The two ends of this net are furnished with ropes, which extend for a considerable distance beyond them. One of the long sides of the net is buoyed up by cork floats, and the other side made to sink by leads. This net is sometimes set and drawn in the sea, in which case two boats are required; each boat takes an end of the net, which is let down into the sea, and stretched between them. They then row in such a way as to enclose with the net a great circle of the sea, and when they meet they commence to haul in the net into the boats, until the circle has become small, when the bottom rope is hauled in faster than the top, so that the

fish become enclosed as in a bag, and are pulled over the sides of the boats.

Often the net is set and drawn from the land. Then one boat takes an end of the net, as far as its length will allow, out to sea, and brings it around with a great sweep to the point of starting, where gangs of men haul it in by the ropes at the two ends, gradually pulling the lower rope more than the upper. Again, two boats may stretch the net between them at a distance from the shore, and sweep inward toward the beach, carrying the fish before them. This method is possible where there is a smooth sand beach. Rocks or rubbish would obstruct and tear the net.

275. *Fishing by Night.*—Fishing is rarely done by day. On the Sea of Galilee it is still usually done at night, as in the time of our Lord. Thus, the disciples said they had toiled all night and taken nothing. How could they expect to catch anything in the morning by daylight?

The fisherman, while fishing, takes off his coat; indeed, he does not mind working entirely naked, but if a stranger or one not of his company comes to the shore, he puts on his coat. Thus, Peter put his fisherman's coat about him because he was "naked."

Dr. Tristram tells of an experience on the Sea of Galilee, near Bethsaida. He inquired of a miller if he had any fish. The miller said yes, and ran toward some rushes, which was really the hut of the fisherman, whose net was spread on the shore to dry. Out of the rushes emerged a man stark naked, who began to prepare his net for a cast. Having folded it neatly, he swam in with it a little way, cast it, and returned by a semicircle across to the shore, when he gently drew it in with a few fishes enclosed. Fishermen with a cast-net at the present day work stark naked, with the exception of a thick woolen skull cap. On the Egyptian monuments persons catching fish and water fowl with nets are depicted naked. The poet Virgil advised plowmen to plow "naked," by which he meant, however, in an under garment only. Peter probably had on a tunic or under garment, which peasants usually wear at labor.

276. *Fish Laws.*—Men were trained and became skilled in fishing long before the patriarchal period. On the Assyrian monuments, which are of a very ancient date, various modes of fishing are represented. Fish and fishermen are mentioned over sixty (64) times in the Scriptures. First of all, man was given dominion over the fish in the sea.[1] Various methods of fishing are mentioned, or are used as illustrations of their message by the sacred writers. The Levitical law permitted some kinds of fish to be eaten, and other kinds were forbidden as food to the Hebrews.[2] Those having fins and scales were counted "clean"; those without fins and scales were counted "unclean," like all reptiles, and were not to be used as food. Fish we know were common in Egypt, for the Israelites longed for the fish of that country. "We remember the fish, which we did eat in Egypt."[3] The fish of the Nile were destroyed by one of the ten plagues.[4] Frequently fish died because the streams dried up.[5] In the time of the captivity, Sidon and Tyre were famous for their fisheries.[6] The prophet foretold the time when the fisherman would spread his nets on the ruins of that city, a prediction which is fulfilled to the letter to-day. The fishermen of the wretched village near the site of old Tyre now dry their nets, as the prophet foretold they would, upon the desolate rocky site.[7]

277. *Modes of Fishing.*—The methods of fishing in ancient times were quite like those which prevail to-day. "He taketh up all of them with the angle, he catcheth them in his net, and gathereth them in his drag (net)."[8] The prophet Isaiah alludes to fishing with a cast-net as well as with the hook, "The fishers shall lament, and all they that cast angle into the Nile shall mourn, and they that spread nets upon the waters shall languish."[9] This exactly describes the modern circular cast-net and the mode of fishing with it. This mode of fishing

[1] Gen. 1 : 26. [2] Lev. 11 : 9–12. [3] Num. 11 : 5.
[4] Ex. 7 : 21; Ps. 105 : 29. [5] Isaiah 50 : 2. [6] Neh. 13 : 16.
[7] Ezek. 26 : 5–14. Compare 47 : 10. [8] Hab. 1 : 15. [9] Isaiah 19 : 8.

with a cast-net also illustrates what the two disciples were doing when the Lord called them to follow him, saying, "Come ye after me, and I will make you fishers of men." [1]

The modern draw, or dragnet, is referred to in the parable of our Lord.[2] The prophets allude to fishing with hook and line. Thus, Amos uses that mode of fishing to illustrate the severity and mode of treating captives: "The days shall come upon you, that they shall take you away with hooks, and your residue with fish-hooks." [3] The remarkable instance of securing money for paying the temple tax will be recalled by every reader. The Lord told Peter, "Go thou to the sea, and cast a hook, and take up the fish that first cometh up; and when thou hast opened his mouth, thou shalt find a shekel: that take, and give unto them for me and thee." [4] Spearing of fish is also frequently mentioned. Thus, in describing the power of leviathan, Job is asked,

> " Can'st thou draw out leviathan with a fish hook?
> Can'st thou fill his skin with barbed irons
> Or his head with fish spears?" [5]

So the Lord called his disciples, by the Sea of Galilee, "to become fishers of men." [6]

278. *Hunting.*—The mode of hunting in Oriental lands has completely changed since the invention of guns and gunpowder. Sometimes, though rarely, traces of the old method of taking wild animals by traps and snares, or driving them into hidden pits, still prevails as in the interior of Africa and some remote corners of Asia. In like manner, the method of taking them by spears or by arrows has largely been displaced by more modern weapons.

The pit or pitfall was found to be a mode of catching and killing the larger animals in Africa by Livingstone. Long lines of hedges were made to approach each other in the shape of the letter "V." The two lines were not joined at the extremity,

---

[1] Matt. 4 : 19; Mark 1 : 16; John 21 : 6.   [2] Matt. 13 : 47.
[3] Amos 4 : 2.   [4] Matt. 17 : 27.   [5] Job 41 : 1, 7.
[6] Matt. 4 : 19; Mark 1 : 17; Luke 5 : 10.

but ended in a narrow lane, many yards long, and at the end of this lane was a deep pit, carefully concealed by rushes and brush. The animals were driven into this lane, and forced into the pit. The net was used to catch some wild game, as birds, from time immemorial, as we know from the scenes sketched upon Assyrian monuments, and also in Egyptian tombs. Even animals as large as the fallow deer were caught in nets or in hidden traps. This method of taking game is frequently mentioned in the Bible. The Psalmist says, "He will pluck my feet out of the net," [1] and again, "In the net which they hid is their own foot taken," [2] and again,

> "They hid for me their net in a pit ;
> Without cause they have digged a pit for my soul. . . .
> Let his net that he hath hid catch himself." [3]

The Psalmist asked to be delivered by Jehovah from snares,

> "In the way wherein I walk
> Have they hidden a snare for me." [4]

The prophet refers to capturing wild beasts in a net, "Thy sons have fainted, they lie at the head of all the streets, as an antelope in a net." [5] The courage required to kill a wild beast taken in a pit is also graphically described, "A valiant man of Kabzeel, who hath done mighty deeds, . . . went down also and slew a lion in the midst of a pit in time of snow." [6] Hunting wild beasts and snaring birds, either for livelihood or as an exercise, or for sport, came natural to the human race from the very earliest time. Thus, Nimrod, a great hero, "Was a mighty hunter before Jehovah," so great was his fame that it became a proverb, "Like Nimrod, a mighty hunter before Jehovah." [7] The father of the Ishmaelites "grew up, an archer." [8] While Jacob was a quiet man, dwelling in tents, his brother "Esau was a skilful hunter, a man of the field." [9] After the exodus the Israelites were not compelled to hunt for a livelihood, but they

[1] Ps. 25 : 15. [2] Ps. 9 : 15. [3] Ps. 35 : 7, 8.
[4] Ps. 142 : 3. [5] Isa. 51 : 20. [6] 2 Sam. 23 : 20.
[7] Gen. 10 : 9. [8] Gen. 21 : 20. [9] Gen. 25 : 27.

continued to pursue it for the sake of securing the much-desired flesh of the hart, and the roe-buck, and other species of deer.[1]

279. *Snares.*—In early times it is quite evident that birds and flying fowl were taken chiefly with snares, and this form of hunting is frequently used to illustrate how the wicked were taken and how the righteous escaped. Thus, "Our soul is escaped as a bird out of the snare of the fowlers: the snare is broken, and we are escaped." [2] The way in which the wicked were taken is also graphically described:

> " As a bird hasteth to the snare,
> And knoweth not that it is for his life." [3]

The false prophets were thus pictured, "As for the prophet, a fowler's snare is in all his ways." [4] The ingenious and iniquitous ways of wicked men to lead others into sin are thus described by the prophet, "Among my people are found wicked men; they watch, as fowlers lie in wait; they set a trap, they catch men. As a cage is full of birds, so are their houses full of deceit." [5]

Many of these methods of hunting were probably known to Abraham before he left the land of the Chaldees, and the Israelites no doubt were further made acquainted with them so that they became familiar with these ancient modes of capturing animals in Egypt, and on their journey through Sinai toward the land of promise.

279a. *Fishhooks.*—Spears and arrows were used in fishing and hunting. When fishhooks were first used in fishing is unknown. They were used in Palestine on the Sea of Galilee in the Christian era, but were not as common as nets. Arrows are noted in the Bible over fifty times. Spears are also mentioned frequently, often called javelins, and were among the earliest forms of utensils for hunting, as also for war.

---

[1] Compare Deut. 12 : 15 with Lev. 11 : 3–7, 13–19, 24–27.   [2] Ps. 124 : 7.
[3] Prov. 7 : 23.   [4] Hosea 9 : 8.   [5] Jer. 5 : 26, 27.

CAMEL—GROUP AND LOADS. P. 192

(Vester & Co)

SYRIAN DOGS. P. 167

XXIV.

TRAVELING IN ORIENTAL LANDS.

It is a common saying that hardly anything is more distinctive of Oriental life than the mode of traveling. It was also said a century ago that little progress had been made in this respect for three thousand years. Then pilgrims from Jaffa to Jerusalem, from Haifa to the Lake of Galilee, from Beirut to Damascus, and thence to Mecca, went on foot, or on mules, or camel back; now they can go by railways. This is significant of the rapid and radical changes in Oriental lands. Let us get a flashlight on primitive Oriental traveling before it wholly passes, never to return.

280. *Caravan.*—I have spoken of the camel, "the ship of the desert," as a typical Oriental scene, and mode of traveling. A caravan of pilgrims going to Mecca a century ago well illustrated Israel's march through the desert to the land of promise. An eye-witness gives us the picture: "The first day we set out without any order in hurly-burly, camels, mules, men, women, and children, struggling to get on, often quarreling, shouting, and gesticulating, a babel of confusion. But when everyone had his place among the great companies of people in the caravan, each company having a leader and a standard, they kept the same place orderly and peacefully. For the caravan was divided into several companies, each having its name, consisting it may be, of several thousand camels, moving one company after another like bodies of troops. They all camp during much of the day because of the heat, and travel in the cool of the evening and by night. Each morning they pitch their tents and rest for hours. The camels are unloaded and the owners take them to water and feed them. The pilgrims lay down to sleep. About four in the afternoon the trumpet sounds a signal for the moving of the hosts. Quickly the tents are taken down,

things are packed, camels are loaded, and the journey begun."
This picture is almost identical with that presented by the
sacred writer concerning the movement of the Israelites through
the wilderness.[1]

281. *On Camel Back.*—Traversing large tracts of wilderness,
sometimes sandy, arid, and without water, the camel becomes
an indispensable mode of travel. Every experienced traveler
unites in testifying to the peculiar disposition of the camel.
It is not an amiable animal, forms no attachment to its owner,
nor does its owner, only now and again, an Arab, form one for
his beast. A traveler can make a friend of his horse, or even
of a mule, but never of a camel. Tristram declares, "I have
made a journey in Africa for three months with the same camels,
but never succeeded in eliciting the slightest token of recognition from one of them, or of a friendly disposition for kindness
shown." Robinson, the American explorer, gives a graphic
description of the habits and uses of the camel: "Admirably
adapted to the desert regions, which are their (camels) home,
they yet constitute one of the evils which traveling in the desert
brings with it. Their long, slow, rolling, or rocking gait,
although, not at first very unpleasant, becomes exceedingly
fatiguing; so that I have often been more exhausted in riding
five and twenty miles upon a camel than in traveling fifty
on horseback." Camels were made "to be the carriers of the
desert." "The coarse and prickly shrubs of the wastes are
to them the most delicious food; and even of these they eat
but little. So few are the wants of their nature that their
power of going without food, as well as without water, is
wonderful. They never appear to tire, they commonly march
as freshly in the evening as in the morning." "Their well-
known habit of lying down upon the breast to receive their
burdens . . . is their natural position of repose." "Hardly
less wonderful is the adaptation of their broad cushioned foot
to the arid gravelly soil, which it is their lot chiefly to traverse."
"They are commonly represented as patient; but if so, it is

[1] See Num. 2 : 1–34; 9 : 15–23; 10 : 1–36.

the patience of stupidity. They are rather exceedingly impatient; and utter loud cries of indignation when receiving their loads, and not seldom on being made to kneel down. They are also obstinate and frequently vicious; and an attempt to urge them forward is often very much like trying to drive sheep the way they do not choose to go. The cry of the camel resembles in a degree the hollow bleating of the sheep; sometimes it is like the lowing of neat cattle, or the hoarse squeal of the swine."

282. *Camel's Habits.*—The camel eats and drinks little, and secretes little; he is a cold-blooded, heavy, sullen animal, having little feeling and little susceptibility for pain. Thistles and briers and thorns he crops and chews with more avidity than the softest green fodder; nor does he seem to feel pain from blows or pricks, unless they are very violent. There is nothing graceful or sprightly in any camel, old or young; all are misshapen, ungainly, and awkward. The young have nothing frisky or playful, but in all their movements are as staid and sober as their dams.

"As the carriers of the East, 'the ships of the desert,' another important quality of the camel is sure-footedness. I was surprised to find them traveling with so much ease and safety up and down the most rugged mountain passes. They do not choose their way with sagacity, as the mule, or even as the horse, but they tread much more surely and safely, and never either slip or stumble. . . . The sounds by which the Arabs govern their camels are very few and guttural. The signal for kneeling is not unlike a gentle snore; and is made by throwing the breath strongly against the palate, but not through the nose. That for stopping is a sort of guttural clucking, which I could never master." [1]

Western travelers see none of the glory or poetry which Orientals put into their ideal of the camel. Palgrave, an experienced traveler, says of the camel, "He takes no heed of his driver, pays no attention whether he be on his back or

[1] Robinson, Researches, vol. ii, pp. 208–210.

not, walks straight on, when once set going, merely because he is too stupid to turn aside, and then should some tempting thorn or green branch allure him out of the path, continues to walk on in the new direction, simply because he is too dull to turn back into the right road."

In kneeling, the camel first bends his forelegs, and falls upon his knees, and then gradually settles down, so that his breast lies square upon the ground. The saddle for loading or riding the camel is made by the Arabs. The frame is usually of cyprus wood, of two parts, to span the back of the camel, and of uprights, between which sits the rider. The comfort of the saddle depends on the width of the span of these wooden arches. The wooden frame is padded with raw-hide skins or some soft material to protect the constant rubbing of the frame. It is girded on with a rope of camel's hair, ornamented with tassels, or by thin leather straps. Dr. Van Lennep says, "In riding the camel the same saddle is used as for loading, a cushion being added for the greater comfort of the rider, who, when proceeding at a slow pace, sits or lies down in every imaginable posture."

283. *The Swift Camel.*—The dromedary is a special breed of camel, prized for swiftness. A superior kind, called "Hajeen," is a thoroughbred, not used for burdens, but reserved for riding. The Orientals regard them as very swift. Riders may push them into a gallop at a speed of some say fifteen to twenty miles an hour, or about two hundred miles a day. Prof. Post sent me a description of his experience through the desert of Sinai. He says, "The dromedary of Sinai is small, very square in build, with delicately shaped legs and head. He is capable of much greater endurance than the larger, clumsier camel of Syria, and eats and drinks less." His power to go without water and his swiftness have been much exaggerated, in Prof. Post's view. He adds, "When unable to find water, he sometimes endures thirst for ten days. We found that our beast drank eagerly at every spring, and even at the bitter salty brooks."

284. *Camel Mounting.*—"Mounting a camel is less difficult than many travelers represent. If there be a ledge of rock, or a bank, he may be bestrode standing like a horse. If not, it only requires a hand to be laid on the pommel behind the saddle, while he raises himself on his hind legs. The action of rising is divided into three stages: a backward undulation, by which the hindquarters receive the whole weight of the trunk, while he disengages his left foreleg, and advances it bent at the foreknee, then a strong forward lunge as he raises his hindquarters to their full height. It is this lunge which surprises the inexperienced rider by the punch in the back and the forward fling. The third stage consists in straightening the left foreleg freely, thus raising the forequarters. He assists himself in this motion by steadying himself on the right wrist until he is nearly erect, when he flings the right forefoot also into position in the act of straightening the other foreleg. The act of kneeling reverses these motions."

"The dromedary walks slowly, not more when loaded than two and a half miles an hour. When light, he may be urged to a gait of three miles an hour. His trot is very disagreeable, and he cannot long endure any pace but a walk." But distance is not computed by miles, but by hours, in Oriental lands. Reduced to Western phrase, an hour is equivalent to about two and a half or three miles.

285. *Going in Crowds.*—A great drawback to traveling in the East is the necessity for journeying in company, or with a caravan. Inns or hotels with rooms and food are rare, or not found, off the European routes. Thus, Prof. Post says: "It took nine camels to transport our party of two and the necessary baggage and provisions for the thirteen days' journey from Cairo to Sinai. . . . Poultry is carried in cages made of the ribs of palm leaves, and balanced on the tops of the loads. Oranges are carried in similar crates." He had a tent for beds and baggage, another for meals and reading and writing, and a third tent for the dragoman cook. Even on more frequented routes than those through the wilderness of Sinai,

roads and paths are not safe to the solitary traveler, for stragglers in advance of or behind a caravan are often attacked and robbed or murdered. Travelers going on a journey must often wait, at great inconvenience, to join a caravan or a company.

286. *Roads.*—Roads in the Orient—there are none. Even the so-called "Sultan's road" Tristram calls "a mere track." Road makers there are none, except the feet of camels and mules which have worn beaten hard paths in the sand and steps in rocks. Thus Prof. Post, out of a lifetime of experience says, paths through the open country lose all trace of regularity. "If a rock fall across the highway, it is no one's business to remove it. The road or path accordingly swerves aside at the obstacle like a stream eddying around a boulder in its course. If an adjacent field presents an easier foot-way, a path is soon made through it. Fences—there are none; a stone or a clump of bushes in the way no one ever clears. If a bridge falls, there is no one to repair it, and a wide detour is soon established to the nearest ford, and back on the other side to the main track again. The Oriental roads are never well defined, never straight. There are many side paths, and short cuts, and detours around the obstacles. It is often quite difficult to determine whether a branching path is a diverging road or a mere side track, and only when followed for a distance can one be certain whether he is still on his course or has been turned into another road. To straighten the path, make it plain, remove the stones, and enable the cavalcade of a great man to pass is the function of his courier." Speedily, the torrents wash out the road again, and it becomes practically impassable. The great routes across the desert and between provinces are little more than paths made by caravans, sometimes marked by "*ahmond*," heaps of stones or bricks. "These are useful to the traveler," say writers of the last century, "for it is as easy for one to find his way amidst drifted snow as to find it on this sandy desert." The prophets seize upon this to teach a lesson: "Set thee up waymarks,

FAMILY TRAVELING WITH DONKEY. P. 200

(Copyright by Underwood & Underwood, New York.)

PALANQUIN LEAVING ORIENTAL INN.

(Copyright by Underwood & Underwood, New York.)

make thee guide-posts."[1] "O my people, they that lead thee
cause thee to err, and destroy the way of thy paths."[2]

This also illustrates the prophecy concerning the Messiah,
and the preaching of John the Baptist in the wilderness.[3] Light
is also thrown upon other allusions to "paths," as in Proverbs
and the Psalms, where the plural form seems strange, until
we learn that it exactly describes the many paths—often a
dozen or more—that mingle and mix together, to make the
one broad way or route. These are due to the peculiar mode
of the camels, following one another, making new paths beside
the old ones. Thus, "Neither do they attain unto the paths
of life," where we would look for the singular, "path."[4] "My
steps have held fast to thy paths."[5]

Roads in Syria and paths and bridges are poorer to-day
than they were in the time of our Lord. The Romans were
road-builders. Their great lines of travel were marked out by
roads, binding their provinces together, which made traveling
easier nineteen hundred years ago than it is to-day in Western
Asia. But the Romans were not Orientals, the typical Oriental
is not a road-builder.

287. *On Foot.*—Traveling on foot and in companies is still
common as it was in olden times in Oriental lands. The
Oriental requires a simple outfit for his journey: a scrip, purse,
and shoes, with a weapon for defense. The scrip is a bag,
usually of leather or of matting, to carry the provisions, olives,
dried figs, thin barley cakes, or, more commonly, barley meal or
parched wheat. The purse is a small leather bag, concealed
under the shirt, and hung by a string around the neck, or his
money and jewels may be carried in his girdle. The shoes
usually are of hide, dressed with the hair on the upper side, with
heels and softer material for the side, and are strapped on the
feet with thongs. As there are no hotels with furnished rooms
and a table in the East, the traveler carries his bed and cover-

[1] Jer. 31 : 21.   [2] Isa. 3 : 12.
[3] Isa. 40 : 3; Matt. 3 : 3; Mark 1 : 2, 3; Mal. 3 : 1; Luke 3 : 4.
[4] Prov. 2 : 19.   See also 2 : 20; 3 : 6; 4 : 11; Jer. 6 : 16; 13 : 15; Lam. 3 : 9.
[5] Ps. 17 : 5; 23 : 3; Job 38 : 20.

ings and sometimes a tent, though he usually sleeps under the stars.

An Arab now travels, even in the desert, with very simple provision. He may have two skin-bags over his shoulder, one full of water and the other of barley meal or parched wheat. Stopping for the night, he picks up a few twigs and roots of the juniper, kindles a fire on a flat stone or two, with his flint and steel, "takes a handful of meal from his bag, mixes it with a little water, rolls it out into a cake of dough, and when the stone is hot brushes it off, puts the dough cake on the hot stone, covers it with coals and ashes, and his cake is soon baked." So Elijah found a cake baked on "coals" of hot stones, and a bottle of water, when the angel awaked him.[1]

288. *Travelers' Supplies.*—Orientals now, as in our Lord's day, do not go on a journey without having either barley bread, or meal, or parched wheat, enough for one or two days' food. This illustrates the feeding of the four thousand.

On the third day Jesus said, "I have compassion on the multitude, because they continue with me now three days and have nothing to eat: and I would not send them away fasting, lest haply they faint on the way."[2] The peasants who flocked to hear him in the desert would have, according to custom, a day's food or more with them. On the third day their supply would be used up, yet the disciples had "seven loaves" and a "few small fishes" left even on the third day.[3]

289. *Children Traveling.*—When traveling in companies now, as in Oriental times, the boys of the transition age would be sometimes with their fathers, and at other times with their mothers and the women. Orientals now traveling in companies usually separate, the men for the most part spending the night by themselves, and the women and children by themselves. A lad who was uncertain whether he could travel as rapidly as the men, would naturally go in the advanced portion of the caravan, or company, with the women, who start first and proceed at a slower pace. The men, starting later, travel more

[1] 1 Kings 19 : 6.   [2] Matt. 15 : 32; Mark 8 : 2.   [3] Matt. 15 : 34.

rapidly. Thus, it was easy for the parents of Jesus to miss him. The mother would naturally think that he had remained to come on with his father; the father, not seeing him, would suppose that he had gone ahead with his mother and the women. It was not until the whole company came together for the night that he would be missed.[1]

290. *Girdle and Staff.*—Orientals now carry coined money, usually gold, because it is more easily carried. "They keep some change in pocket or purse, carrying the greater portion in the girdle. These girdles are made of leather, or of woven silk, wool, or cotton. They are quite wide, and a portion is made double, so as to form a long pouch, in which the money is placed, and the girdle is fastened about the person with stout straps and buckles. Sometimes it is long enough to go twice around the waist. Everyone East wears a belt or girdle of some description." Every traveler also on foot in the Orient has a staff. There is an Arab proverb, "The staff of the old man is his third foot."

291. *Ships.*—The typical Oriental sailing vessel, as a mode of travel or of transporting goods, has largely given place to steamships. Rarely may an old style of Eastern sailing vessel be seen now. Some may be found in localities along coasts not reached by steamers. Mr. Haddad observes, "Sailors in these ships do not study navigation in the schools; they have no maps, no instruments to measure distances, and few possess a compass. They know the route by experience, they find the course during the day by the sun, and at night by the moon and stars. When these are obscured by clouds, they depend upon their intelligence and experience. They make the voyage successfully for long periods. Sometimes they still have misfortune in storms, as Paul did in his day."[2] "Some ships, which do not hold more than four thousand bushels of grain, traverse the Mediterranean Sea, from one end to the other, summer and winter."[3] In ancient times the Phœnicians, living on the sea, were famous for

1 Luke 2 : 41–51.   2 Acts 27. See also 2 Cor. 11 : 25.
3 Compare Jonah 1 : 3–5 with Num. 24 : 24; 1 Kings 22 : 48; 2 Chron. 9 : 21; 20 : 37; and Isa. 60 : 9.

shipbuilding.[1]   Solomon and Hiram had a navy of ships "on the Red Sea." [2]

The ships so often mentioned in the Gospels upon the Lake of Galilee were in reality small boats; either row-boats or boats having a small lateen sail.   Over fifty years ago Dr. Thomson said of the Lake of Galilee and the Arabs on its shore, "They have no more use for boats than for well-made roads; both disappeared together when the Arabians conquered the country." He predicts, "Both will reappear together as soon as a more civilized race rises to power."   The tax-officer of the district told me that a few years ago he listed nine boats for taxation on the lake.   Thus, the fishermen on the Lake of Galilee, who were said to be fishing "in a ship with Zebedee their father," were in fact in a small boat, as were all the "ships" on that lake in the time of our Lord.   They were either fishing boats or small sailboats.[3]

But the vessels named in the story of the Acts were large sailing vessels, although some of them had oars, either for steering or for rowing.[4]

292. *By Mules.*—In Oriental lands to-day, as in olden times, persons of rank travel upon mules.   Thus Deborah's song says,

> "Tell of it, ye that ride on white asses,
> Ye that sit on rich carpets,
> And ye that walk by the way." [5]

They still ride also in a sedan-chair, carried by men or mounted on two wheels, and drawn by men, like the *jin-riksha* of Japan. The travelers of the last century also describe a more luxurious mode of traveling by a *tachterwan*, a species of tent bed placed on a frame and supported in front by one animal—either horse or camel—and in the rear by another camel instead of by men. They also travel by a species of tent bed placed crossway on the back of a mule, or arranged like two childrens' cradles fitted in

[1] Ezek. 27 : 3–9.   [2] 1 Kings 9 : 26–28; 10 : 11.
[3] See Matt. 4 : 21; 8 : 24; 14 : 24; Mark 1 : 19; 4 : 38; 8 : 14; Luke 5 : 7; John 6 : 21; 21 : 6.
   Acts 20 : 38; 21 : 2; 27 : 2, 30, 40; Ezek. 27 : 26, 29.   [5] Judg. 5 : 10.

PANNIERS ON DONKEY, SYRIA.　　P. 200

the same way panniers are on the back of the camel. Some of these were enclosed with curtains and are described as very comfortable. Possibly young Rachel was riding in a similar manner when she "had taken the teraphim, and put them in the camel's saddle [or 'lister'] and sat upon them."[1]

293. *Footman Runner.*—Royal persons or persons of high rank when riding are still attended by a servant on foot.[2] Thus, Elijah ran before the chariot of Ahab as men now do. Almost every traveler in the Orient speaks of seeing instances of this kind in India and other parts of Asia, as well as in Northern Africa. Harmer saw runners on foot move with great speed in Barbary, which gave a new meaning to him to Job 9 : 25. All writers from Herodotus to the present day speak of the endurance and velocity with which these runners will accompany a man riding on horseback, or in a chariot, and of the swiftness of messengers sent to deliver messages on important business. They will easily keep up with a rider on a camel, a mule, or in a chariot all day, without showing fatigue.

[1] Gen. 31 : 34.   [2] See 2 Kings 4 : 24; Eccles. 10 : 7.

XXV.

WARFARE.

SOME think Oriental nations are constantly in a ferment, if not in warfare. In this generation they have been in a high state of turbulence. Archers, the use of bows and arrows, of slings, catapults, and battering rams, of coats of mail, of greaves, shields, helmets, and war chariots have passed. With them also has disappeared the need of walled cities for defense. The ancient weapons of the Orient, the dagger, scimitar, sabre or sword, club and spear, are, however, still common. The Circassians use bows and arrows on secret military expeditions or when their powder fails.[1] The method of warfare among primitive tribes throws some, though scant, light upon the methods which were common in the days of the sacred writers.

294. *Warrior.*—A warrior or sheikh of to-day would, like Abraham, be armed with a spear, and a sword, and dagger, but he would also have a pistol, or a musket, and would depend largely upon the latter now, though still having the other weapons of defense common to ancient times. A wandering Arab upon his fleet steed, brandishing his spear, is still a picturesque character when dashing across the arid desert. To this day he delights to carry a dagger, brandish his sabre, and twirl his spear. The spears used by the Arabs have handles about twelve feet long and nearly two inches in diameter. The head of the spear is of pointed steel or metal, sharpened on both sides like a dagger. Its head is about a foot long. Sometimes on the other end of the spear is a sharp spike, three or four inches long, which can be thrust into the ground, the spear standing upright. It can then easily be picked up by a rider on horseback. The Arab rider

[1] Dr. Van Lennep, p. 680.

is skilled in grasping it when riding at a rapid pace, and is also skilled in hurling it so as to transfix an approaching enemy.

This long spear or lance, stuck in the ground, marks the place where the leader of the band or the sheikh is to be found. If in the open air it stands by his side, or it may be at his tent door. Thus the spear of Saul marked the place where he was sleeping.[1] A shorter kind of spear is used for footmen, but of the same general character. This short spear, with the javelin, is an ancient and common weapon.[2]

295. *Body Guard.*—In the last century Oriental monarchs maintained a military body guard. Sometimes the guards are slaves and sometimes they are nobles or princes of the country. Thus, the Sultan formerly had lads taken or stolen from their parents, and brought up as Moslems in military service. They might be the children of Christians killed in war. This custom has come down from early times.[3]

296. *Oriental Sword.*—The Bedouin and other Arabs of to-day always go armed. In the Orient of olden time, as now, the sword is the symbol of power.[4] The Oriental sword is of two kinds; the *Sârem*, or curved sabre, about two feet long, with hilt of wood or horn, the sharp edge on the concave side, and another with the sharp edge on the convex side. The scimitar, or "Damascus blade," a thin, highly tempered sword, is also curved, and of marvelous strength and lightness, made of two masses of fine wire, differing in hardness and temper, so blended together as to give the appearance on its sides of microscopic flowers. The process of manufacture is said to be a secret, a genuine "Damascus blade" bringing a fabulous price, from five hundred dollars upward. An Oriental sword, called *Yataghan*, is also common among the Arabs.[5]

297. *The Dagger.*—The Oriental without a dagger would be regarded with wonder. The dagger of the fellahin of

[1] 1 Sam. 26 : 7.
[2] See Judg 5 : 8; 1 Sam. 13 : 22; 17 : 45; 2 Chron. 11 : 12; Job 39 : 23; Jer. 46 : 4; Hab. 3 : 11.   [3] 1 Sam. 13 : 2; 14 : 52; 1 Chron. 27 : 1.
[4] Deut. 33 : 29.   [5] See Pal. Quar., 1905, p. 116.

Syria is two-edged, slightly curved, from nine to eighteen inches long. In other Eastern lands daggers were straight or slightly curved at the end, two-edged, with a hilt and sheath. With such a two-edged dagger Ehud slew Eglon, King of Moab.[1] A similar dagger or "knife" Abram had when he was about to offer Isaac.[2] The "pen-knife" King Jehoiakim used to cut in pieces Jeremiah's parchment was a "sheath-knife" or "sheathed dagger," probably with a convex edge.[3] Or it may have resembled the Egyptian closed knife, used also as a razor.

The Bedouins of to-day have the type well described by the words of the angel to Hagar concerning Ishmael: "He shall be as a wild ass among men; his hand shall be against every man, and every man's hand against him."[4] The peasant or fellah at his plow has a dagger in his belt, a sword at his side, or a gun swung over his shoulder for fear of the wandering Bedouin. The laborer and the traveler alike usually have a leathern girdle full of daggers and pistols. Arab bandits, descendants of Ishmael, and their spies scour the land, and watch springs of water for companies of traders and travelers poorly defended, whom they may swoop down on to capture, spoil, and rob them.[5]

The modern Oriental warrior is of stern character. He bears privation and misfortune with stoic indifference—to revenge himself or his friends. The Arab poetry, like that of Homer, tells of battle, of warriors of iron character dashing suddenly upon foes and performing marvelous feats of personal valor.

298. *African Warriors.*—In the regions of Central Africa travelers have lately found primitive customs, including military armor and modes of warfare, strikingly illustrative of many of the Old Testament narratives. These primitive tribes are armed with spears, swords, bows, and poisoned arrows, and are mighty hunters. Some have immense shields

---

[1] Judg. 3 : 16.   [2] Gen. 22 : 10.   [3] Jer. 36 : 22, 23.
[4] Gen. 16 : 12 (R. V.).   [5] John Teller, Pal. Quar., 1901, pp. 189, 198.

ORIENTAL SWORD MAKER.   P. 203

(Copyright by Underwood & Underwood, New York.)

of buffalo hide, and great clubs, called Knob-Kerry. The
natives of Uganda divided the country into provinces, each with
a chief, answerable to the king. These chiefs formed a council
with the king at the head. The organization was so complete
that at the sound of the king's war-drum the whole adult
male population was transformed into an army, with marvelous celerity, ready to march whithersoever the king commanded.

Another pastoral people near the source of the Nile were
grouped in clans, having a large number of trained warriors,
six feet or more in height, "straight as an arrow," physically
developed, high cheek bones, "beautiful nose," "fierce nomadic
warriors," each armed with a large heraldic shield marking
his clan, and brandishing spears, or skilled in the use of poisoned
arrows, ready and watchful to swoop down upon the enemy,
sometimes so blood-thirsty as to let scarcely one escape to tell
the ghastly story. It is needless to add that these African
clans still arm themselves with spears, knives, sticks, clubs,
bows, and arrows for the fights, as of old.[1]

Warlike customs among many primitive Oriental tribes
are much the same now as in ancient times. The victors
slay the vanquished, search the dead and wounded, taking
possession of whatever they find. They destroy or carry
away all valuables from a sacked city or hamlet, having no
mercy on the aged, invalids, women, or children. This is
specially characteristic of Moslems when attacking those of another faith. Their fanaticism, cruelty, and bloodshed make
them the terror of any land. They remind us of the story
of the horrid siege of Samaria by the Syrians,[2] or of the destruction of Jerusalem,[3] or of the sweeping destruction of the Canaanites in the conquest of their land by Joshua.

299. *Covenant of Peace.*—The modern way of making peace
among the African tribes closely resembles that of four thousand
years ago. Among the African Masaba peoples, after a fierce

---

[1] Purvis, "Through Uganda to Mt. Eglon," p. 73.
[2] 2 Kings 6 : 24 ff.   [3] Matt. 25, Josephus, Bk. vi.

and fruitless war among the clans, neither side likely to win, peace is proposed and sanctioned by sacrifice. The sacrificial animal is cut into two pieces where the battle took place. Where two clans at war find that neither is likely to be master, they agree to a peace compact, which no man nor woman would dare to break. To sanction the covenant a dog is brought to the border, cut in two, where many fights have taken place. One half of the dog is placed on the territory of one clan, and the other half on that of the other clan. The warriors of each clan march in procession between the halves, which are then spurned by both parties. Handshaking and merriment follow, and from that time the clans are friendly.[1]

In precisely similar manner covenants were sanctioned in ancient days. Thus, even Jehovah is represented as saying, "I will give the men that have transgressed my covenant, that have not performed the words of my covenant which they made before me, when they *cut the calf in twain, and passed between the parts thereof*." [2] Again, in the days of Abram, a compact was sanctioned by sacrificial animals that were cut in two, and each half laid over against the other half, a flaming torch passing between the pieces after dark.[3]

300. *Spoils*.—The Arabs usually carry all the spoils to the chief, or sheikh, to divide according to well-established rules. If they capture camels, cattle, sheep, money, jewelry, or household goods, such as rugs, cooking utensils, and the like, they take all to the chief of their tribe. The spoils are placed in a pile, and he takes a share of them; the remainder he divides among his followers. If one has no sword, to him he gives a sword, those who were daring in scouting or fighting are rewarded, and those who have otherwise risked their lives to discover the strength of the enemy or his location, also have special reward. This throws light on the award to Caleb and Joshua, of David and his band, and upon many other like cases in Scripture.[4]

---

[1] Purvis, "Uganda to Mt. Eglon," p. 292.   [2] Jer. 34 : 18.
[3] Gen. 15 : 9-17. See Purvis, "Uganda to Mt. Eglon," p. 292.
[4] See Josh. 14 and 15; 1 Sam. 30 : 14-25.

301. Warrior Customs.—There is a trait in the Oriental soldier that amazes the Western mind; that is his great frugality, and his capacity to endure hunger and thirst without complaint. The economy of an Oriental army, particularly without any commissariat, with only bread and olives, or meal and cheese, often without tents, sleeping on the ground under the canopy of heaven, make the problem of moving an Oriental army vastly simpler and more economical than in Western warfare. Witness the economy in this respect among the armies of the Russo-Japanese War.

The severity in dealing with captives and with forms of revolt shocks our sense. Thus, Morier relates that "a pretender to the Persian crown was mockingly mounted upon an ass (the royal beast), with his face toward the tail, the tail in his hand, a mock crown on his head, a sword by his side, and was thus paraded through the camp, a crier going before, and proclaiming, 'This is he who would be king.' He was then stripped, scourged, spit upon, and finally his eyes put out." [1]

This instance well illustrates the treatment of Zedekiah by the Assyrians, and of Jesus by the Jews. [2]

[1] Morier, vol. ii, p. 351.
[2] See 2 Kings 25 : 7; Matt. 27 : 27-31. Compare also 2 Kings 19 : 28.

XXVI.

MECHANICAL ARTS.

302. *Metal and Wood Workers.*—The "lost arts," once known
to the Orientals, but now absolutely lost to the world, would
fill a long chapter in the history of mechanical arts. We must
not overlook this fact. Moreover, we will do well to remember
in looking for light from modern Oriental life upon the arts
referred to in the sacred writings that the Orientals of three
thousand to four thousand years ago were relatively far more
advanced in inventions, in artistic and skilled work than now.
Thus, they seem to have been familiar with processes for making bronze flexible, for mixing durable and brilliant colors and
pigments for mural paintings, for making glass malleable or
flexible, not now known to Orientals nor to us. Of course,
they were familiar, as they are now, with gilding, plating, and
covering wood and ivory figures with gold and other precious
metals. Layard found ivory figures covered with gold-leaf,
or traces of it, in Assyria. An Egyptian mummy has been found
wrapped in a similar way.

The development of mechanical arts began originally in the
East, but their origin is buried in obscurity. The earliest needs
of man would be food and clothing. Food would be easily
supplied there by natural fruits and grains, and would require
little skilled labor.[1] According to the Genesis account, garments to clothe the race were made from leaves of trees, sewed
together by thread, made from the fibre of plants. Such cloth is
still made from plants, by primitive tribes, in Central Africa.
The primitive garment was "the girdle" ["aprons" of the A.
V., or things to gird about him, margin] after the expulsion
from Eden.[2]

Very early, how early we know not, man learned to use the

[1] See Social Intercourse, xiv. [2] Gen. 3 : 7; see xv.

METAL WORKERS   P. 209.

IN IRON, COPPER, AND BRASS—SICKLE SHARPENER ON LEFT.

(Copyright by Underwood & Underwood, New York.)

POTTER'S WORKSHOP, SYRIA.   P. 209

(J. E. Hanauer.)

various metals. Thus it is said that, "Jubal: he was the father of all such as handle the harp and pipe." The term "father" is here applied, as I have elsewhere explained, to one who is the head or leader, showing that Jubal was distinguished in this work, but probably not the first. He was rather the head of a large company of those who were skilled in the making of musical instruments. So also the sacred account mentions Tubal-cain, or "Tubal the smith," as the "whetter" or "forger of every cutting instrument of brass and iron" or copper bronze and iron. The rendering "iron" is questioned, as that of "brass" is also disputed. The true rendering may be copper and bronze, for wherever brass is mentioned in the Old Testament it is now believed to designate bronze, and not modern brass. Thus, Tubal was a smith, making tools for farmers, carpenters, builders, and weapons for defense.

303. *Workshops Rare.*—Skilled Oriental artisans, not influenced by Western ideas, do not have shops in small villages as with us. Those who follow trades, as smiths, carpenters, builders, or joiners in small villages are wandering persons, going about as journeymen. Thus, Rev. F. A. Klein (who discovered the Moabite stone) tells us that in some villages there is not a single artisan.[1] The fellahin are now dependent on German mechanics, copper-smiths, silver-smiths, gun-makers, and cover-makers, who travel from place to place as they find work. On the far side of the Jordan there are smiths, however, in some smaller villages, where the surname "haddad," smith, or forger, is quite common. The blacksmith, or worker in iron, is called in Arabic *Hadîd*, which corresponds to the Hebrew *harash barzel*, literally "worker in iron." [2] The worker in brass and copper is called in Arabic *nahhâsh*.

304. *Metal Vessels.*—The better class of Arabs have copper kitchen utensils, and even the poorer classes now have a kettle of copper. Some of these vessels are lined with zinc to prevent corroding with acid foods. In almost every

---

[1] Zeitschrift Ger. Pal. Ex. Soc., 1881; see Eng. Pal. Quarterly, 1881, p. 297.
[2] Isa. 44 : 12 with Gen. 4 : 22.

household now there will be a large kettle with two handles
a little wider at the bottom than at the top, used to boil water,
and to cook large quantities of food, such as rice, or a whole
sheep, since the peasants rarely cook small quantities of meat.
This kettle has no cover, and is put on an iron tripod, and no
doubt is like that used by the prophet at the religious feast.[1]
The peasants also have a common, every-day kettle, smaller
than the caldron, which has a cover, and may be one of the four
mentioned in the above passage as *kiyyôr*. The other common
metal dish is the frying-pan, sometimes of copper, but now
more often among the poorer classes of iron. Various kinds
of trays and bowls of different sizes used for washing the hands
are a common outfit in the village houses, and usually with a
copper jug.

305. *Silversmiths.*—The gold- and silversmiths in the larger
towns are found in one street. They make the gold plates,
earrings, corals, bracelets, and ornaments worn by nearly all
classes. For, as heretofore stated, the wealth of individuals,
and especially of maids and girls, consists in the ornaments
upon their persons. The metal worker also is skilful in making
spears, known as *hârbet*, a short spear now carried commonly by
dervishes. The Bedouin also carry long spears.

306. *Carpenter.*—The Oriental carpenter or joiner in a
country like Palestine has not wood enough now to make large
things, but he fits up doors, windows, cradles, low tables,
small chairs, chests for the women, and the like. Many of
these articles are made in imitation of Western furniture, and
do not strictly belong to true Oriental life. They are impor-
tations. The Arab carpenter has one indispensable tool always at hand, the adze, which he calls *kaddûm*. In Egypt
it is called *mukshut*. The plane is not an Oriental tool; it
was introduced from Europe. The next indispensable tool
for the Arab carpenter is the saw, Arabic *munshac*, Hebrew
massâr.[2] The awl, or the auger, is not an instrument like
those in use with us. It is turned by a handle and string,

---

[1] 1 Sam. 2 : 14.   [2] Isa. 10 : 15.

resembling a whip. The leather string is twisted once around
the handle of the iron borer, and pulling back and forth drives
it into the wood. The carpenter makes wooden locks and
keys for the houses, as well as windows and doors. The
hammer, pliers, pincers, or tongs; the vise, the file, and the
rule, or square are common instruments now among Orientals,
both with wood and metal workers.

307. *Crude Tools.*—To Western eyes the tools of both the
metal and wood workers of the Orient seem very crude and
primitive, yet their products are sometimes marvels of skill
and genius. Every observer and student of history is compelled to conclude that the evolution of Oriental invention
and skilled workmanship, either in wood or in metal, has been
an evolution backward.

308. *Oriental Skill.*—For the Oriental formerly knew how to
move immense blocks of stone, like those of Baalbec. He did
also plan and build the great pyramids, things which he looks
upon as impossible now. The skill to accomplish these things
is among the lost arts. The durable and the brilliant tints
within the wonderful tombs, tints which have remained apparently as fresh and strong as the day they were painted, over
three thousand or four thousand years ago, cannot now be
reproduced by any known art.

The works of great art which the world still admires and
copies, those of Phidias and the great masters, are not the
production of this century, but of nearly twenty-five centuries
ago, and in the East. Modern engineers and artisans sit
before these wonderful productions in biblical times and
lands puzzled even now to understand how these marvelous
achievements were done in former times. How long the
East has known some other skilful arts is unknown. Thus,
Egypt over a century ago, was famous for extensive and successful incubators, its hatcheries turning out millions of young
birds from eggs by artificial methods.[1]

As an evidence that the supremacy of the East in arts and

[1] See Lane, "Modern Egyptians." vol. ii, p. 6.

arms, once so marked, and long ago lost, it is worthy of note, that even in the last century Eastern looms were still weaving the celebrated silk fabrics and costly rugs from the Orient, which brought fabulous prices in our Western markets. They remind us of the tapestries and "luxurious hangings" of the days of Bezaleel, and of Solomon, described in Scriptures.[1] It is unnecessary to point out the causes which have led to this decline in Eastern art. No doubt the scientific inventions of the West during the past century have aided in dispelling the charm of Oriental productions.

The exclusive regulations of arts and trades in the East tended also to promote their perfection on the one hand, and to destroy their permanence on the other. To this day certain rare arts are monopolized by families, classes, and races in the East, and the secret is never revealed to other than their children, who succeed them in these arts. So was it in the time of Solomon and Hiram, whose chief artists learned the trade from their fathers, and never allowed it to go out of their family or guild. To such a guild belonged Demetrius and craftsmen of his order. No modern "artisan guild" or "labor union" was ever so strict in limiting journeymen, who might learn the trade, and in guarding the secrets of it as were these ancient Oriental trades, craftsmen, and labor guilds.

[1] Ex. 35 : 30-35; 2 Chron. 2 : 13, 14.

INLAID PEARL WORKERS.

SITTING AT WORK.

(Copyright by Underwood & Underwood, New York.)

XXVII.

TRADES.

THE old Semitic proverb, "Whoever does not teach his son a trade, is as if he brought him up to be a robber,"[1] is a sentiment widely prevalent among Orientals. There is a saying in Damascus, told by a native, "to be master of a trade is like a band of gold about the arm." Skilled manual labor, therefore, is counted worthy and honorable. A learned professor even may sometimes be found in his workshop devoting part of his time to watch-making or as a jeweler.

309. *Honorable and Humble.*—There are some exceptions to this. The trade of the shoemaker, or tanner, is not highly esteemed. If you ask such a person what his occupation is, he will apologetically reply, "May God exalt your state, I am a shoemaker"; or, "Saving your presence, I am a cobbler." In keeping with this sentiment, all tradesmen try to have boys or inferiors to do the coarser work. A cook must always have a scullion; just as with us, a bricklayer or mason must have a hod-carrier, so in the Orient.

310. *Master Craftsmen.*—Large industries in some cities, such as silversmiths, have a master craftsman, who may attain great influence. Mr. Haddad, a native Syrian, speaks of such a person elected as a ruler, or arbitrator, over those in that trade. He may be recognized by the government, and so be entitled to test the gold or silver articles manufactured, and to stamp them as pure or up to the proper standard of purity. He will represent his fellow craftsmen in courts, and be responsible for their protection and for their behavior, and may arbitrate their disputes. Such a master craftsman was Demetrius among the silversmiths of Ephesus.[2] The silversmiths make rings, bracelets, necklaces, ear-rings, nose-rings,

[1] Kidd, 29. [2] Acts 19 : 24, 25.

set precious stones, make crowns or coronets, girdles of varied
design, gold and silver bands for the ankles, with little silver
bells attached, and all shapes and forms of beautiful jewels
and jewelry which the Oriental artisan so skilfully devises,
including cups, lamps, curtains, candlesticks, altar pieces,
and ornaments of every sort to adorn the person or to decorate
the house.

311. *Sit at Work.*—All Oriental workmen sit while at work.
An Oriental workman never stands if he can help it. The
silversmith has a small anvil, vise, and a funnel-shaped furnace, a skin bag for bellows worked by two handles, and a
boy to work them. The furnace is heated usually with charcoal. The smiths are skilled in the use of the blow-pipe.
They are often very skilful in engraving, ornamenting, and
chasing on silver and gold.

312. *Pay in Advance.*—Skilled and trained workmen in
manual trades usually require pay in advance in the East.
They have little or no capital, hence workmen like carpenters,
masons, and stone dressers, after a very old custom, expect
money to be provided. When the temple of Jerusalem was
repaired in the reign of Joash, and again in the reign of Josiah,
the narrative indicates plainly that the laborers and skilled
workmen were paid in advance, not only for their work, but
money was put in their hands to purchase the material for all
those repairs.[1] This old custom still lingers in the East,
though it is gradually being displaced by the Western practice
of contractors. Or, perhaps, it is more accurate to say that
the older Babylonian plan of master builders, taking the
responsibility of the work, is being revived among the more
progressive peoples of the East.

313. *Trades Guilds.*—Trades unions are not common in the
Orient, but trades guilds are. It is common for workmen of
like occupation to herd together, to be grouped in quarters near
to one another in Oriental cities. Thus, Aquila and Priscilla
and Paul were of the same craft, "tentmakers," hence they

[1] See 2 Kings 12 : 11; 2 Chron. 24 : 12.

drifted naturally into the same quarter of Corinth, and became colaborers, not only in tent-making, but in gospel work.[1]

Guilds exist among the silversmiths of the Orient to this day. Similar guilds are formed by the fruiterers, drug-venders, and even muleteers and merchants, who gather in one corner, or stop at the same khan in a city, thus being together for mutual protection, information, and advantage, or are within call for this purpose.

314. *Tent-making.*—Tent-making is still an independent and popular occupation in the East, and often has a special market for these articles. It was once a far more popular trade than now. It is said that many celebrated and learned men, and even kings, preferred it to a life of ease or of amusement. An Oriental king, after disposing of questions of state for the day, it is said, retired with his wife to a humble room in the palace, and together they would weave baskets of palm leaves, and send them secretly to market for sale. No one who sold or bought them knew who made them.

315. *"Bargains."*—The "bargain counter" and "bargain shop," that lowers the dignity and degrades the ethical and social ideals of the best trade in civilized lands to-day, had their earlier counterpart in the Eastern bazaar. Any person is regarded as "green," if not idiotic, who would pay what is asked for any article in an Eastern shop. The salesman there always asks a price he never expects to get, and the buyer never expects to pay. The original price is lowered once, twice, thrice, so that for what a hundred was asked, thirty is often accepted with perfect satisfaction. Such is the perverted and deep-seated character of this bargain business in the Orient that no purchaser is ever sure that he has not paid too much for what he buys. No matter what he buys, the price must be reduced to make a sale, even if it is the merest trifle; in the price, though trifling, there must be a reduction. It is thoroughly debasing there to the morals and to the honesty of buyer and seller.

Native workers in colored cloths, like purple and fine linen,

[1] Acts 18 : 1-3

worn by persons of wealth and distinction, are being displaced
in modern times, since these fabrics are now being largely im-
ported and made by machinery.

Payments are now made chiefly in coin, but barter and exchange are also widely prevalent in the Orient. Formerly
in the East coins of gold and silver were weighed. This was
like an inspection or test and to see whether the coins were full
weight, as required by law. If short of weight, the coin would
be refused, or discounted, and taken at its real value.

316. *Basket Makers.*—Basket manufacturers are plentiful in
the East. The baskets are of three kinds: (1) the *küffah*,
woven of palm leaves, and in the shape of a fez. It has two
handles, one on each side, and one loop or handle is longer than
the other. The longer loop is passed through the shorter one,
so the basket is drawn together, partly closing it. This is
used for provisions, and holds an amount about equal to our
bushel. (2) The *sell*, made of bamboo or twigs, resembling
rattan, and shaped like a teacup. These are used for fish, fruit,
grapes, or figs. It is much larger than the first-mentioned
basket. (3) The large basket, or *zembeel*, made of palm, hemp,
or flax, is used for grain. It is the largest basket of these three,
and was probably the one used to let Paul down by the wall
when he escaped from Damascus.[1] The smallest, or hand
basket, is the one that was used in gathering up the fragments
at the feeding of the five thousand.[2] The medium basket,
number two, is the one that appears to have been used in gathering the fragments at the feeding of the four thousand.[3]

[1] Acts 9 : 25.   [2] Matt. 14 : 20.   [3] Matt. 15 : 37.

ORIENTAL LATHE AND CHAIR MAKER.   P. 210

(Copyright by Underwood & Underwood, New York.)

XXVIII.

MUSIC AND MUSICAL INSTRUMENTS.

ON ancient Hebrew music modern biblical scholars find themselves in a quagmire, and confess that little is known of the nature of the music of Hebrew singers and players on musical instruments.

317. *What is Good Music?*—It is of great importance, then, to gather the little information possible on Oriental music and musical instruments, in order to throw light upon the many biblical narratives, whose chief charm consists in allusions to this obscure, but very interesting feature of life in Bible lands.

Scholars infer that the Psalms were chanted, but did these chants resemble in any respect what we designate by that term? Hitherto the Western mind has looked on the Oriental as possessing little musical taste or skill. Their performances are counted wild, weird, and wanting in musical discernment. But the Oriental returns this criticism with interest, for he looks upon European and Western music as peculiar, strange, wanting in delicacy of tone, and not fitted to give real pleasure to his ear. Neither party can rashly condemn nor harshly criticize the taste and skill of the other.

318. *Oriental Musical Scale.*—Western opinion in regard to Oriental music has changed in recent times. Thus, it has been discovered that the trained Arab of Egypt has some aptitude, and a delicate, if peculiar taste, in distinguishing and making gradations in his music and song. He requires a division of whole tones of the scale into thirds, rather than into semi-tones alone. He regards the Western system of music as sadly deficient in its number of musical sounds. The Oriental peasants attain a peculiar skill in executing these easy gradations in chanting and singing, using a musical song as a relief in their work.

Thus, the native boatmen of the Nile swing their oars in rowing to the notes of a song. The monotonous labor of working the shadoof, for raising water, is relieved by similar chants. The porter, staggering under his mountain load of trunks, the boys and the girls with bricks and mortar, or running of errands, the man at the saw, or swinging the sickle, or in any kind of labor, often regulate their motions, and brighten the dulness of their work by some chant or by the cadences of some popular ballad and song.

Why has the Oriental such a different point of view, and so widely varied a judgment in music? Partly because of the structure of the musical scale. In Oriental music the sweetness and charm centers closely about the melody. Their more delicate gradations of sound, as compared with Western music, give a peculiar softness to the melody, which, in some measure, compensates for the lack of other parts in a harmony or symphony.

This radical difference in the structure of their musical scale was long a puzzle to musicians of the West. They found that Oriental melodies seemed to be set in the minor key, and were, of course, without symphony or harmonizing parts. Even so, they were unable to reproduce Oriental music on Western musical instruments. The stringed and wind instruments of the West required to be made over to reproduce Oriental melodies even. Why was this? Because the Oriental musical scale differs from that used in the West, and also because the Western musical octave has only tones and semi-tones, while the Oriental scale has tones, semi-tones, and quarter-tones.

319. *Hindu Musical Scale.*—Thus, the musical octave of India has seven chief notes, as with us, but while we have twelve semi-tones, that of India has twenty-two intervals, that is, audible sounds. Observers and writers are agreed that the intervals between the whole tones in the Oriental scale are not equal in the same sense that they are in the Western scale. Whether the intervals are according to a fixed proportion between the semi-tones, thirds, and quarter-tones they are not

agreed. The music thus produced is generally in unison, and is confined to an air or melody.

Some observers assert that the first, fourth, fifth, and eighth tones of the Oriental musical scale correspond closely to those of the Western musical scale. Thus, Dr. Henry J. Van Lennep, out of his lifetime experience as a missionary in Syria, has tabulated the number of vibrations of notes in the European scale, as compared with those in the Oriental musical scale, to show that the four chief tones in the two scales are substantially alike in respect to pitch. He also has noted the naturally and extremely fine quality of the Oriental voice. They sing in modes of time unknown in Western music, often alternating one kind of measure with another. This mixed-measure singing seems to delight them. It is the general testimony that attempts to express Oriental music by our system of notation is a failure. We cannot express it on our instruments, for as one facetiously says, "We must always begin by tuning our instruments wrong if we perform their music at all." Their tones, semi-tones, and quarter-tones, and trills upon a single note are the despair of all Western writers of music on paper. Even their intonations in common conversation are such as utterly to baffle the power of a Western voice to reproduce.

Oriental music has changed marvelously during historic times. Thus, Dr. D. O. Allen, in his history of India, notes that music was far more cultivated in ancient times in India than in modern days. And we must not forget that music has changed not a little in past generations, and has really grown to be an art in Western life within the past few centuries. Even now we are not agreed in many things concerning the highest class of music. While we have reduced the art to scientific accuracy in many respects, yet even in the pitch of a single note the vibrations are not counted the same by all classes of musicians. We have the old classical pitch of 415 to 430 vibrations, the French pitch of 435 vibrations, the concert pitch of 440 to 455 vibrations. For the "a" above middle "c", or applying it to the middle "c" we have the old pitch of 256 vibrations, the French pitch of 261 vibrations, the concert pitch of 270 vibrations.[1] The pitch or key, of course, depends upon the number of vibrations per second. The greater number of vibrations, the higher is the pitch. An English professor of music gives four different keys or pitches to treble "c." In like manner music has changed among the Orientals, but from their mode of treating the scale and of dividing the tones we may gain some light upon the allusions to music and musical instruments in the Bible.

320. *Musical Instruments.*—The educated Moslem of the East looks on the study of music as unworthy of a man of sense. The prophet Mohammed condemned it, classing it among the amusements which led to frivolity and vice, yet his followers to-day often chant, rather than recite, the sacred book, the Koran. As evidence that Mohammed was not wholly wrong, Lane, in his study of the modern Egyptians, found many professional musicians in Egypt dissolute, and some of them scarcely less disreputable than professional public dancers, but they were not all so. Female musicians were called *'Awa'lim*, singular *'A'limeh*, meaning a learned female. These professional female musicians are not to be confounded with the public dancers, however. The latter belong to a different tribe, or, at least, have a different origin, and were formerly known as the *Ghawazee*. The cultivation and prevalence of music differs in Oriental lands as with us, but among them all the taste prevails, while the development of the ballad, the song, and of musical instruments is adapted to the peculiar conditions and training of the various peoples.

321. *Three Kinds.*—Oriental musical instruments may be divided into three classes: (1) stringed instruments; (2) wind instruments; (3) instruments of percussion, as drums, tambourines, metal bars, bells, and the like. Before Western

---

[1] Scientific investigation shows that the lowest simple sound that can be distinguished by the ear is caused by fifteen or sixteen vibrations in a second. In practice, the pipe made to sound the lowest note by organ builders is thirty-two feet long, making about that number of vibrations per second. The highest note beyond which the ear cannot distinguish a single sound requires about 48,000 vibrations in a second. The limit of the human voice in music is approximately between eighty-seven vibrations a second for the lowest note, and about 4200 vibrations for the highest note.

ideas influenced Oriental peoples there were various forms of the viol, or "violin," but wholly different in shape and appearance from our instrument of that name. For example, the Egyptian viol was given a name which is supposed to be Persian, *kemangeh*, believed to signify a bow instrument. This was about a yard long, the sounding body was a part of a cocoanut, with a fourth part of the nut cut off, and the rest hollowed out and covered with the skin of a fish. Upon this rested the bridge, while the neck of the stick was of ebony, inlaid with ivory, and of a cylindrical form. The cords consisted of about sixty horse-hairs attached to a ring, just below the sounding body, where they were lengthened with a piece of lamb's gut (not cat-gut), attached to a peg. The bow, about the same length as the instrument, is made of wood, and strung with horse-hairs. The Arabs also have a stringed instrument something like a dulcimer. The cords of this instrument are also of lamb's gut, three strands to each string, and altogether twenty-four treble cords. The strings are shorter at one side of the instrument than at the other, something like the strings of a modern piano. This instrument the player puts upon his knees or lap, he sitting squat upon the floor and playing the instrument with two plectra, one plectrum upon the forefinger of each hand. The plectra were thin pieces of buffalo's horn and held on the finger by a ring or thimble. Besides these the Arabs have a kind of guitar or mandolin. These instruments have seven double strings (two strands to each string), and they, too, are of lamb's gut and not cat-gut. The double cord of the lowest string is that which corresponds to the highest cord in European guitars. Next comes one of a fifth above, then the seventh, second, fourth, sixth, and third. In this case the plectrum is a slip of the vulture or some other bird's feather. The instrument is held against the breast and played not unlike a modern mandolin or guitar with us.

322. *Wind Instruments.*—There are various kinds of wind instruments common among Orientals—one resembles the modern flute, another is similar to a clarinet. Some of the pipes are

made to produce musical sounds by blowing through a very small aperture of the lips, pressed against the orifice of the tube, so that the wind is thrown within the tube, with more or less force, producing sounds an octave higher or lower at the will of the performer. The boatmen of the Nile have a kind of double reed pipe. One of the reeds is much longer than the other, and serves as a continuous bass. These pipes produce harsh sounds resembling the sounds of a bag-pipe. There is also rarely heard a sort of bag-pipe, the bag being made of goat's skin. Whether this is an Oriental idea or borrowed is an open question. Possibly the "organ" of the patriarchal era was the bag-pipe.[1]

323. *Of Percussion.*—Of the musical instruments which are beaten with sticks there are a great many. The tambourine is played sometimes with the hand and sometimes with something attached to the fingers. The kettle-drum may have a parchment face, and is usually beaten with two slender sticks. The performer may carry it suspended from a string around his neck or, if large, it may be placed upon the floor. Besides these there are cymbals, castinets of copper, of brass, plates or bars of metal of different lengths, to produce sounds of different pitch. The Occidentals are familiar with the musical sounds of the Chinese and Japanese gongs.

324. *Songs.*—Lane found that the popular songs of the peasants in Egypt were sung with a distinct enunciation and a quavering voice. Here are some specimens:

" O ye beauties ! fear God,
  And have mercy on the lover for the sake of God.
  The love of you is ordained by God :
  The Lord hath decreed it against me."

" Every night long my moaning ceaseth not
  For a solitary gazelle that hath taken away my soul.
  I vow that, if my beloved come,
  I will do deeds that 'An'tar did not."

[1] See Gen. 4 : 21; Job 21 : 12; 30 : 31; Ps. 150 : 4.

"A lover says to the dove, 'Lend me your wings for a day.'
The dove replied, 'Thy affair is vain': I said, 'Some other day
That I may soar through the sky, and see the face of the beloved:
I shall obtain love enough for a year, and will return, O dove, in
        a day.'"
"The night! The night!" &c.

Dr. A. A. Bonar and R. M. McCheyne [1] tell of many years
ago, when crossing the desert, the drivers being weary, proposed
to camp for the night. The dragomen desired to go further.
Upon this the young Arabs proceeded without a murmur, and
in order to cheer the way commenced their native dance and
song. One of them, advancing a little before the rest, began
the song, dancing forward as he repeated the words; when the
rest, following him in regular order, joined in the chorus,
keeping time by simultaneous clapping of hands. They sang
several Arab songs in this way, responding to one another,
and dancing along the firm sand of the seashore in the clear,
beautiful moonlight. The travelers remark: "The response,
the dance, and the clapping of hands brought many parts of
the Word of God to our minds. We remember the song of
Miriam at the Red Sea, when the women went out after her
with timbrels and with dances, and Miriam answered them,
that is, Miriam sang responsively to them." [2] In the song of
David before Saul, and of the women of Israel after David's
victory over Goliath, the women answered one another as they
played and said: "Saul hath slain his thousands, and David
his ten thousands." [3] The Psalmist also exclaimed, "O
clap your hands, all ye people; shout unto God with the voice
of triumph." In another Psalm he exclaims, "Let the floods
clap their hands: let the hills be joyful together," that is, as
in a full choir. See also the responsive form of Psalm 136.

325. *The Viol.*—Lieutenant Lynch also, in his expedition,
notes the sad and solemn tone of the music produced by an
Arab bard singing sadly to the sound of his *rebabeh*, a kind

---

[1] Narrative of Mission to the Jews, p. 61 (Dr. A. A. Bonar and Robt. M. McCheyne).
[2] Ex. 15 : 20, 21.
[3] 1 Sam. 16 : 23; 18 : 6, 7; compare 2 Kings 3 : 15 and Is. 5 : 12.

of one string viol, and he adds, "the music, although more
varied in character and modulation, was essentially the same
in its prevailing sadness, . . . the sound of tabret, and harp,
of sackbut and psaltery, the flute, the viol, and the instrument of two strings are heard no more in the land; the '*rebabeh*,'
with its sighing one string, befits the wilderness and the wandering
people who dwell therein. . . . Not even the Emir, although
he threw all the mirth he could command into his voice, and
touched the string with quite elastic fingers, striking out notes
and half notes with musical precision, his dark eyes flashing
and his white teeth glistening, and his body swaying to and
fro, nodding his head to the music of his minstrelsy, as if to
triumph over the bard, though he won applause with every
verse, he could not change the tone; there was the same sad
minor running through the song.   These low complaining tones
lingered in our ears long after the sounds had ceased and the
Arabs were gathered in sleep around the smoldering watch-
fires."[5]

Lynch's Expedition, p. 244.

XXIX.

ORIENTAL WRITING.

ORIENTAL writing is in contrast, and almost opposite, to the manner prevailing with us. Arabic writing runs from the right hand to the left, and most of the people of Western Asia write after a similar manner. In Eastern Asia the lines in writing and printing are often vertical rather than horizontal. The signature and seal are usually at the beginning, and not at the end, as with us. The date of a communication or document is commonly at the end, not at the beginning.

326. *Public Scribes.*—Formerly, Moslems forbade the printing of the Koran. They held it a desecration of the name of God to pass it under the press, and that printing increased errors. Scribes wrote copies of their sacred book. Now the Koran is printed. Public writers of letters and documents are a necessity among a people where so many are illiterate. The scribes are found near the mosques and courts, as Jewish scribes frequented the temple courts and the synagogues in earlier days. Literary men, says Mr. Haddad, now often write themselves, or have a copyist re-write documents in a better form. Such copyists or scribes are around government offices, the markets, and the courts.

327. *Samaritan Law.*—The Samaritans also have a written copy of their sacred book of the law of Moses, which they guard jealously. Many years ago, Dr. Post was allowed to enter the sanctuary at Nablūs, and to see the three sacred copies. The most sacred of the three, however, was then exhibited unwillingly and hesitatingly, for fear of the jealous feeling of the sect. Even the faithful among the Samaritans were not allowed to look upon it except once a year, and then only in the hands of their high priest. The Moslems are not allowed to touch the Koran with unwashed hands. In

more recent times they have become apparently less cautious.
The Samaritan Bible, that is, the five books of Moses, written
on gazelle-skin parchment, is kept in a costly case, with a cover
of green Venetian fabric, within the Samaritan synagogue at
Nablūs. It is an inferior parchment that is now so readily
shown by the rabbis to visitors on application and payment of
a small sum.

328. *Seals*.—Every Oriental document is attested by a seal.
Such seals are universal in the East. The seals may be of
brass, engraved with the name or monogram of the owner, a
little scroll work, the seal being tied by a string, or worn on the
finger as a ring. To make the seal impression, the finger is
smeared with ink, rubbed over the face of the seal, and the
paper is pressed between the seal and the forefinger. Sealing-
wax was rarely used.

Dr. Edward Robinson relates how, after a long talk, and
much clamor, he agreed with Sheikh Beshara to furnish his
party with dromedaries and camels. The contract was at
once written by a scribe, upon his knee, and signed and sealed
in a very primitive manner. Arabs of the towns usually had
a signet ring to serve as a signature. But Bushara had none,
so he held up one of his fingers, the point of which was daubed
with ink, and he then gravely impressed it upon the paper,
which to him was as binding an act as if he had sealed it with
a gold or jeweled seal. Dr. Perkins records similar customs
of scribes in Persia, as Harmer does also in Barbary, Lane in
Egypt, and Malcolm in Southern Asia. Lane tells us that
regular scribes wore a silver, brass, or copper case, with receptacles for ink and pens stuck in the girdle. The prophet Ezekiel
had a vision of a man in linen clothes, with a writer's ink horn
by his side.[1] Dr. Perkins says the profession of scribes was
an extensive one in Persia. The higher classes avoid the
drudgery of the pen, and peasants are too ignorant to do their
own writing. The lower class of Persian merchants usually
keep their own accounts, write their own letters, and use their

[1] Ezek. 9 : 1-4.

own seal. The chief merchants carry on their business in cipher-characters, like government cipher-despatches, every one having his own cipher-alphabet. At that time there were no regular mails in Persia, and letters were entrusted to couriers, who might be bribed to betray the secrets of the letters to commercial rivals, hence they would avoid writing in the current language.

329. *Traditions—How Kept.*—The Orientals partially over-came the apparent inconvenience of keeping records by com-mitting things to memory. Mr. Haddad tells that when writers are or were comparatively few, people were obliged to commit things to memory, such as sayings of the wise, historic facts, and business matters. It came to pass that a certain class made a profession of doing this, and of handing down the facts from generation to generation. This class became permanent witnesses, and were, therefore, required to be honest, veracious, and trustworthy, so that the things committed by and to them would agree in the main with those reported by others of a like class. In modern times in Turkey, three groups or divisions of persons of this kind are said to exist. These hold in memory and recite written and unwritten matters. First, those who commit to memory religious books and matters among Moslems, Jews, and Christians. They can recite whole books from beginning to end, often without a mistake in a word. Second, those who recite the sayings of Mohammed, not recorded in the Koran. Third, those who recite history and noted poems.

330. *Records.*—Records and documents of importance are often lost and found in after years. Mr. Haddad reports that a noble Syrian family had inherited an estate hundreds of years ago. The products of the estate were to be shared among the descendants, but the property could never be sold. The mem-bers of the family who knew the provisions of the will passed away, the document was lost, and the descendants fell to quar-reling over the division of the income. Lawyers and judges were consulted, and their fees absorbed the chief portion of the

inheritance. Finally, the old public record hall fell into decay, and to rebuild it, the documents and papers were removed from the closets, where they had been piled together for hundreds of years. They were not arranged in any systematic order, so a document could be easily lost. In sorting over the old documents, by chance, a book with a copy of the lost will was found and reported to this Syrian family. All agreed that the document was genuine and not a forged one. The paper, style of writing, and other proofs showed that it was genuine, since a fraudulent record could not have stood the tests applied. This is a striking illustration of the account of the lost book of the law, which was found in the temple among the piles of documents and was read to Josiah the king, and recognized as the law of Moses.[1]

331. *Books.*—The Oriental book was a roll, such as the Samaritan law is written upon, and it could be easily written on both sides. Writing on the back of a book of the modern form would have no meaning. Hartley saw two rolls written on both sides in a Greek monastery. Dr. Buchanan found an old copy of the law in India, written on a roll of leather about fifteen feet long. These rolls are wound on wooden axes, and often enclosed in a silver or copper gilt cylinder, which opened at the side. On feast days, these rolls were carried in solemn procession. Such rolls are often alluded to in Scriptures.[2]

332. *Letters.*—An Oriental letter is written with a long reed pen.[3] This pen is carried in a tube. A large piece of paper is required for a letter in good form. The letter has the seal or signature at the top. They begin to write from the right hand side of the page. The opening sentence is a flowery and complimentary introduction, in high-sounding words, seasoned with extravagant and fulsome phrases and pretensions of love, no matter whether to a friend or an enemy. Usually, as Dr. Thomson observes, this rigmarole has no meaning, or is an egregious lie, a mere formality. Following this usually there

---

[1] See 2 Kings 22 : 8–23 : 3; 2 Chron. 34 : 14 ff.
[2] See Jer. 36 : 2, 21; Ezek. 2 : 9, 10; Zech. 5 : 1–3; Rev. 6 : 14; 2 Tim. 4 : 13.
[3] Judg. 5 : 14; 3 John 13.

is an epitome of the communication, which is to be answered, often repeating it word for word. Examples of this form are common in the Bible. The letter is dated at the bottom, but often no place is mentioned, and no address given. Thus, the mother of a servant girl wanted two wooden bowls, and a small Hungarian trunk sent to her from Jaffa to Bethlehem. The girl was in Jaffa. The letter to her, from the mother in Bethlehem ran thus:

"To the most honoured and excellent lady, the respected Catherina; God liveth and endureth for ever. Amen!

"After having settled on the principal question, that is, your dear health and security, which is with us the essential cause of writing, and the occasion of our prayers; firstly, if your question about us be admitted, we are,—God be praised,—in perfect happiness, and do nothing but ask about you and the security of your health, which is with us the essential cause of writing, and the occasion of prayer." [After several sentences, referring to health again and that of the members of the family, comes the real request.] "Send us two wooden bowls, without mistake, by the kind camel driver,—my contentment rest on you." [Salutations are then sent to several of the family, and then the second request.] "Send him [your brother] a Hungarian trunk, like the trunk of Tufaha, the daughter of your uncle, Jirius. For its price is from us, and when you will face us we will repay you its price. What we now want we have told you, and if you want anything tell us. God liveth and endureth!" [Then follows four special sentences of commendations and salutations from various members of the family, which close the letter.]

This letter would require two pages of writing.

333. *How Written.*—The paper Dr. Van Lennep used in the East was thick, in large sheets, and polished by rubbing. It is not ruled with a ruler and pencil, but by successive foldings, a margin being left at the right side of the page, and a line, slanting somewhat upward toward the left, unless the sheet is written on both sides, then the lines are written straight. The paper is held in the left hand, which rests upon the right knee in such a manner that the pressure of the reed on the paper is sustained by the two fingers of that hand. The Oriental never rests his paper while writing upon a desk or table. He is independent of mechanical contrivances, to which the Occidental has become a slave.

As before stated, the signature of a letter or document is not
written, but stamped with a seal.   State documents have the
name and titles of the sovereign inscribed at the top in a peculiar
style, called *tourah*, or imperial cipher.   These are stamped
with an official seal, as described above.   If special importance and weight are attached to the document, it is sometimes
sealed or marked with blood, or burned at the four corners.[1]
See references to seals on letters and orders.[2]

Formerly, letters were folded, and put up in envelopes opened
lengthwise, to receive their contents at one end, and were
closed with two seals.   The address was written across (not
lengthwise of) the envelope.   The messenger usually carries
such a letter on his head, between the cap and its lining, hence
the Oriental proverb, "Upon my head."

334. *Reed Pens, etc.*—How widespread and uniform the
general type of Oriental writing was is shown by what Lane
tells us he saw nearly a century ago in Egypt.   The ink used
there was thick and gummy.   The scribes wrote with reeds,
not with quill pens, as Arabic characters, like most of the characters in Oriental languages, cannot be easily made with quills
or metal pens.   The paper was thick and glazed.   Scissors
were a necessary part of the apparatus of a writer, to trim the
edges of the paper, since torn edges were considered in bad taste.
The Egyptian places his paper on his knee, or on the palm of
his left hand, rarely upon a kind of pad.   He rules his paper by
laying under it a piece of pasteboard, with strings stretched
and glued across it, and slightly pressing the paper over each
string.   The Oriental ink-horn and reed pen of later times are
close patterns to those in use thousands of years ago.

About half a century ago, foremost biblical critics were posi-
tive that Moses could not have written any part of the Pentateuch, because they declared that the art of writing was then
unknown.   This assumption is now exploded and laughed at.
For writing has been found in Egypt of earlier date than the

[1] See Churchill, "Lebanon," vol. iv, p. 150.
[2] 1 Kings 21 : 8; Esther 8 : 8, 10; Job 14 : 17; Is. 8 : 16; 29 : 11; Jer. 32 : 14, 44; Ezek.
28 : 12; Dan. 9 : 24; 12 : 4, 9; Rev. 22 : 10.

time of Abraham, and extending through the reigns of all the Pharaohs. Cuneiform writing in Babylonia has also been brought to light, probably more than a thousand years older than the age of the Hebrew patriarchs. The bundles of letters found at Tel-el-Amarna indicate how widespread was the knowledge of writing before the days of Moses. Dr. Griffis also tells of an interesting discovery that at the earliest introduction of writing into Japan, men devoted their studies to the Chinese language, and left their own language to be cultivated by women. It is said that a large proportion of the best writings in the past age of Japanese literature is the work of women.[1]

Modern Pens in the Orient.—It is not uncommon now for travelers to see Orientals using *steel* pens. Reed pens are slowly passing into disuse, since steel pens are now so cut as to adapt them for writing Arabic. The ancient ink-horn is likewise fast disappearing in the Orient. Arabs even may occasionally be seen using a fountain pen! In fact, many Oriental utensils, habits and manners are passing away before the swift advance of Western customs. Orientals are lamenting the disappearance of their long-cherished ways and manners, but yield doggedly to the inevitable, mourning that their loved characteristics in a few years will utterly have vanished from among them.

334a. *Hieroglyphic and Cuneiform.*—The Oriental's skill in writing extends far back into prehistoric times. The hieroglyphic, or picture writing, of Egypt, on obelisks, and the cuneiform, or wedge-shaped writing, on clay tablets, of old Babylonia, formed immense libraries that have been buried for millenniums and in recent years dug up, adding much to our knowledge of those remote peoples. The code of laws of Hammurapi, the oldest in the world, was thus preserved, as elsewhere noted.

[1] Mikado's Empire, p. 213.

XXX.

NOMADS and primitive races have no commerce and no shops. Yet they trade, by barter and exchange, in rude and simple ways. Among more settled tribes in an Oriental village the first shop started is usually a *bakkal*, grocer's stall, who sells bread, cheese, olives, salt and dried fish, wood, iron, and earthenware utensils for the passing traveler. Sometimes the village will have a *haddad*, blacksmith, a coffee house, a baker, a cobbler, or a butcher.

335. *Shops.*—Oriental shops are all after a similar pattern—the workshop and the place to store goods usually being in the same room or building. Dr. Van Lennep, out of his long observation, describes one of these places. On the street is a platform, about two feet high, and along the whole front of the shop. A small door opens to a room back, the goods and best articles are displayed in front, as they are now in the windows of our great department stores. On the platform is a *sejadeh*, or rug, or thin mat. Upon this the keeper sits cross-legged. He keeps himself busy with his accounts, or displaying his goods, keen to address passersby, inviting them to look at the special beauty of his articles.

Buyers and sellers meet in the Oriental village "market," on a chief street. Shop and store-rooms line this street, which the Arabs call *sûk*.[1] Here the peasant is found, with his animals ladened with food-stuffs and his country produce. The gardener is there with his small fruits. All the shop-keepers are on or near this market street or center. Prof. Elihu Grant tells us an Oriental shop in a Syrian village is a small room, six to twelve feet square, has a door, but rarely a window, a counter, or bench, and shelves and bins along the

---

[1] Matt. 20 : 3.

walls, where sugar, flour, oil, matches, candies, spice, starch, coffee, rice, and dried figs—but no wrapping paper—may be found. For liquids, the buyer brings his own dish; his other purchases he carries away in the ample folds of his skirt or in a handkerchief.

336. *Buying.*—Oriental buyers and sellers are alike keen at bargains. They haggle over prices with great heat. They cool, then are swept into a frenzy of strife; again they grow calm, but the haggling and controversy and argument begin over again, becoming more heated than before, and so excited as to appear soon to come to blows. At last, however, they find a common basis, and the sale is made with flattering compliments to one another, and to the rapturous delight of both parties.

This "striking a bargain" is a tedious process to the stranger. The native Oriental takes pleasure in the exercise, and sees great possibilities before him. He assures you the bargain shall be just as you like, wholly. Is he not a servant of God? He cares not for money, but for your good-will and happiness. That is the sweetest thing of life, the love and favor of brothers. You offer a price, and he says, "What is such a trifle as that between us? Take it for nothing." But he does not *mean* a word of it. A native once offered a young gazelle found in the wilderness to Prof. Grant. He said it was a "present." The professor offered him forty cents for it; he promptly demanded sixty.

337. *Bazaars.*—The shops or bazaars in some Oriental villages are found in clusters. Each group of shops in the *sûk, agora,* or market, has a supply of special articles or necessaries of life, belonging to similar classes. Thus, every considerable Turkish town, says Van Lennep, has a bazaar or *bezesten,* a sort of arcade: a stone structure, open at both ends, a narrow alley or street running through it, covered with an arched roof, the sides pierced with openings or windows. This covered street on both sides is lined with shops, narrow and shallow. Dealers in similar goods and articles flock

together here, as do the artisans of like trades in Oriental cities. Such shops can yet be seen in Constantinople, Damascus, Cairo, and Bagdad. In ancient days they were in Jerusalem, Babylon, and Noph.[1]

338. *Markets.*—In inland towns and cities the markets and market-places are often in the open air as well as under cover. Great bazaars or fairs are held on certain days of the week. Several towns or villages each select a different day for the bazaar or market, offering at such times everything for sale; cattle, sheep, horses, mules, chickens, butter, eggs, vegetables, fruit, jewelry, garments, as if the whole town were for the day turned into a fair or exhibition, where everything was for sale. The day thus appointed is often a Sunday, or a Friday, the Moslem Sunday, since these are holidays in Turkey. On such days, peasants and people come together in larger numbers than on other days.[2] The Oriental "bargain counter" has been described in the section on Trades.

339. *Credit.*—The shopkeeper does not always get cash from the native buyer. Indeed, as Prof. Post tells us, debt is almost universal in Syria. The peasant sows borrowed seed, on borrowed land, plants and reaps with borrowed tools, and lives in a borrowed house. In an abundant harvest even, the amount of the crop left by the tax-gatherer barely pays the debt accumulated in making and gathering the crop. When the buyer pays cash for his purchases, after a true Oriental manner, his payment is in coin, or rings of copper, silver, or gold, such as are now common in China. In biblical times we find allusions to this kind of payments. See Ezra 2: 69, where the term *adarkonim* signifies Persian coins, similar to the Greek *darics*. The Persians are said to have got the idea of coining from Lydia, at the capture of Sardis, 564 B. C. Earlier Lydian coins were of electrum, but Crœsus changed this to coins of gold and silver, probably about 568 B. C. Examples of these coins are now known. This throws light on the passage in Gen. 43: 21, where the rings were weighed;

the phrase literally meaning "bundles" or "strings of money." So in the record of 2 Kings 22 : 9, where the scribe reported to the king that the servants had "melted" [gathered] the money.

340. *The Café.*—The Palestine Exploration reports the common method of shopkeeping peculiar to Syria and Palestine. The grocer, called *samman*, keeps all kinds of dry fruits, and olive oil, while the perfumer, on the perfumers' street, has all kinds of spices, usually in a very small room, so small that the perfumer can reach almost any of his articles without getting up from his seat. In fact, many of his goods are stowed under his seat, such as cinnamon, pepper, and spices. These are in little oval boxes, with a label in Arabic marking the contents of the box.

The café is usually at the corner of some street, and is the meeting place of all strangers and natives when they have finished their business. Everybody is here, friend and foe, so that the café is the institution of the Oriental town. Some are to be found near the gates, where is also the *khan*, for travelers to leave their animals, while the owners go about the town doing their business. When a customer stops at any of the shops and is shown what he calls for, he is quite often offered coffee and a pipe, *narghileh* ("smoking bottle"), from the nearby café, where men resort, but no women are admitted, because it is a kind of bourse, or place for discussing the markets and sales. Hence, the Eastern café is a wide-spread institution, found everywhere in the Orient.

341. *Women Shoppers.*—Formerly women of high class in the Orient remained at home; they rarely went out shopping. This led to a peculiar class of women-sellers and buyers, who went from house to house, making sales, and acting as intermediaries or merchandise brokers. Prof. Post found this class very common when he first went to Syria. The custom is gradually giving way now, and many women do their own buying and selling, due to the invasion of Western customs.

342. *Silos.*—The Arabian peasant brings his grain from the various places of concealment, for he is compelled to hide his

wheat and other grains, lest the marauding tribes of Bedouins or the tax-gatherer, whom he fears, may plunder him. Arab tribes are said to possess large hordes of wheat and other grain concealed in what are called *silos*, which Tristram tells us are underground pits, eight feet deep, carefully cemented, and bottle shaped, with a narrow neck, large enough to admit a man. They are plastered with cement, and the ground leveled over them to prevent discovery, and the secret is only known to the owner. It may have been to such *silos* that the ten men referred when they said to Gedaliah, "Slay us not: for we have treasures in the field, of wheat, and of barley, and of oil, and of honey." [1]

These *silos* are carefully guarded, but left unvisited or un-opened for months, lest some one should discover and plunder them.[2] (See Storehouses.)

343. *Shops in Clusters.*—As further proof that the shops and bazaars are usually in clusters in Oriental cities, Dr. Griffis tells us of streets in Japan lined with open shops. The chief occupation of the shopkeepers seemed to him to be toasting their fingers. One shop was full of ivory carvings, some of them elegant works of art, real puns in ivory, and some were historical tableaux. In Tokio he found one street devoted to bureaus and cabinets; another was full of folding screens, yet another street was filled with dyers' shops, with their odors and vats. In still another street nothing was on sale but bamboo poles, and "enough of those to make a forest." The Oriental habit of like shops and like trades clustering together is typical in Japan. There are many passages of Scripture that require a knowledge of this fact in Oriental life to become in-telligible to Western readers.

344. *Some Odd Customs.*—Again, of the reverse way the Ori-ental does everything, Japan is a conspicuous example. As elsewhere in the Orient, the bamboo worker saws the cane by pulling the saw toward him instead of pushing it from him as we do. The carpenter pulls his plane toward him; the black-smith works his bellows with his foot, while he holds and ham-

[1] Jer. 41 : 8.   [2] Eastern Customs. Tristram, p. 251.

mers his iron with both hands.   The cooper holds his tubs with
his toes, and all the workers sit while they work, as do shopkeepers also.   Why do they do things contrariwise to us?   Are we
upside down, or are they?   The Oriental says we are.   They
call us "crab-writers," because to them our writing goes backward on the page; our printing is "crawfish" work, because it
goes across the page from left to right, and not right to left, or
downward properly, as their writing does.   Even Japanese
screws turn the other way from ours, and their locks turn to the
left, when ours turn to the right.   Are the Orientals or we
turned the wrong way about?

The custom of having shops in clusters or groups, Dr. D. O.
Allen says, prevails in India.   The small villages in his day had
a few shops for the sale of grain, tobacco, coarse cloths, and the
like, while larger villages had appointed market-days, or fairs,
after Oriental custom, to which traveling traders and people
from hamlets resort.   Streets are narrow and crooked, few being
wide enough for carriages to pass.   Merchants and bankers are
on the principal street of large towns and cities, or about a public square.   They sit cross-legged, on a carpeted bench, or on a
floor raised about two feet above the ground, and covered with
a rug.   They are very courteous, lending money to small traders,
and advancing it to farmers on their harvest crops as security.

345. *Fairs.*—Similar fairs are described by travelers in
Africa, and are usually held outside the towns, in front of their
principal gate.   Slaves, sheep, bullocks, and live stock in great
numbers were for sale, with wheat, rice, tamarinds in pods,
groundnuts, ban beans, and indigo.   Leather was offered in
great quantities, skins of a large snake, and pieces of crocodile
skin as ornaments, for the scabbards of daggers, were also on
sale.

Morier attended similar fairs in Persia, where were also
gathered sellers of all sorts of goods in temporary shops or tents,
such as the sellers of barley and flour, at the gate of Samaria
after the famine.[1]   Layard noticed little shops for the sale

[1] See 2 Kings 7.

of wheat, barley, bread, and other breadstuffs at the gate of
the modern town of Mosul, opposite the site of old Nineveh.
It was "at the gate" that Boaz called the elders and people
to witness that he had bought all that was Elimelech's.[1] Allusions to trading and traders of a similar kind may be found
in Job 5 : 4; Prov. 31 : 23; Ps. 127 : 5; and Lam. 5 : 14, as
also at an earlier period in Gen. 23 : 10, 18; 2 Chron. 18 : 9.

[1] Ruth 4 : 1-3.

SELLING FISH, GALILEE LAKE.

(Copyright by Underwood & Underwood, New York.)

MEASURING GRAIN—FULL MEASURE. P. 232

(Vester & Co.)

XXXI.

FROM time immemorial, primitive peoples have been grouped into two classes—those having temporary and movable, and those having permanent dwellings, tents, and caves. This division is recognized in the early Genesis narrative. Thus, Jabal is called "the father of such as dwell in tents and have cattle," and "Cain was a tiller of the ground," and "he builded a city."[1]

346. *Cave Dwellers.*—Whether prehistoric man dwelt in dens, caves, or cliffs is a question which lies beyond the scope of this work. Natural caves and rocky and cliff-dens exist in great numbers throughout all Western Asia. Many of them bear evidences of having been occupied by man at different periods. Tyrwhitt Drake tells us of Syrian troglodytes, who inhabit old caves with their cows, sheep, and goats. The walls of these caves are seldom smoothed, are circular or oval, and rarely six feet in height. The center is occupied by the cattle, the portion reserved by the human part of the community is marked off by a line of stones or a slightly raised narrow dais. The state of the cave after a heavy downpour of rain, added to the general uncleanliness, the slimy damp of the walls, the mosquitoes, the vermin, the reek of men and beasts, make an ordinary pigsty a palace in comparison. The indolent, able-bodied rascals, dignified by the title of reasonable beings, who own this byre, are too lazy to build themselves huts. The cave dwellers, Mr. Drake says, are sunk but little lower than their house-sheltered brethren.

347. *Rock Refuge.*—Van Lennep tells us of shepherds who stable their flocks in these caves of Western Asia, and people oppressed by tyranny and war forsake villages and dwell for a

[1] Gen. 4 : 2, 17, 20.

time in these wild and inaccessible places to escape from their
oppressors. Bandits and outlaws make these caverns their
abode, as in olden time, and from these they sally forth to commit robbery and murder. David and his outlaws escaped from
Saul and dwelt in the cave of Adullam, whither he gathered
malcontents of every sort.[1] Extensive habitations of this kind
are still found east of the Jordan and in Arabia. Porter describes with much swelling rhetoric the giant cities of Bashan-
land, and the wonderful cliff city of Petra is attracting troops of
tourists in our day. Similar extensive rock excavations, with
apartments and rooms, may be found in Lycia, on the coast of
Asia Minor. The Persian town of Sherazûl, near where
Alexander gained his victory over Darius, is also largely dug out
of rock.[2] Similar caves exist in various parts of Palestine, bearing evidences of having once been dwelling-places of man, thus
confirming references thereto in the Scriptures.[3]

348. *Nomads.*—These cave dwellers led a nomad life, and
many of them are still found in the East, following much the
same kind of life that their ancestors did, six thousand or eight
thousand years ago. A large class of Arabs of the desert, widely
known as Bedouins, dwell either in caves or in tents, and
roam over wide areas. The other class of peasants, or fellahin,
dwell in huts and hamlets, and abodes that are a step toward a
more permanent type of dwelling, but scarcely possess more
comforts than the cave dwellers themselves. Drake describes
these fellahin as living in miserable huts, dark, dirty, and
comfortless. In the mountains they are built of mud and stone,
generally roofed with beams of rough timber, on which bushes
and a couple of feet of soil are laid. Roofs require careful
rolling before rains, or the water sinks in, and causes them to
collapse. A few pans and jars for cooking, a few rush mats,
or if the man be well off, a cotton quilt, is a catalogue of the
furniture. They seldom eat meat, except when an animal is
to be killed to prevent its dying a natural death.[4]

[1] 1 Sam. 22 : 1, 2.   [2] Tavernier, p. 73.
[3] Josh. 10 : 16 ff ; Judg. 6 : 2; 1 Sam. 13 : 6; 23 : 14, 25, 29; 24 : 3, 4.
[4] Pal. Survey, Special Papers, 312.

349. *Tents.*—The tent, and the hut or house, as I have said, are the product of two kinds of life and society—the nomad, or pastoral, shepherd and herdsmen, and the settled farmer or dweller in some village. Each of these modes of life and of dwellings is found widely in the Orient now.

Buckingham tells of the Bedouin tents which he found to be "almost universally made of black or brown hair cloth. When made in camp the cloth was often a mixture of goats', sheep's, and camels' hair, in various proportions. The tent cover was of black goats' hair, woven into cloth about a yard wide, and as long as the tent. These long strips were stitched together, and he found from experience they would keep off the heaviest rains." [1] Such tents are graphically described by the author of Song of Songs:

> "I am black, but comely,
>   O ye daughters of Jerusalem,
>   As the tents of Kedar,
>   As the curtains of Solomon." [2]

Of the setting up of an Oriental tent, Buckingham says, "It was formed of one large awning, supported by small poles (twenty-four in four rows, six in a row), the ends of the awning being drawn out by cords, fastened to pegs driven in the ground. Shaw also saw and used tents put up in a similar way. He says they were kept firm and steady by bracing or stretching down their eaves with cords, tied to hooked wooden pins, well pointed, and driven into the ground with a heavy mallet."

350. *Family Tent.*—The usual shape of an Oriental tent is oblong, rarely round. If intended for a large company or family, it is divided by awnings or curtains into two or three apartments; one for males, another for females, and sometimes a third room for servants or for cattle. Layard tells of a sheikh's camp at Nimrūd, in which the tall, robust, courageous, and intelligent chief received him. At the entrance to his capacious tent, of black goats' hair, he was met and led to the apartment

---

[1] Buckingham's Notes, p. 37. [2] Song of Sol. 1 : 5.

16

divided by a goats' hair curtain, and assigned to men. This reception apartment was also occupied by two favorite mares and a colt. Camels were kneeling on the grass outside the tent, and horses of strangers were hitched by halters to the tent pegs. Carpets and rugs were spread for the guest, while on both sides were long lines of men, seated on the bare ground within the tent, the sheikh at the farthest end, also on the ground, out of respect for his guest. He could only be prevailed on after excuses and protestations to share the rug with the guest. In the center of this motley group crouched a half-naked Arab, blowing the dying embers of a small fire of camels' dung, or pounding roasted coffee in a copper mortar, to fill the huge pots that stood near by.[1]

351. *Tent Apartments.*—This picture of the shape, the setting up, and the divisions of a modern Oriental tent might well fit the character of the tents of thousands of years ago. Abram led a pastoral life and "pitched his tent" where good pasture was found. When that was used up, "he removed . . . and pitched his tent" in a new and more suitable place. Likewise his nephew Lot had "flocks, herds, and tents," moving about with his uncle, until he parted with him and settled in Sodom.[2] In like manner Isaac "encamped [pitched his tent] in the valley of Gerar, and dwelt there."[3] According to Oriental custom, his son Jacob likewise was a quiet man, dwelling in tents, as his father and grandfather did before him, but in contrast to Jacob, Esau was a huntsman, a freebooter, after the type of the modern bandit of desert Arabs.[4] It shows us how fixed was this type of life, and how close the Oriental adheres to custom, to read that centuries after the Rechabites and the people of Kedar and other nations likewise dwelt in tents, because it suited their mode of subsistence.[5]

The figure of setting up a tent was used by the prophet as an emblem of the security which Jehovah would give to his people, "I will fasten him as a nail (literally a "tent peg") in

[1] See Nineveh, vol. i, p. 56.   [2] Gen. 12 : 8; 13 : 3, 5, 18.   [3] Gen. 26 : 17.
[4] See Gen. 25 : 27.   [5] See Jer. 35 : 7, 10; 49 : 29; Hab. 3 : 7.

a sure place." [1] The captives under Ezra were given a temporary safety, which he compares to a "nail" or "tent pin" in his holy place.[2] Again, in a vision of the coming glory of God's people, the prophet compares it to "a tent that shall not be removed, the stakes whereof shall never be plucked up, neither shall any of the cords thereof be broken." [3]

352. *Groups of Tents.*—The Oriental tent not only has apartments under one cover, but sometimes separate tents are assigned as a mark of honor, or for distinction, or for convenience. These seem to have had their counterpart in patriarchal times. In the Genesis narrative it is said, "Laban went into Jacob's tent, and into Leah's tent, and into the tent of the two maidservants," hunting for his stolen gods.[4] "And he went out of Leah's tent, and entered into Rachel's tent," but failed to find the teraphim or household gods. But his grandfather, Abram, dwelt in a single tent, for when the angels visited him, Sarah was in the woman's apartment and overheard their conversation through the curtain.[5]

When several tents were in camp together, whether in peace or in war, they usually were grouped in some systematic order. Burckhardt tells that when there are few tents in a camp they are arranged in a circle, called *dowar;* this is for better protection. When there are many tents they may be placed in a row by the side of a stream. Robinson saw a nomad encampment of these tents arranged in a sort of square, the tents were black, but not large; were open at one end, and the sides were turned up so that he could see they were filled with men, women, children, calves, lambs, and kids; for the band had about six hundred sheep and goats, mostly goats, and a few cows.[6]

353. *Hebrew Tent Life.*—Tent life occupies a large space in patriarchal and early Hebrew history. The sacred writers seem to delight in drawing symbols and figures from it to illustrate their spiritual teaching. It appeals to minds in every age and clime. Thus, Dr. Thomson goes into rapturous dreams, as

---

[1] See Isa. 22 : 23, and compare also Zech. 10 : 4.
[2] Ezra 9 : 8.   [3] Isa. 33 : 20.   [4] Gen. 31 : 33.
[5] Gen. 18 : 1–10.   [6] Researches, i, p. 485.

he introduces a traveling friend to his house-tent, pitched among oleanders and willows, his cot and luggage on the left, and those of his friend on the right side of the temporary abode. He looked with wonder and alarm at the "hundred and one" articles that the dragoman, Salim, gathered and stowed away on mules, just as every traveler has done, and was amazed to see his muleteer, Ahmed, sound asleep, his old cloak over him, lying on the bare ground, a stuffed cap on his head, and a stone under it for a pillow, just as Jacob slept at Bethel.[1]

354. *Beside Ruins and Groves.*—Tent-camps are so often by some old ruin, town site, or grove that Thomson says wherever you see a clump of large oaks in Palestine, you may be sure that there once stood a city, and there, too, is the Bedouin's tent. One class of Arabs, a generation ago, tilled the soil, paid taxes, but were contemptuously disowned by the genuine sons of the desert. This Arab aristrocrat of the desert would scorn to intermarry with the "miserable wretches" who dwelt in houses, and earn their bread by honest toil. Yet, even these Arabs live in squalor and inexpressible filth, but are prouder than Jupiter.

Probably the peasant's proverb, "To your tents, O Israel,"[2] may have sprung from the tillers of the soil who dwelt in tents rather than in villages. Thomson tells us again how gladly he would escape from the village, with its crowded houses, filthy within, and infested with every sort of vermin, to enjoy the sunlight, the groves, and the sweet air of the open country, the proper heritage of the tent-dweller. Old Isaac dwelt thus in tents, sowing the land, and reaping the same year a harvest of a hundredfold.[3]

355. *Charm of Tent Life.*—Again and again does the traveler in the Orient, like Dr. Thomson on the charming plain of Jezreel, break out in rapturous joy over the luxury of travel, on bright days, in the cool air, over the fragrant hills and in the valleys, robed with green, and brilliant with flowers, hearing the chorus of birds' songs out in the open country, or in a tent under the clear blue sky. Then comes "the night so

[1] Gen. 28 : 11.   [2] 1 Kings 12 : 16.   [3] Gen. 26 : 12.

solemn, almost sad, and yet are very sweet . . . every harsh
sound subdued, and the soul called to rest or reverie. It is
bliss merely to lie still and breathe . . . while bygone memories,
historic associations, and recent experiences chase each other
through all the labyrinths of this fairy land." And to this day,
the Bedouin Arabs, the modern Midianites, sweep over the
plains of Jezreel, robbing right and left, as in the days of
Gideon.[1]

356. *In the Tent Door.*—Thus, travelers in Oriental lands
now witness many interesting scenes, strikingly reminding them
of their counterparts, so often alluded to in the Bible. That
beautiful scene when Abraham sat in the tent door, in the
heat of the day, and received the strange messengers, and
besought them to accept his hospitality, and that other tragic
scene, in which Sisera was met by Jael, and persuaded him
to turn into her tent, which he would not enter without express
invitation, and would be thrown off his guard when she offered
him food, as a pledge of hospitality and protection, have had
their frequent counterpart (save in the murder) in the experiences of modern travelers. Burckhardt notices that his murder,
under these circumstances, was a clear violation of the most
sacred laws that bind the dwellers in tents, though it is a ful-
filment of the threatened doom in Judges 4: 9.

357. *Tent Furniture.*—The furniture of a tent is of a simple
kind. Curtains or rugs, which separate the different apartments and which cover the ground, the wheat-sacks and
camel-bags, piled around the middle posts of the tent, like a
pyramid; the pack-saddles upon which the sheikh and the
guests recline, the camel-driver's stick, the butter and water
skins, the leathern bucket in which the water is drawn from
the deep wells, the copper pan used in cooking, the hand-mill,
the mortar in which the wheat is pounded, the towel which
is spread under the mortar to save any flour that might fall,
the wooden bowl into which the camels are milked, the wooden
water-cup, the wooden coffee-mortar, the coffee-pot, stones

[1] Judg. 6 : 2–5.

on which the pan is placed over the fire, and the feeding-bag for the horses—these form the furniture and treasures of an Arab's tent. These necessities offer him luxury when weary and a royal feast when hungry.[1]

357a. *"House of Hair."*—In some remote parts of Arabia the Bedouin dweller of the desert has his "house of hair," or black tent. (See illustration facing title page.) This nomad regards himself as "guest of God," and also "steward of God," to welcome to his house all stranger pilgrims—wanderers over God's great earth domain. When the pilgrim wonders over this hospitality, as Rev. William Ewing did in the last century, the Bedouin nomad in primitive simplicity says, "Are we not all guests of Allah?" and thus entitled to share the free gifts of a common Father? So Abraham, Isaac, and Jacob's history evidence similar ideas and customs of their era.

---

[1] For the counterpart of this picture, see Balaam's poetical description of Israel, Num. 24 : 5, 6. And a similar poetical sketch of the tents of Cushan in affliction, and the curtains of the land of Midian that trembled, is in Hab. 3 : 7.

XXXII.

ORIENTAL HOUSES.

358. *Houses.*—In Syria houses are usually built of stone or sun-dried brick. Timber is too scarce and costly there, and has been so for ages. Houses in the villages are usually partitioned into two or three apartments. The front room, in which is the door, is the common family room. To the family it is sitting-room, bed-room, dining-room, and reception-room, unless they have an upper room, which can be used as a reception-room. A doorway leads from this to the second room, which may be used to store supplies before winter sets in. People do not there have access to shops daily for purchases. Farm produce is stored in this second room. In the third room, in the rear, there may be kept cut straw and other fodder for the cattle. Here will also be found wood and charcoal and farming implements. Sometimes one of these rooms is used for domestic animals, horses, donkeys, or cattle. Thieves usually try to enter one of the rear rooms, by digging or breaking through the wall of the house when the people are asleep. Householders keep watch-dogs, which are let loose at night, and in case of special danger some one of the family is on watch all night.[1]

359. *Peasants' Houses.*—Many peasants' houses and some in the towns have only a single room. Such a room is often large in size, as Dr. Post tells us; the roof is supported by pillars, made of blocks of stone, one above another. Sometimes these are plastered, and often there is a little shelf-like projection in the plastering, on which a lamp is placed. Bits of colored pottery are pressed into the plaster as ornaments. The plaster is also ornamented by lines and figures and bits of scalloped edging, pinched out while the plaster is in a plastic state.

[1] This illustrates the parable in Matt. 24 : 43; Luke 12 : 39.

These single-roomed houses have but one door and often no windows. The smoke from the fire finds its way out through the door, and through sundry holes left in the wall for this purpose.

360. *Building Material.*—In Egypt the village houses are still built of sun-dried bricks, made of wet earth, rarely clay, mixed with straw and chopped hay. The mixing is often done, as of old, by treading upon the earth and straw with the feet. When well mixed it is put into molds, and set out to dry in the sun. Farmers and country people build their houses out of these sun-dried bricks. The work of making the bricks is still counted a bitter service.[1]

In Syria and Western Asia the ordinary houses are also built of stone or sun-dried bricks. Sometimes the stone may be hewn, or put in the wall in a rough state, and cemented with mud or mortar. Van Lennep tells that almost every house in the country in Western Asia is made of crude or sun-dried bricks. Occasionally one meets with a bridge, a khan, a church, or a mosque built of hewn stone, to which may be added some half-dilapidated structures, and crumbling walls, and battlements of citadels. The blocks of stone have been brought from some more ancient ruin. The traveler becomes used to this patchwork of old inscriptions turned upside down, and of carved stones arranged haphazard in the walls, columns of various materials and dimensions belonging to different orders of architecture, standing in a row, and forming the portico or the building. Other dwellings are made of mud bricks, and this was as much the case in ancient times as now. Where porous limestone is found, it is cut into regular blocks with a saw, and used in the erection of buildings.[2]

361. *Rooms of House.*—Houses of poor and rich in Syria are usually mixed together. There are no quarters for the wealthy, and separate quarters for the poor, says Mr. Haddad. You may find a fine palace, beautiful outside and inside, and close to it a little cottage of a very poor family. Even a poor

---

[1] See Ex. 1.   [2] Van Lennep, p. 421.

invalid may sometimes have a booth or hut in front or beside the door of a wealthy man's house. He may live on gifts of passers-by, or of visitors to the rich man's house; nobody objects.

362. *The Roof.*—The most important and most frequented portion of the house next to the reception-room is the roof. The roof is made in various ways. Mr. Haddad speaks of a common way in Syria, to lay beams across from one side to the other of the walls, then a mat of reeds on the top of these beams, then some bushes of a thorn, and finally, a coating of clay or earth, and scatter sand and pebbles on the top of the earth, then they roll it with a roller of stone, to make it compact, so that the rain will not run through. Sometimes a little space three or four feet square is cut in the roof, with separate pieces, made like the rest of the roof, or covered with mat or tiling, which can be taken up when desired. It might have been such a place in the roof that was used in letting down the paralytic on his rug or quilt, which would be the only bed an Oriental in such condition would be likely to have.[1]

These roofs are flat, and the terraces or parapets around them are low, and made of dried bricks, or stone, just like the wall. If a higher terrace is required, it is made of lattice-work to screen the women of the household. In summer the people of Palestine, Egypt, and Mesopotamia usually sleep upon the housetops. The servants sleep on bedding or the ground in the court below. The very poor people often sleep in the streets, the open squares, the market-places, and courts, rolling themselves in a coverlet, a rug, or their outer garments, and screening their faces.

Many occupations are carried on upon the roof. Here the wheat is washed and spread to dry, the flax is prepared, and vegetables and fruits to be stored in winter; wool and cotton when washed is spread out upon the roof, clothes are hung there to be dried; as now, so has it been of old. Rahab hid the spies sent by Joshua under the stalks of flax, which she

[1] Matt. 9 : 2; Mark 2 : 3; Luke 5 : 18.

had laid upon the roof to dry.[1] Luke tells us that the paralytic
was let down through the tiling or tiles.   This might mean
that the center portion of the roof over the court was covered
with a mat or matting or tiles.[2]

363. *The Court.*—The court in the better class of Eastern
houses is often a pavement of stone, marble, or pebbles, taste-
fully designed.   There may be a fountain or well in the court, a
little garden with flowers, shaded by orange, lemon, or citron
trees.[3] This court would be shut off from the street; the house
being built around the court, the windows of the house would
be opened upon this court, and not upon the street.   But the
windows are without glass, closed at night with a single shutter
of wood, and fastened inside with a hook.   Sometimes the
door or space for a window would be closed by a heavy rug or
piece of carpet, hung from the top of the opening with a heavy
slat of wood fastened to the bottom, to keep it stretched in its
place like a door.   When one is to enter, this screen or curtain,
called *perdeh*, would be lifted, perhaps on each side.[4]

364. *Entrance.*—The door is the entrance way to the house.
It is usually made of some solid material.   In the giant cities
of Bashan-land, or modern Hauran, the door is often a single
block or slab of basalt-stone, nine or ten feet long.   Similar
stone doors are found in the gardens of Urumiah, in Persia,
as Dr. Perkins tells us.   The hinges of these doors are simply
a projection, above and below, fitting into holes in the stone
threshhold, and highly polished, so that they can be opened by
a simple push with the finger.   Outside doors have simple locks
of iron or wood, usually the latter.   The key of the lock is a
piece of wood several inches long, with pegs at one end.   It is
not put in a keyhole, but there is an opening at the side of the
door large enough to admit one's hand.   The key is applied
to the wooden bolt within, its pegs fitting into corresponding
holes, and by displacing another set of pegs allows one to draw
the bolt aside and unfasten the door. [4] This key is fastened to

[1] Josh. 2 : 6.   [2] Matt. 10 : 27; Luke 5 : 19; 12 : 3.   [3] 2 Sam. 17 : 18.
[4] See reference to this in Ps. 24 : 7; compare also Ex. 39 : 38.
[5] See Lane, Modern Egypt., vol. i, p. 24.

a string or cord, and carried over the shoulder or attached to the girdle.[1]

365. *Gates.*—Oriental gates and large doors are provided with small doors, through which a man can pass by stooping, as Dr. Post tells us. These small doors are like a panel in a gate. The little door is used on ordinary occasions, the large door or gate is opened on extraordinary occasions. Similar arrangements are found at the gates of walled cities and towns for night service. Doors are not opened without a previous parley between the porter and the visitor. If the visitor cannot give a satisfactory account of himself, he is viewed through a window overlooking the gate. Thus, when the disciples were gathered in the house of Mary at Jerusalem for fear of the rulers, Rhoda took just such precautions as a servant in an Oriental house would take to-day.[2] Dr. Post tells of his experience in being challenged, as Peter was, by a Moslem servant and being compelled to wait outside the gate while the servant ran in to tell some one of the household, and to get an order to let the doctor in.

366. *Sleeping Rooms.*—In the one-roomed house all the family, says Dr. Thomson, parents, children, and servants, sleep in the same room. As they make very slight changes in their long loose clothing, and often none at all at night, the impropriety of the custom as it would appear to us, is lessened, but the practice does not tend to promote the highest social purity. Sometimes under the same roof may be father, sons, and grandsons, for the sake of economy, but it leads to confusion and lack of independence in family discipline. This custom of all the family sleeping in one apartment is alluded to in the parable of the friend at midnight. When asked to lend three loaves, the friend replies, "Trouble me not: the door is now shut, and my children are with me in bed; I cannot rise and give thee."[3] Out of this custom grew also the law requiring that a garment taken for debt should be restored to the owner before sundown.[4]

---

[1] See an allusion to this carrying the keys upon the shoulder in Isa. 22 : 22.
[2] Acts 12 : 13, 14.   [3] Luke 11 : 7.   [4] Ex. 22 : 26, 27.

367. *Beds.*—In Oriental houses sleeping rooms are furnished not as with us. Thus, Lane says that in Egypt the bed in daytime is rolled up, and placed on one side, or in a near-by closet. This closet in winter is a sleeping place. In summer many people sleep upon the housetop, a mat or carpet spread upon the raised part of the stone floor, and a *dewan,* or divan, constitute the furniture of a room.

368. *Plan of Egyptian House.*—The plan of an Egyptian house is irregular. The apartments are of different heights, so that a person has to go up or down two or more steps to pass from one room to another. The aim of the builder is to render the house as private as possible, particularly that part of it which is occupied by women. He never makes a window to overlook the apartments of another house. It is also planned so as to make a secret door, from which the tenant may make his escape in case of danger, either from arrest or assassination. There is also a hiding place for treasures, called a *mukhba,* in some part of the house. In Egyptian towns, shops occupy the lower part of a house in a street or thoroughfare, the upper part being used as a dwelling. Sometimes the upper part is divided into several apartments or lodgings for different families. There is one entrance and one staircase to the several apartments. They are not furnished.

369. *Of Bricks.*—The Egyptian houses of the lower order, as of peasants, are built chiefly of unbaked bricks, cemented with mud. Some of them are mere hovels. The greater number comprise two or more apartments; very few are two stories high. The ceiling is low. In one of these apartments of peasants in lower Egypt there is an oven at the end, farthest from the entrance, and occupying the whole width of the chamber. It resembles a wide bench or seat, and is about breast-high, made of brick and mud, the roof arched within and flat on the top. The people of the house, who seldom have any special night covering, during the winter sleep upon the top of this flat oven. The rooms have small holes high up in the walls to admit light and air; some-

times these holes have a grating of wood. The roofs are formed of palm branches and palm leaves, or of stalks of millet, laid upon rafters of the trunk of the palm, and covered with a plaster of mud and chopped straw. The furniture is a mat or two to sleep upon, a few earthen vessels, and a hand-mill to grind corn. In villages, large pigeon-houses of a square form, but with the walls slightly inclining inward, like many of the ancient Egyptian buildings, or of the shape of a sugar loaf, are constructed upon the roofs of the huts, with crude brick, pottery, and mud. The pigeon-houses are sometimes of oval form, with a wide mouth, and a small hole at one end, a pair of pigeons occupying each separate place. Again, many of the villages of Egypt are upon eminences of rubbish, and a few feet above the inundations of the Nile, surrounded by palm-trees, or having a few of these trees near-by. The rubbish consists of the ruins of former huts, and seems to increase in about the same degree as the level of the alluvial plains and the bed of the river.

370. *Syrian Housetops.*—In Syria and Mesopotamia in summer the family sleep upon the housetop. Dr. Tristram was so entertained frequently. When there was a porter, he says, "We were literally locked out for the night, and had to summon him to admit us for our ablutions in the morning. In humbler families the master of the house locked the door below, and followed us up the steps to the roof of the empty house." Sometimes there is a guest-chamber on the roof, such a chamber as the woman of Shunem had her husband build for the prophet "on the wall." That means that the "chamber" was reached from the outside by steps on the wall, so that the prophet might be free to go and come, and to have privacy. Tristram tells us of such guest chambers in Syrian towns now.[1] Perhaps it was in such a room that Nicodemus sought Jesus by night.[2] A room like this could be reached just as the prophet's room at Shunem by outer steps without the observation or knowledge of the inmates of the dwelling. Moreover, such a room on the

[1] See also 2 Kings 4 : 8.   [2] John 3 : 2; 19 : 39.

roof was just the place to have suggested the figure which Jesus
used. The breeze blowing over the roof would give emphasis
to the illustration, "The wind bloweth where it will, and thou
hearest the voice thereof, but knowest not whence it cometh, and
whither it goeth: so is every one that is born of the Spirit." [1]

371. *"Upper Room."*—Again, such a large upper room, or
alliyeh, might have been the one where the last Passover was
held. The disciples inquired for the *kataluma,* literally the
"resting place." The ordinary resting place of an Eastern
house is a shelter-place upon the roof, opening into the court-
yard. It would have couches or mats, a low table; the guests
would recline upon the mats when eating. No doubt, Peter
at Joppa retired at noon to a room on the housetop for prayer,
as Daniel in Babylon had done before him.[2] The flat roof
had a parapet which shielded the visitor from observation,
and protected him from falling off the roof, as required by the
Deuteronomic law.[3] When Jesus healed the paralytic, he
was probably in the *lewan,* a room on the ground floor, looking
upon the court. Thus, the dust and dirt that might fall from
opening the roof would fall into the court, and not into the
room where Jesus stood.

372. *Mud Walls.*—Dr. Thomson notices the frail houses
or huts built of loose stones and mud, with roofs that will
"drop through" in a single winter because of neglect, and
then the walls wash down by the rain into shapeless heaps,
illustrating the proverb in Eccles. 10: 18, and the statement in
Job 15: 28, of houses which are ready to become "heaps." The
prophet also uses the same careless method of building to describe the destruction which will come upon the people, because
they build a wall and daub it with untempered mortar.[4]

373. *Staircase.*—An outside staircase to an Oriental house
is quite common. Thus, Dr. Robinson says the house was
built around a small court, in which cattle and horses were
stabled, then a stone staircase led up to the roof of the house
proper, on which at the northwest and southwest corners were

---

[1] John 3 : 8, R. V.   [2] Acts 10 : 9; Daniel 6 : 10.
[3] Deut. 22 : 8.   [4] Ezek. 13 : 10, 11.

high single rooms, like towers, with a staircase inside, leading to the top.[1]

Dr. Shaw states that in Barbary the stairs are sometimes placed in the porch, sometimes at the entrance into the court, when there is one or more stories, and are afterward continued through one corner or other of the gallery to the top of the house, whither they conduct us through a door. We may go up or come down by the staircase without entering into any of the offices or apartments, or interfering with the business of the house.[2] A similar experience is narrated by Drs. Bonar and McCheyne of a century ago. "The house has a staircase from the flat roof down into the street, by which the owner could descend and escape, without passing through the house, if danger called for it.[3]

374. *In India.*—Captain Hall notices a similar plan of the houses in India: "My friend, the Hindu, got on his feet, cast the long folds of his wrapper over his shoulder, stooped down, and having rolled up his mat, which was all the bed he required, walked into the house with it, and then proceeded to the nearest tank to perform his morning ablutions." Another Syrian traveler of a century ago states, "We had now to retire to rest, not on a bed raised from the ground with posts and canopy, but upon the floor. From a large receptacle in the room two thick cotton quilts were taken out, one of which was folded double as a mattress, and the other as a covering, with large flat pillows for our heads." This reminded him of the command, "Take up thy bed and walk." Shaw describes a different experience: "At one end of each chamber there is a little gallery, raised three, four, or five feet above the floor, with a balustrade in front of it, with a few steps leading up to it. Here they place their beds, a situation frequently alluded to in the Scriptures, and illustrating Hezekiah's turning his face when he prayed toward the wall, that is, from his attendants. So also Ahab turned his face toward the wall to conceal from his attendants his disappointment.[4]

---

[1] Researches, iii, 302.   [2] Barbary, i, 379.
[3] Mission to the Jews, 147.   [4] 1 Kings 21 : 4; 2 Kings 20 : 2.

XXXIII.

KHAN, CARAVANSARY, INN, STOREHOUSE.

375. *Kinds of Inns.*—Public lodging places in Oriental lands are of three kinds—khan, caravansary, and menzil. A khan is a building, generally in or near a town, to shelter travelers, but without furniture, landlord, food, or fodder. A caravansary is a lodging place, a somewhat pretentious building, often in remote places and under the control of the government. The better class of caravansary sometimes appears to the stranger like a castle or fortress; the wall is high, the building extends several yards on each side of the square or court, which it encloses. Commonly, it is built of brick or stone. In the center of the front wall is the entrance, usually an archway, over which may be chambers under showy domes. On each side, under the arched roof of the portico, may be keeper's rooms, sometimes shops, where articles required by travelers are kept for sale. Entering the archway, the traveler sees a porch extending on each side of the interior of the quadrangle, leaving a spacious court in the middle. The arched recesses in the wall around are like apartments, divided from each other by walls, but open in front, paved, rarely having a place for fire. In the middle of each of the three sides of the building is a larger apartment, not divided, used for the travelers to smoke, while they gossip or tell tales. Sometimes along the outward wall of the building, back of the apartments, is a series of cell-like places for servants and poor people or for animals, but usually the animals are within the court.

376.—*Bare Lodges.*—The traveler furnishes his own bedding, cooking utensils, and provisions. At the angle or corner of the square, flights of steps lead to the roof or to the second story of the building. Such buildings may be found in Persia and in other Oriental lands.

Buckingham found such khans or caravansaries in Damascus

nearly a century ago. There the court was paved with flat
stones, polished and neatly put together; in the center was
a large fountain flowing and the walls of black and white
stones were profusely ornamented. Two Scottish travelers,
Dr. A. A. Bonar, and R. M. McCheyne, found an old dilapi-
dated khan in the last century between Sidon and Tyre. As
night came on, one company and another, with mules and
tinkling bells, filled the khan, till the square presented quite a
lively appearance. They pitched their tent on the roof of
the old ruin where the grass had been allowed to grow.

377. *Castle Khan.*—Dr. Thomson, journeying from Tabor to
the Jordan, found a khan et Tejjar (inn of the merchants)
near Sulam. In fact, there were two khans, one on a hill about
a hundred feet square, with octagonal towers on the corners.
It was both castle and khan. Another larger khan was in the
valley below. It had a fountain within the walls, vaults and
magazines on either side, and was fitted up with rooms for travelers and for the storing of merchandise. The place was deserted, and no inhabited house in sight. Caravans did not
spend the night there for fear of Arabs watching to rob. Thomson adds, "I have never halted there for half an hour without
having some of these rascals pass along and scrutinize my party
closely, to see whether or not it would do to attack us." In his
day a great fair was held on Monday of each week at the khans.
Thousands of people assembled from all parts of the country to
sell, trade, or purchase. Cotton comes from Nablûs; barley,
wheat, sesamum, and corn from the Hûleh, the Hauran, and
Esdraelon. Horses, donkeys, cattle, and flocks, with cheese,
leben, semen, honey, and other articles from Gilead and
Bashan-land. These are mixed up with such things as chickens
and eggs, figs, raisins, apples, melons and grapes, and all sorts
of fruits and vegetables in their season. Peddlers are there
with packages of fabrics, the jeweler with his trinkets, the tailor
with his ready-made garments, the shoemaker with his stock,
from rough and hairy sandals to yellow and red morocco boots,
the farrier with his tools, nails and flat, iron shoes, driving a

17

prosperous business for a few hours, as does also the saddler. Every one is crying his wares at the top of his voice; chickens cackle and squall, donkeys bray and fight, and the dogs bark. Every living thing adds something to the many-toned and prodigious uproar. It is an excellent opportunity to see Syrian manners, customs, and costumes.

378. *Persian Khans.*—Layard describes the khans on the road between Bagdad and sacred places, as large edifices built by Persian kings or wealthy and pious men for pilgrims. These have large open squares, generally with raised platforms, of brickwork for travelers to sleep on during summer, and are surrounded by small apartments or cells for winter use. Behind them spacious stables for horses run around the whole building, and within these stables, on both sides, are other cells for travelers.[1]

Dr. H. C. Fish found a similar old khan a generation ago between Ramleh and Jerusalem. If was built of stone, and covered quite an area, having beside the ground floor a second story, reached by stairs on the outside. On the upper floor travelers who have the means take their quarters, paying a pittance for the use of the furniture there, which consisted of a few rickety chairs and tables, and two or three verminous cots, dignified as beds. Baedeker's Guide wisely advises the traveler never to resort to a khan, caravansary, or a hut of the peasants (the latter generally built of mud) except as an absolute necessity, because they swarm with fleas and other vermin. If compelled to use them he should see that the straw matting which covers the floor is taken up and thoroughly beaten, and the whole place carefully swept and sprinkled with water. Every article of clothing and bedding belonging to the inmates should be removed to another room. The tents of the Bedouin are free from bugs, but are terribly infested with lice. Scorpions also are plentiful in Syria, but they seldom sting unless irritated. If the bed is slightly raised from the ground the sleeper is quite safe from their attacks.

[1] Nineveh and Babylon, 478.

The huts of the peasants, described above, which are offered for the use of travelers, are sometimes called menzils.   North of Beisan is a large khan, el Ahmar.   It may have been along this road and by this khan that the Ishmaelites came with their camels, bearing spices, and balm, and myrrh, going to carry them down to Egypt, and to whom Joseph was sold by his brothers.[1]

379. *Syrian Inns.*—Prof. Post, out of his experience, describes the Oriental khan or inn as a range of vaulted chambers around a large open court.   These chambers have only small high windows, no glass for ventilation toward the outer side, but are quite open toward the court.   Along the walls are stone mangers for the mules and asses, and doubtless in one of these the babe was laid.   This was not a sign of Joseph's poverty, or of Jesus' humiliation, but because a great number of pilgrims crowded the rooms above the vaulted chambers.   Prof. Post adds, "It is quite common for well-to-do people to sleep in the vaulted chambers with their beasts of burden, or in the open court, or on the grass outside the khan.   The khan, or inn, mentioned in the parable of the good Samaritan was one of the rarer kind where the guest lodges, and can buy from the keeper what his own foresight has not provided.[2]

380. *Bethlehem Inn.*—Thus, the "inn" wherein there was no "room for them," Mary and Joseph, was one of the unfurnished chambers, above or around the court of the khan, not itself so much better than the vaults where the cattle are housed. These chambers are bare walls, with a stone or composition floor and blackened roof, as cheerless and unhomelike as one can conceive.

381. *India Rests.*—Dr. Russell describes similar resting places in India, where part of the court is planted with trees and flowering shrubs and the rest paved.   In one end of the square is a basin of water, and close to it upon a stone platform, two or three feet above the court, is a small pavilion, sometimes a divan upon it, or a larger divan is in the court, opposite the basin

[1] Gen. 37 : 25.   [2] S. S. W., July, 1878.

looking to the north, and protected from the sun. The fragrant plants give a sweet scent to the air. In similar manner are the royal palaces constructed. The Persian palace had a series of courts, one of which was named the inner, and the other the outer; the former of which was reserved for a private audience with the sovereign.[1]

382. *Storehouses.*—Storehouses are not usually pretentious buildings, as with us, but secret underground pits or places secure from bandits and from the rapacity of tyrannical rulers. The rich man of the parable who would build larger barns, strictly storehouses, to store his grain, his goods, and his other treasures, no doubt including his coin and his gems, would build them in some hidden spot or underneath the ground.[2] Other storerooms were built of a pretentious character, as in Egypt. Thus, the buildings erected at Pithom by the Israelites appear to have been large storehouses above ground. Yet, Dr. F. J. Bliss, the explorer, suggests that some of these granaries may have been large pits dug in the hard ground, with narrow mouths, similar to the pits in which the wandering Arab stores his corn to-day. He adds, "Pits of this kind, but smaller, containing perhaps the stores of a single family, were recognized in our excavations at Lachish and elsewhere. These were filled up quite solidly when we excavated them, but their circumference of hard earth was distinctly preserved. In one case at Lachish a chamber was found full of charred barley, which had been stored away some three thousand years ago, and burned before it ever could be used."[3]

383. *Store Pits.*—Mr. Haddad also says storerooms in the private houses are still built in Syria as in olden days. The roofs are flat and level, the walls usually of stone. In the houses they leave a little square space between two beams, covering it with a thin slate, stone, or tile, above which they put the thorn bush, a layer of clay, and of cement. They divide part of the room with partitions, one space for wheat, another for barley, another

---

[1] A graphic description of these courts is to be found in the book of Esther 4 : 11, 16; 5 : 1, 2; 6 : 4.
[2] Luke 12 : 18. [3] S. S. W., May, 1907.

for corn.   They carry the sacks of grain to the top (roof) and from that opening they empty them into the bins inside the room.   These houses have stone stairs at the outside of the house. Up these stairs the sacks of grain are carried, and emptied into the space below.   After all their grain is put in through the opening they replace the tile and cement upon the opening as before.[1]   Sometimes these pits are in the court of the house, as already stated.   To give greater security, the storehouse pit may be under the women's apartment.   Tristram tells that in Arab *dowars* these wells for barley and grain are found under a wattled chamber, in the village square.   This custom is clearly referred to in 2 Sam. 4 : 6, "they came thither into the midst of the house, as though they would have fetched wheat."   It was in such a well or grain storehouse that Jonathan and Ahimaaz were hidden from Absalom.   The messengers "came to the house of a man in Bahurim who had a well in his court; and they went down thither.   And the women took and spread the covering over the well's mouth, and strewed bruised grain thereon." After Absalom's servants had gone, the messengers came out of the pit and reported Absalom's conspiracy to David.[2]

[1] S. S. W., 1906; see "Silos," under Section XXX.   [2] See 2 Sam. 17 : 15-20.

XXXIV.

PROPERTY, TAXES, RIGHTING WRONGS.

384. *Personal Rule.*—Government by the people is an idea foreign to Asiatics. Oriental rulers have ever claimed a divine right to rule, hence Oriental peoples refer all acts and responsibilities of government to the ruler; he is absolute sovereign. Of necessity, he must rely upon others to examine petitions, recommend appointments and pardons, and execute his will. But the typical Oriental ruler takes no counsel of legislatures, parliaments, or cabinets. In Turkey the Sultan has a grand vizier to execute his will, yet he may repudiate and disown any of his acts. Joseph was, in fact, the grand vizier of Pharaoh.[1] The ruler reserved the right to express his will to any petitioner. Any subject to whom he held out the scepter could present a petition, and was morally sure of having it granted. A marked instance of this is given in the book of Esther.[2]

385. *Divine Right.*—The chief system of government, of which the Oriental has any idea, is by an autocrat or despot. Less than a generation ago, Prof. Post, out of a life-long residence in Turkey, declared, "that universal suffrage, trial by jury, rotation in office by election, would seem unmitigated evils for Turkey. Several generations of popular education are yet needed to enable even Christians in Turkey to grapple with the problem of self-government." He adds, "Certainly all who live among Asiatics are convinced that the divine right of government is the safe doctrine for them. Any such ideas as the social compact, or any approach to popular institutions is regarded as anachronism and a disaster for them." Perhaps he might modify this extreme statement now. Under even such conditions, he conceives that rulers are a terror to

[1] Gen. 41 : 41.   [2] Esther 5 : 2–4.

the evil doer, since an honest man with good sense and industrially disposed, is treated fairly well in countries as misgoverned as some of those in the East seem to be. It may be a truthful man has an advantage sometimes more marked for being surrounded by a company of liars!

386. *Head of All.*—An Oriental ruler thus regards himself as the head of all the kingdoms of the earth. The former Sultan of Turkey was addressed as "king of kings, and lord of lords." It is said that when he traveled in Europe he put Turkish soil in his shoes that he might not tread upon the soil of his hosts, because if he should do this, they would become part of his dominions, according to his theory. All rulers of the East, says Prof. Post, are addressed in terms of flattery, which would be regarded as ironical in the West, and all Oriental kings assume a style which would be counted as absurd and make them a laughing stock in Europe. This habit comes down through the ages. Thus Cyrus, king of Persia, declared, "The Lord God of heaven hath given me all the kingdoms of the earth."[1] A forcible illustration of the arbitrary and tyrannical acts of Oriental rulers is given me by Prof. Post. The Pasha, controlling the Beirut district, wished to make a road near the college, taking in a portion of the college land. He had the trees cut, the roads staked out without the slightest attention to the protests and entreaties of the property owners. When the president of the municipality was asked why the property had been taken without compensation, he replied that there was no use in remonstrating against the orders of the governor-general. Mr. Haddad states that Damascus makes a heavy appropriation every year to repair the roads for the Haj caravan to Mecca. Boatmen, muleteers, and other persons are impressed into the service with little or no compensation; forced gifts of money, horses, clothing, and provisions are also exacted.

387. *Not Law, But Custom.*—The people of the East have little idea of observing law or of keeping contracts to the

[1] Ezra 1 : 2.

letter. In fact, custom rules the Asiatic mind, as fashion rules
that of the West; the custom changes not, while fashion may
change.   It is customary for a ruler's decree to be unalterable.
Thus the king responded to his counsellors when they appealed
to him, accusing Daniel of breaking the law.[1] The common
people do not say "it is unlawful," they say more forcibly,
"it is not our custom." They would not answer, "it is not right,
or wise, or good, or desirable," they would simply declare
"it is not according to my, or our, custom." That ends all
debate.   An American was seen talking with a bride, chatting
freely with her, her eyes open, her face radiant, when an
Arab guest entered, and she closed her lips and eyes, and stood
quite impassive.   When asked why she did this, she answered,
it was a great disgrace in the eyes of the natives for a bride to
manifest any feeling but shame, but added, naïvely, "You
know it is not *customary* to be ashamed before the Franks."
She regarded all Europeans and Americans as Franks.

In this century the spirit of liberty is spreading among Eastern
peoples, and many of them are waiting for an opportunity to
throw off the yoke of tyranny.

388. *Possessions*.—The various plans of acquiring and
holding property were briefly treated in XVIII.   I may
add here that in Syria, as in most of the Orient, outside of
cities and towns, the apparent land owner is not a true pro-
prietor.   He has been called an "eternal mortgagee."   He
must pay the government a tenth of the land product every
year.   This tithe is collected in kind, that is, in grain, oil,
wines, or fruits.   No matter what proportion is taken, the
payment is always called a tithe, although it may be one-fifth,
or one-half even, of the produce.   Renting out land is a mode
of farming prevalent in the East.   The tenants may contribute
their work in terracing and planting a vineyard, tilling the soil,
trimming the vines, and the labor, the caring for the vintage,
the treading the wine-press, curing the raisins, or carrying the
grapes to market.

[1] Dan. 6 : 12.

389. *Tenants' Rights.*—They usually receive one-fourth to one-third of the produce, or an equivalent in money. Often the landlord loans them money on the coming harvest, and deducts the sum with ruinous interest from the produce. Such landlords are generally absentees, and send agents to superintend the division of the product. This custom will illustrate the parable of the wicked husbandmen.[1] In Syria the rentals of all land are on the *cottier* principle, who rent their property also on the idea of permanent tenancy, with *metairial* rights. The tenant farmers are often real squatters, but in the chaotic state of law seriously contest the ownership of the property. The disappearance of direct heirs may, in some cases, embarrass questions of property in farming land. Contests involving issue of ownership are among the most common in the Turkish courts.

390. *Rights in Cities.*—Upon the character of property holdings in Syria Prof. Post remarks, "Properties in cities change hands frequently, adding to the risks of commerce and manufactures, and the great diversity of employments and opportunities. The more patriarchal and agricultural states have commerce and manufactures. Hence, the greater improbability of regaining through some other channel property lost in any other way. In the country, with but one channel for industry, the tendency would always be to absorption of real estate by the most gifted, so each generation would witness an extension of the properties of the large land holders at the expense of the smaller, with little chance of those who had lost ever regaining their patrimony. Such a state of things tends to tyranny and the degradation of the working class, as the history and the present state of Turkey abundantly shows."

391. *Inheritance Customs.*—In Turkey sons cannot be disinherited, as in Europe. Prof. Post says some rich families in Beirut have sons in Alexandria, Paris, and London, yet such is the unity of the family tie that these absent sons remain partners of the parent firms, and return with their share of the for-

[1] Matt. 21 : 33–41.

tunes made, to build their homes beside the paternal mansions. One such family has a half dozen palatial houses on the highest hill of the city and within a few rods of each other. This throws light on the parable of the prodigal son.[1] On the other hand, the arbitrary interpretation of the law or custom of inheritance has furnished cases of indefiniteness as to the heirs as well as to the master of any property. The twist of the law, or caprice of the ruler, might make a man's family beggars.

392. *Taxes.*—Taxes in Oriental lands, especially in Turkey and elsewhere, are farmed out to be collected by those who purchase the privilege. True, the law technically limits it to one-tenth. You ask how can the collector get more than this? Quite easily. The publican or tax collector has the government behind him. He sends spies to watch and prevent everybody from using their harvest products until he has his share. For example, he has assumed the taxes to be collected in a given district at a certain sum. He employs every agency in his power to make the taxes yield their utmost.

393. *An Example of Robbery.*—Suppose the taxes of a given province to be $50,000. He agrees to pay that sum to the government. He goes to that province, takes up his quarters in a town, the people hasten to him with presents of wheat, milk, eggs, rice, to conciliate him. He has horses and horsemen who must be fed at the expense of the tax-payers. If they do not use him and them well, he will abuse them, and extort twice or thrice his due. Complaints to the government are forestalled by bribes, and no redress is to be obtained from his exactions. While the tax is but a tenth of the produce, the amount taken from the poor farmer may amount to one-half or even two-thirds. For, he will not give the farmer permission to harvest his produce without bribery, he will not let the people eat their own fruits in their greatest need, nor allow them to feed their hungry animals that work in the field. He sometimes compels the owners to muzzle their animals, he accuses the peasants of stealing their own fruits, and then they are fined twice the price of

[1] Luke 15 : 11–32.

the fruits. Half of the fine from this robbery is given to the complainant, and the other half to the tax-gatherer. For all these things the tax collecter or publican of the East is the most odious of human kind, and supremely hated. In Egypt there are personal taxes besides the land rent, and these taxes were formerly collected by the aid of a hippopotamus whip. All these modern customs throw great light upon the narrative of Zacchæus and his interview with Jesus.[1]

394. *Suffer vs. Suits.*—In many countries of the Orient it is more advantageous to suffer a wrong than to attempt to have it officially righted. For, being judged in Asia is a calamity, whether the case is decided for or against the litigant, says an old resident and native. If in his favor it must be in virtue of a large gift, and if against him it may be in total disregard of justice or equity. The magistrates or judges have small salaries, living almost wholly from bribes. Thus, the chief justice of Cyprus before its annexation to England received a salary of one hundred dollars a year. The Turkish government received four million piastres a year. When it came under English supervision, it paid twenty-four millions, though the population and resources of the island had not increased materially in the two years.

395. *The Victim.*—The judge is not the only one who inflicts loss upon the prisoner. The unfortunate man must pay all his expenses while in jail and a large backshish to the officers in charge for such privileges as are allowed. Of the delays in Turkish justice a resident writes, "Should you have lived in this century in Turkey, and had to go to Constantinople with an appeal to the Sublime Porte, you would think the Roman Courts fine in comparison. Many cases had been delayed five, eight, twelve, and sometimes eighteen years, and the one who had appealed has been spending his money, not knowing when the end of that case will come. If you went to the Sublime Porte during the last part of the nineteenth century you would see thousands crowded around that palace, from all

[1] Luke 19 : 2-10.

the states of the Empire, some free, some of them in prisons, waiting from month to month, and years may pass before they are given trial or their cases heard. Physicians who spent the best part of their lives in studies, and were near reaping the fruit of their labors, were obliged to go to the capital to register their diplomas permitting them to practice, but some of them were detained for years. They spent their money, and through their grief and sorrow from not practicing their profession lost much of their ability and knowledge, and if, after all, they got permission, they would go to their homes broken-hearted, without the means to start in business, their lives ruined by delay. These facts illustrate the case of Paul's appeal to Cæsar.

396. *Criminals—Bribes.*—In the case of one accused of crime, the accuser usually conducts his own case, but there is little making of speeches. It chiefly depends upon the judge, who is, accordingly, the recipient of the lion's share of bribes. A long resident of the Turkish Empire states that bribery is so much a feature of Asiatic government that salaries are expressly adjusted with reference to it. It is charged that bribery is universal among the officials in the Turkish Empire. No one is ashamed of it, they all practice it, while all condemn it in theory. A great bishop would bribe a *zeptieh* just as the chief priests and elders bribed the Roman soldiers.[1] Mr. Wad-el-Ward, a native of Palestine, declares that the recently deposed Sultan was a usurper not a descendant in the direct line of the prophet as he claimed, but was of the nomad Tartars. Positions were to be bought by the highest bidder in Constantinople. He declares that the former Pasha of Jerusalem, having fifty to a hundred servants and twenty wives, and a correspondingly large family, received only $500 a year. He is said to have secured the position by paying $50,000 for it. Of course, he could easily find ways to recoup himself whenever a complaint appealed to him for justice. In a controversy between two persons the one that pays the most is morally sure of his case. As in the collection of taxes, the officials have the authority to extort any amount by oppres-

[1] Matt. 28 : 11-15.

sion and cruelty, so an official in a province may claim that a village has committed some offense through some citizen, and if an assessed amount is not paid over to the official, he sends mounted police, who stay in the town until the amount is paid.

397. *Extortions*.—A similar kind of extortion is carried on by customary gifts to a governor or official of a province. This custom throughout the Orient has not changed for thousands of years. A present of lambs is a special sign of respect as a free-will offering to the official and is not intended to imply any necessity or compulsion from either side. To offer a sum of money is not considered as great a respect as to offer a lamb, because the latter gift has a peculiar significance in the East. When a host wishes to honor a distinguished guest, all that he may do for him is as nothing to that of killing and serving the choicest lamb of his flock. Mr. Haddad says, "I once heard a lieutenant-governor upbraiding a man who brought him a poor lamb as a present, telling him, 'the dogs would refuse to eat the meat of that lamb, if they were able to find any meat on its bones, for it appeared to be nothing but skin and bones. As a mark of respect it fails to answer, and you rather insult me than honor me by offering such a poor lamb.'"

398. *Debtors*.—In Oriental lands it is generally allowable to imprison one for debt. How poor the security for debts is may be indicated by the high rate of interest demanded, usually from twelve to sixty per cent. But according to Moslem law interest cannot be demanded or received, so the creditor requires the debtor to count in interest with the principal, and agree to pay the full sum for both principal and interest as having already been received. When pay-day arrives he is usually unable to meet his promise, then the value of a new note, with interest added, is given, and this promise goes on until the man who owed fifty owes five thousand, and his whole property is swept away by the remorseless creditor. Debt is nearly universal among all Asiatic races. It is the custom to-day, as thousands of years ago, for creditors to charge a high rate of interest, and hence, those who loan money are

hated and usually denounced. Farmers are ruined by debts, and sometimes they or their families are reduced to slavery. Under the Turkish law to this day a man will shut up his debtor in prison, but he must make some provision, of about twenty cents a day, for feeding him, and the time is limited to about one hundred days. A debtor, however, can be arrested many times in succession for the same debt, if it continues unpaid.

399. *Prisons.*—Oriental prisons are dark, foul, and noisome places. A resident of Turkey says the prisons in Syria and Palestine are chiefly those that were built by the Greeks and Romans; a few have been constructed by the Turkish government in a little different style. They are great buildings of stone, the walls from three to six feet thick, and they usually are divided into three parts; the inner one has no window, the second part has one window, and the third has one or two windows. The inner room has no opening, except the doorway, which is closed by a heavy iron door, with heavy locks. The prisoners are obliged to sit on the damp floor, where the air is foul and oppressive, and a dim light straggles in through the grating over the door. This inner room is intended for the worst of criminals, who are chained to the wall by fetters around the wrists, ankles, and sometimes the neck. Guards are stationed at the door or by the room itself. In the middle room is a window, heavily barred, with little ventilation, where the prisoners are also bound by chains attached to the wrists, but they are allowed to move about the cell, though a strict watch is kept on them. Sometimes they have a mat to sleep upon. In the outer apartment are prisoners for debt and the like, who may be allowed bedding of their own. Prof. Post tells of a jail in Beirut which consisted of a series of unpaved vaulted rooms under the administrative apartments. The rooms are on a level of the large open court of the Seraglio, and are lighted by low windows, barred with iron gratings. The prisoners are huddled together in the filthy apartments, with little distinction between those charged with grave and light crimes, and with no hope of a speedy trial, unless they

have influential friends or money influence.   It is not common for the government to provide nourishment for the prisoners taken on suspicion, or for debt, or for those upon whom sentence has not been pronounced.

400. *The Jailer.*—Usually the compassion of the jailer depends upon the amount of backshish which he receives. Solitary confinement is too expensive for Asia.   The prisoners are thus thrust together in a lonesome, stable-like dungeon. There is little inquiry into the conduct of the jailer.   The high officials are not in any way interfered with in their plans of plunder, and the jailer may discriminate in favor of one prisoner without fear.

Prisoners are not always committed on suspicion of crime, but often at the arbitrary will of a ruler, or at the instigation of some man, and their imprisonment is then for a term limited only by the caprice or the cupidity of the ruler.[1]

400a. *Despots, and Tax Extortion.*—The tax collector, hated by the Oriental, is not popular with the Occidental.   Why is he so generally ostracized by all the world?   The statement of his historic acts throws much light on the question.   There is an underlying suspicion that in the West, as ever in the East, he is skilled in methods of extortion.

This extortion began by despots in primitive times.   The despot's decree was law.   Samuel told the Israelites what extortions they would suffer at the hands of a king.[2]   Their lives also were subject to his decree, as in the days of Ahasuerus and Esther.[3]   Under Roman rulers the law nominally limited the pay of publicans to a tenth.   To this John the Baptist refers in Luke 3 : 13.   But even those who aimed to be just, as Zacchæus, were ostracized and hated.[4]

---

[1] See Matt. 5 : 25, 26.   [2] 1 Sam. 8 : 14, 15, 17.
[3] Esther 3 : 13.   See also the story of Jezebel and Naboth, 1 Kings 21 : 13, 14.
[4] Luke 19 : 7.

XXXV.

RELIGION AND MORALS.

401. *Orientals Devout.*—It is a common saying, man is a religious being. But every Oriental counts himself exceptionally devout and emphatically a worshiping creature. Religions are many and countless in their diversities. Thus, in Syria the first question asked a man in court is, "What is your religion?" Government enrolls the entire population according to religious devotions. No greater insult can be offered an Oriental than to say he has no religion. Some kind of religion is part of his inheritance; his patrimony.

There is no end of names and salutations framed out of, or which include, the name of God. Holy days, social worshipers, intermarriages, prayers, fastings, feasts, vows, pilgrimages, shrines, weleys, charms, relics, saints, tombs, and sacred sites without number, and everywhere and in every home, and always apparent, speak of the stress the people universally lay upon what they call religion and a display of worship.

402. *Not Pious.*—It is the united testimony of missionary travelers and students in the Orient, out of long experience and observation, that the Oriental attaches secondary value, however, to practical piety. Thus, Dr. Post says of the sects in Syria, that if a man is true to the externals of religion, he is not debarred of its privileges on account of immoralities. He tells of a Moslem hung for murder in Beirut some years ago who was accorded religious honors of the most pious kind, for though a murderer, he was none the less a Moslem believer.

403. *Not Moral.*—Morality is at a low ebb. Lying is almost universal. While many Syrians, says Dr. Post, tell the truth at times, and a few do it nearly always; it is admitted that no native will tell the truth at once and simply if it is disagreeable. "As a physician," he says, "I am daily asked by

272

friends of my patients to tell the sick that he will soon be well
or that he doesn't need my services. If I cannot tell these
falsehoods, the friends will tell them for me, and appeal to
me before the sick man to confirm them." He was called to
a desperate case of illness in Lebanon, and asked to tell the
sick person that his illness was very trifling, or that he was
visiting near by, or, if he would not do that, to say that he was
provoked, as a physician, to be called to see one who had no
need of his services. And dozens of other ways were proposed
of deceiving the sick under like circumstances.

Natives generally do not expect to keep promises or agree-
ments. A carpenter, muleteer, or peasant will promise to
do something for you, or meet you at a certain time, just to
please you, when he knows he has another engagement or
another job begun that will surely prevent him from doing so.
Therefore, life insurance companies decline to take policies
on Oriental lives because of the difficulty of getting trustworthy
testimony in case of accident.

404. *Profane.*—Perjury, profanity, and cursing are conspicuous vices among Orientals, and often as ridiculous as they
are wicked. Impurity, obscene language, and the like are
widespread evils. To offset this catalogue of social evils
and vices they have the love of children and love of parents;
winning and beautiful traits of character, a marked contrast
with their vices.

405. *Display in Worship.*—Oriental worship and devotion
are largely external acts, apparently for display, hence hypoc-
risy is a notable sin, the normal state of man in the East.
Some declare that everybody is a hypocrite there. Fasting,
for example, is a mere exchange of time and kinds of nourishment. Moslems have some delicate and choice viands of the
year for the night festival of the month of Ramadan, the great
month of fasting. The Moslem fasts all day and gorges
himself all night.

406. *Saints and Holy Men.*—Holy men and saints are
among the most familiar of spectacles in Syria and the East,

18

as well as in India. Their devoutness is external. One of
these sallow, lean, sour-faced, fanatical dervishes, or sheikhs,
walking with fixed downcast eyes through the crowd, muttering his prayers, while the passers-by reach out for his hand,
or the borders of his garment, to kiss and bow low in reverence
before him, are common sights. It is nothing that the holy
man is dirty, ill-mannered, surly, ignorant of everything
but his narrow circle of ideas, proud, cruel, and vindictive;
he is a holy man, belongs to the saints, and so is revered. It
is, perhaps, charitable to add, that through constant mental
suggestion he has transformed himself into this strange fanatical stage, self-deceived into supposing that the more he
despises the world and the comforts of it, the more holy he is,
irrespective of his inward and spiritual disposition and character.

407. *Belief in Unseen.*—It is widely conceded that true
religion had its origin among Orientals. For all the great
religions, those most widespread in the world, had their origin
in the Orient. The chief sacred books of the world are primarily Oriental. If it be not absolutely true that no race or
tribe is entirely without religion, yet it is true, as Darwin
asserts, that belief in unseen or spiritual agencies seems to
be universal even with the most civilized races. This belief
in spirits is termed animism, and is almost if not quite universal in the human race. It is foreign to my purpose to state in
detail the various forms in which it expresses itself, or is found
to exist in the various Oriental races.

408. *Nature Worship.*—The great variety of forms of nature
worship arises from the belief in some invisible spirit, and
reverence for the invisible or incomprehensible powers at
work in nature. It is also aside from my purpose to treat in
detail the question of how various forms of worship have
arisen. This much both reason and divine revelation appear
to make clear. Man was conscious that his friendship with
God had been interfered with. He was not in that friendly
relation with the Supreme Being which gave him comfort

and confidence. The Oriental is a conspicuous example of this attitude. A careful observer in Syria [1] says, "All believe in God from Damascus even to Beersheba. There are no materialists, although they seem to doubt about some things incomprehensible to them. They further believe Scripture is given of God, that angels accompany every human being, one on each shoulder, that a judgment day is inevitable, that destiny is written on every man's forehead at birth, and no accident can annul it." [2]

409. *God's Friend.*—To put himself in friendly relations again with God, the Oriental would make a contract or covenant, just as one man would make a covenant with another. I have described some of the forms of covenant which men made among themselves in a former section. Such covenants required to be ratified in a solemn and sacred manner. This ratification of the new contract or covenant of friendliness into which man entered with God to establish the new relations for protection, and for guidance, and help, led to the various forms of offerings, sacrifices, and altar services, and other forms of worship which have come down to us. It was natural that these offerings should be made at the door of his tent or dwelling. In patriarchal times the head of the family would make such offerings for the household.

410. *A Covenant.*—Some would go further than this, and affirm that the Old Testament and the New point to a primitive rite of a covenant made at the door as a basis of common religious ritual, and that gleams of the same germinal idea show themselves in the best features of all the sacred books of the East. [3] So, too, the Karens of Burmah have folklore traditions that reflect an apparent trace of the Genesis narrative, covering tales of the creation of woman from the rib of the first man, of the sin of the first human pair, of punishment for it, and of some hope of deliverance through "white foreigners" from the West. [4]

[1] P. J. Baldensperger.   [2] Pal. Quar., 1903, p. 309.
[3] See Trumbull, Threshhold Covenant, p. 228.
[4] See also Dr. Brown. "Nearer and Farther East," p. 216.

411. *An Expression of Worship.*—The covenant, however, became largely an external expression of worship, and stood for much of the devotion of the worshiper. Thus, another scholar writing of the primitive races of Syria says, "Among Christians and Moslems religion does not extend beyond keeping feasts, fasts, and saying prayers. Application of religion to practical life is almost unknown."[1] Moreover, women among Orientals are specially exempt from the practice of religion in common life, and are said not to think about it. A native of Jerusalem says women do pray sometimes, but not as a rule, for Moslem law virtually, if not actually, forbids prayers for women, but prayers are mere repetitions, two to five times of the same sentence; if missed one day they can be repeated the next day. To the very devout, there are five prayers a day, morning, mid-day, afternoon, sunset, and evening. The exceedingly devout would also add a prayer at midnight. This writer adds, "As a whole, women are very careless in observing prayers. There may be some modern Miriams and Deborahs, and some who lead the singing at funerals or as mourners, yet these singers are usually very wicked. In a modern Oriental town women will with disdain speak against a Bedouin woman to this day, just as Miriam spoke against Moses because of his Ethiopian wife."[2]

412. *Religious Membership.*—It has been well said, Eastern life cannot be understood apart from religion. The native Oriental has little conscience as to doctrine or morals, says Prof. Grant. Church membership is what citizenship is to us. Religion is used to secure patronage, immunity, some kind of self-advantage. A moral life and religious growth do not of necessity enter into the conception of religion in the Eastern mind. Out of his experience in village life in Palestine, Prof. Grant tells us some villages are mostly or altogether Moslem, others mostly or altogether Christian. In Syria the Moslem population greatly outnumbers the Christian, though the Christian population is no inconsiderable portion. There are

SAMARITAN HIGH PRIEST AND OLD PENTATEUCH ROLL. P. 225

(*Copyright by Underwood & Underwood, New York.*)

ANCIENT ROCK ALTAR, ZORAH.   P. 277

JUDG. 13 : 19, 20

(*J. E. Hanauer.*)

several small villages outside Bethlehem, in Palestine, for example, where the Christians exceed the Moslems. He points out what other travelers have noticed, that a Christian village is known from afar by its more prosperous look, and Christian quarters of a mixed village are distinguished by the same favorable marks.[1]

413. *Ecclesiastical Organizations.*—These villages have strong ecclesiastical establishments, and church life in the country is the political life, and church dignitaries are skilful and clever in politics. The Moslem stands strong for his faith, the Greek Christian will scorn the thought that Christ and the Bible are for Moslems. In fact, "religious sects in the Orient remind one of volcanic islands; they are either ablaze with the fierce fires of an eruption, or else they are overlaid with the ashes of an extinct fire. Between crazy fanaticism and cold inanition, there are no warm impulses of unselfish evangelism." Even the Semite peasant drifts in his worship to-day as in the ages past. He sometimes has only the veneer of some new faith to escape persecution. The Palestine peasant thus has worshiped Baal, Jehovah, Moloch, Jesus, and the Moslem Allah. Underneath these forms of worship students discover a basic religion which runs much the same through all the changes. It is a species of superstition mixed with external devotion.

414. *Pillars of Worship.*—It is not uncommon to find pillars, or images, or obelisks, like the sphinx of Egypt, which must be connected with the religious sentiment of the people of the Orient. These objects of worship were set up frequently by the Hebrews at various periods and in different parts of the kingdom.[2] The prophet denounced this form of idolatry and mixed Jehovah worship in the severest terms.[3] They even used the jewels of gold and silver which God had given them to make into images of men, and for this judgment was pronounced upon Jerusalem.[4] Some suppose that the sphinx of

---

[1] Peasantry of Palestine, p. 44.
[2] See 1 Kings 14 : 23; 2 Kings 3 : 2; 10 : 26, 27; 18 : 4; 23 : 14; 2 Chron. 14 : 3; 31 : 1. [3] See Ezek. 7 : 20. [4] Ezek. 16 : 15-34.

Egypt was an object of idolatrous worship. Many images of a similar character of marble and stone have been found in Syria. There is one about five miles northwest of Baalbec called El Kamoua. It is a column of sixteen square stones, surmounted by a carved stone crown, the whole pillar is about sixty-five feet high, and was probably worshiped in olden times. Another is to be found west of the city of Haman, which is more like a stone building, and, as has been mentioned, shrines are abundant everywhere throughout all Syria and Asia.

Symbols of Horror.—Rending the garments and putting on sackcloth, and sitting in or sprinkling ashes on the head, are common Oriental acts, signifying horror, and also repentance, as well as deep mourning and sorrow. Consult Matt. 26 : 65; Mark 14 : 63; Acts 14 : 14; Jonah 3 : 5–8; Neh. 9 : 1; Ps. 30 : 11; 35 : 13; Esth. 4 : 1. Compare page 117, ff.

414a. *Custom Overriding Law.*—In primitive times favorite practices arose that were handed down in the biblical era from one generation to another, until the custom modified and overrode not only the civil, but also the moral law, and some commands of God. This "tradition" or "custom" grew more persistent after the Exile. Hence Jesus charged the rulers in his time with making the law of God of none effect by tradition or custom.[1]

[1] Matt. 15 : 3, 6. Cf. Mark 7 : 3, 5, 9; Gal. 2 : 8 and 1 Pet. 1 : 8.

XXXVI.

PRAYERS AND VOWS.

415. *Use of God's Name.*—No part of the human race is more devout than the Oriental. Every mention of God's name by him was once counted a prayer. The Arab, Prof. Post tells us, has the name of God on his lips from morning to night. The mystic power of that name is part of his religious consciousness. If a man slips and falls he instinctively ejaculates "Allah" (God). If you ask him how he is, his answer is prompt, "God bless you," which means "I am well." If a child is greatly admired, they say of it, "The name of God is on you." If you ask one whether he will do a certain work he answers, "If God wills"; you ask, "Are you well?" again the answer, "As God wills," and if you say, "I hope you will do this better the next time," again his answer is, "As God wills." You exclaim, "What a beautiful view!" the Arab responds, "As God wills." He never loses sight of the First Cause in speaking of second causes. Thus, the doctor tells him, "I hope to restore or help your sight," he answers, "If God wills," or the doctor says, "There is no hope," and again his response comes, "As God wills."

416. *Personal Names.*—While the Hebrew would never utter one name of God, that is, Jehovah or *Javeh*, always substituting *Adonai*, yet that first name of God he made a part of a great class of proper names of persons and places, as, Abijah, Ahaziah, Isaiah, Jeremiah, Azariah, Benaiah, Jacob, Jahaz, Josiah, Moriah, Obadiah, Urijah, Zedekiah. In a similar way proper names abound in Arabic, compounded of the name of Allah. Again, the other prominent Hebrew name for God, "El," is likewise widely used as a part of proper names. Thus, for example, we have Daniel, Eleazar, Eldad, Elijah, Elihu, Elkanah, Ezekiel, Israel, Peniel, Uzziel, and scores of

279

other similar compounds showing the frequency with which
the Semitic languages introduced the various names of God
into names of persons and places.

417. *God a "Charm."*—Furthermore, the name of God was
and is still used as a talisman, charm, or protection against evil.
The Arab of to-day exclaims "Mushallah"—"What hath
God wrought," believing that the mere mention of the name
of God will avert the evil eye, the eye of envy or jealousy.
The Koran begins with this clause, "In the name of God, the
Merciful, and Gracious," and often in Christian books in the
Orient the first sentence runs, "In the name of God, the Father,
and the Son, and the Holy Ghost." Oriental Christians and
Moslems use the name of God in ejaculations. Thus, Prof.
Post tells us sometimes it is with a yawn, or in a fit of passion,
or to still a noisy child, or to start a donkey, to stop a mule,
or to hurry a workman.

418. *Prayer.*—Prayers, petitions, and appeals to God enter
into every action and expression of life in the Orient. It has
run into superstition, fanaticism, and folly, as well as wickedness.
It still continues, as in our Lord's day, when it called forth his
severe rebuke in respect to vain repetitions. They still think
they will be heard for their many and vain repetitions.[1]

419. *Gestures in Prayer.*—Gestures and attitudes in prayer
are a large part of this form of worship among Orientals.
Thus, the Moslem begins his prayer standing, then bows, then
kneels, then touches the earth with his forehead between his
flat hands. He cultivates the habit of abstraction in devotion
and prayers. Many are the cases recorded of those who have
attained this great power in their worship. Ayesha, a favorite
wife of the prophet Mohammed, said that when she and the
prophet were talking together, and the hour of prayer arrived,
he seemed like one who did not know her, and she as one who
did not know him.

420. *Praying in Public.*—Thomson tells of a Moslem
spreading his cloak or Persian rug toward the south to say or

[1] See Matt. 6 : 7.

perform prayers in public, amidst all the noise and confusion of a street. He first raises his open hands till the thumbs touch the ears, shouting "God is great" and other short petitions. Then the hands are folded together near the girdle, and he recites a passage of the Koran, then he bends forward, resting his hands upon his knees, and three times repeats a formula of praise to God most great. Again he stands erect, crying, "God is great." He drops upon his knees and bends forward until his nose and forehead touch the ground between his expanded hands, he repeats the same phrase three times, muttering rapidly short formulas of prayer and praise. Then he brings himself up upon his knees, and settles back upon his heels, mumbling very sundry grunts and exclamations, according to his taste and habit. He has now completed one regular Rek'ah. He repeats this same process two and sometimes three times, with precisely the same postures. All this is the result of habit and training; the smallest children will imitate it to perfection. After all, there is an air of much solemnity in their form of worship, especially in the mosques.

421. *Prayer by Moonlight.*—Thomson again tells of having heard the same prayers by moonlight on the wild banks of the river Orontes, near Hamath, and these prayers were by as villainous "a set of robbers as ever could be found in that lawless region." In his peasant life of Palestine Grant tells of the peasants and villagers going through the exercise of prayer five times in the twenty-four hours, sometimes with preliminary bathing, always with the formulated utterances and the prescribed prostrations. Even the horseman dismounts, spreads his cloak for a rug, and performs his devotions.[1] Soldiers in the barracks offer prayers. The Effendis pray whoever may be about.[2] Near the springs at El-Bireh are small stone platforms for use when the hour of prayer comes.

422. *Custom Universal.*—These customs are well-nigh universal in Asiatic countries, extending through India, into China, and throughout Central Asia. In Thibet and some

[1] Comp. Ps. 55 : 17.　　　　[2] Comp. Matt. 6 : 5.

mountainous regions of Asia they have reduced the matter
to a mechanical science. A small wheel, with flanges which
can be moved either by wind, water, or by hand, is set up.
On the flanges are written prayers, and the motion of this
wheel is supposed to confer the same merit as reciting the
prayers by him who sets it in motion. Another form is that
of an egg-shaped barrel upon a spindle, composed of endless
sheets of paper pasted one over the other, with a different
prayer written on each sheet. At the bottom of this barrel is
a cord, which gives a rotary motion to it, like that of a child's
whirligig. It is made to spin rapidly, and thus the person
who plies this prayer-mill gains all the merit of the prayers
written on all the papers at every revolution of the barrel.
Buddhists and monks in monasteries used to have portable
ones by which they performed their devotions.[1]

423. *Prayer Beads and Cylinders.*—Dr. Allen tells of a mode
of praying in India in which the worshiper assumes a specified
attitude, carefully adjusting his feet, hands, eyes, and body to
meditate upon some god whose name is repeated in prayer.
To aid him in this he has a string of fifty to one hundred beads,
pearls, or berries, and each time a prayer or the god's name
is repeated a bead is removed, so he knows when the intended
number of repetitions is completed. Many hours are often spent
at this exercise, and the practice reaches back many centuries.
No wonder the Saviour forbid these vain repetitions.[2] Sir
Monier-Monier Williams saw a hideous old woman sitting on
the ground inside the entrance to a Buddhist temple, revolving
a prayer cylinder by means of a cord in one hand. He also
tells us the Thibetans have a prayer of six syllables, and no
other prayer is repeated so often by human beings in any
quarter of the globe as is this mystic form. It is put on a roll
or rolls and placed within a cylinder, which is made to revolve,
and is supposed to have the same efficacy as if the prayer was
actually spoken. Each revolution of the cylinder is credited
as merit, storing so much prayer force for the benefit of the

[1] Lyman Abbott, Dictionary of Religious Knowledge.   [2] Matt. 6 : 7.

person who revolves the cylinder or has it done for him. Williams also describes large barrel-like cylinders set up close to each other in a row at the entrance of a Buddhist temple in Darjiling. No one could pass without giving them a twirl, and by a sweep of the hand he might set them all twirling at once.

424. *Repetitions.*—Lane tells of a worshiper standing with his face toward Mecca, his feet close together, saying inaudibly prayers of so many rek'ahs of the prescribed number. He found there were differences in the attitudes of the four great sects of Moslems during prayer. He notes seventeen different postures in one prayer course. The prayers are said as nearly as possible at the time prescribed. They may be said after that time, but not before. They consist largely in repetitions, "God is most great," "No God but God and Mohammed, his Apostle," "The absolute glory of God," "The eternal one," "The desired," "The existing," "The single," "The supreme," "There is none like God," "The bountiful," and similar phrases are repeated over and over again in the prayers. Meanwhile the worshiper is constantly changing his posture, swaying his body, or bowing to the ground, then standing up and bowing again. Among the most devout, if there is any wandering of the eyes or mind, a cough, or an answering of a question, the worshiper must begin over again, and repeat all his prayers with due reverence. It is counted very sinful to interrupt a man engaged in devotion.

425. *At Mosque.*—On preparations for prayer, Dr. Trumbull tells how his dragoman in a mosque went to the fountain, and with special ejaculations washed his hands three times in the name of "God, the Compassionate, the Merciful." Then he rinsed his mouth three times with similar ejaculations, his nostrils, his ears, his face, his head, his neck, his right hand, and his left hand, his right foot, and his left foot, each three times, with the same ejaculations repeated three times.

426. *Order a Merit.*—His prayer is with his face toward Mecca, his feet close together, his hands open and uplifted,

bowing, kneeling, and prostrating himself in succession. If
he made any slip in the prescribed number of washings or
ejaculations, or the order of them, his entire prayer was nul-
lified and must all be done over again. In the desert where
no water could be obtained he could use sand in place of
water for ceremonial cleansing. Allusions to these cere-
monials and forms are frequently found in Scripture.[1]

427. *Prayer Places.*—On places for prayer, Prof. Grant
tells of mothers praying at shrines and sacred trees for their
sick children, and of tying bits of rag to keep the prayers in
the minds of the saints.[2] At Ram-Allah the women go to a
kibleh—prayer place—to offer prayers to *Ibrahîm, Khalil-
Allah*—Abraham, friend of God—for the recovery of a sick
child. They also pray at these places for offspring. The
natives pray for rain, and often see in any long drought, or
any great flood, or any marked and strange weather change
a heavenly sign of some great portent, possibly the return of
the Messiah.

428. *Prayer Postures.*—Various postures in prayer have been
common in the East from the earliest times. Abraham's servant bowed down his head and worshiped Jehovah.[3] Joshua
prostrated himself and "fell to the earth upon his face" in
prayer.[4] David, on the other hand, prayed *sitting* on the
ground before Jehovah.[5] Solomon prayed *standing* before
the altar of Jehovah, and "spread forth his hands toward
heaven."[6] Yet Daniel "*kneeled* upon his knees three times a
day, and prayed," his window being open toward Jerusalem.[7]
Nehemiah seems to have uttered short ejaculatory prayers
while engaged in temporal business.[8]

429. *Dervishes.*—"Dervish" is a Persian word, meaning
"the sill of the door," that is, those who beg from door to door.

[1] Compare Gen. 32 : 25; Ex. 29 : 19–21; Lev. 8 : 30; Eccles. 9 : 10; Isa. 6 : 7; Jer. 1 : 9;
Matt. 8 : 15; 9 : 20; Mark 7 : 33; Luke 22 : 51; John 12 : 3. On postures also, compare
Gen. 17 : 3; 18 : 22; 24 : 48; Num. 16 : 22; Josh. 5 : 14; 1 Kings 8 : 22; 1 Chron. 21 : 16; 2
Chron. 6 : 13; Ezra 9 : 5; Ps. 95 : 6; Matt. 17 : 14; Luke 22 : 41; Acts 7 : 60; 9 : 40; 20 : 36;
21 : 5.
[2] Grant, p. 93. [3] Gen. 24 : 26. [4] Josh. 7 : 6.
[5] 2 Sam. 7 : 18. [6] 1 Kings 8 : 22. [7] Dan. 6 : 10.
[8] See Neh. 2 : 4; 5 : 10; compare Dan. 6 : 10 with Ps. 55 : 17.

The equivalent Arabic word is "fakir." They are different from the ulemas, being a religious order, but there are various numbers of these dervishes or fakirs belonging to no society, who are simply mendicants or devotees, existing by professional jugglery throughout Turkey, Egypt, Persia, Hindustan, and Central Asia. There are numerous classes of them among the Buddhists as well as among the Moslems. They boast of the saying of the prophet "Poverty is my pride."

430. *At Prayer.*—These various postures in prayer run into fanatical extremes, and have developed certain Oriental holy men, known as dervishes. There are several classes, the dancing, whirling, and howling kind. They wander over the country, and exhibit their exercise on Fridays (the Moslem Sunday) in the open air or in halls, attracting persons of all classes and all lands to see them. Mr. Basmajian, a native Armenian, describes the howling class as consisting of a score of holy men, who begin by a most slow motion, shouting the name of God so wildly that their voices lose all semblance of human sound. When thoroughly excited, streams of sweat roll down their faces, their eyes roll, their tongues hang out, while they gasp for breath; their chins fall loosely on their breasts, their hands hang from their shoulders, and they become motionless. After a few minutes of deep silence, a sobbing is heard, which swells and spreads, till the whole company of dervishes is sobbing, and the sobs deepen into a low cry, and the low cry into a wild burst of grief. Tears roll down their faces and the breasts of the sobbing crowd are wet with weeping.[1]

431. *Beggar Dervishes.*—Van Lennep tells of the beggar class of dervishes, who claim charity as a right, and are the most impudent beggars in the world, inviting themselves into the houses, and at the tables of the rich, who dare not be rude to them for fear of the common people, who venerate them. They are usually filthy, covered with rags. They often carry odd and strange articles to draw attention, such as the bone

[1] Religious and Social Life in the Orient, Basmajian, p. 122.

of a sawfish. During battles in war time these dervishes follow the army like a pack of hyenas, killing and plundering those of the enemy left wounded upon the field. They are proud of some unusual article of dress, like a curious cap or fez. They carry a steel rod, about two feet long, with a curved cross-piece at one end, on which they rest in sleeping, especially if they have made a vow not to lie down during the month of Ramadan. Or they wear a leopard's skin, like the ancient Egyptian priests. Probably some of the false prophets among the Hebrews were of this class of begging dervishes.[1]

432. *Howling Dervishes.*—Van Lennep describes the howling dervishes which he saw, who commonly met on Tuesdays and Thursdays in the evening. They would sit upon the floor in a circle, the chief having a little mattress, slightly raised above the rest. They began their devotions by chanting and recitations, pronouncing ninety times each of the ninety-nine names of the deity, bowing the head every time, while the chief counted the numbers on a long string of beads. As they go on they become more and more excited, bowing lower and lower, until they come to the last and greatest name, "Hoo." Then they spring to their feet, hold each other's hands, and begin to dance in a circle in a most frantic manner, bending their bodies double, then raising them, and bending them backward, crying in unison, "Hoo, hoo." Soon they pull off their upper garments, leaving their chests bare, drop their caps or turbans, and as they never shave their heads nor cut their hair, their locks now fly loosely about their faces and shoulders. Some one outside the circle strikes the timbrel, beating time, which adds to the excitement. The devotees perspire at every pore, their cries grow frantic, but ere long they faint with exhaustion; the sound gradually dies away in a groan, until they drop one by one, apparently more dead than alive, as if they had fallen in a fit.

433. *"Dancing" Dervishes.*—The Old Testament has allusions to scenes something like this in religious services, which

[1] See 1 Kings 22 : 12.

are designated as dancing.[1] These modern dervishes also
have other fanatical performances, calling upon God, and
cutting themselves with knives and swords so that the blood
runs, piercing their nearly naked bodies with wooden or iron
spikes, from which they hang small mirrors. Exhausted
with pain and loss of blood, they faint away. Thus, the
priests of Baal called out and cut themselves in the scene at
Mt. Carmel when contending with Elijah.[2] The Hebrew
seemed to have been carried away with this excitement, though
it was expressly forbidden by the Mosaic law.[3] Van Lennep
would trace some resemblance between the modern dervish
association and the early schools of the prophets over which
Samuel presided, but this is open to question.[4]

434. *Mystics*.—The orders of dervishes are supposed to
have sprung from a class of mystics who were followers of the
prophet. They sprang up about the twelfth century. At
first it is said that great thinkers and poets, particularly among
the Persians, joined this movement, but the dervishes have
degenerated now. The soul of the early movement is gone,
and nothing remains but the external mechanism of worship,
the throwing of one's self into ecstasy, and rendering the body
insusceptible to external impressions. The Orientals, however, venerate these dervishes just as they do insane persons,
and by some they are reputed to be able to work miracles.[5]

[1] See 1 Sam. 10 : 5, 6; 19 : 23, 24.   [2] 1 Kings 18 : 28 ff.
[3] See Jer. 41 : 5 compared with Lev. 19 : 28 and Deut. 14 : 1.
[4] For a full graphic description of the various classes of dervishes, see E. W. Lane,
"Modern Egyptians."   [5] See Baedeker's Palestine. p. 72.

XXXVII.

OFFERINGS AND SACRIFICES.

435. *Votive Offerings.*—Offerings, sacrifices, and votive gifts were, and are still, common to all Oriental religions. The origin of this custom is hidden in obscurity. They were doubtless prompted by a divinely planted impulse in the human soul to recover lost friendship with God. Covenants, vows, offerings, sacrifices, and votive gifts are only different expressions of man's desire to put himself right with God. The offering or sacrifice seemed a fitting seal to a covenant of peace and friendship. Such a contract seemed to call for an added assurance, a solemn oath or attestation indicating that it would be religiously kept. The idea was deeply ingrained in the Oriental mind that the gods as well as kings are influenced by offerings and sacrifices. Homer thus represents his heroes and divinities.

436. *Thanksgiving.*—In the early dawn of human history votive offerings were made out of gratitude. Thus, the ancestors of the Greek, made such offerings as a form of thanks for protection. In successful war the spoils were often given as votive offerings for the success. Similar expressions, called votive tablets, were put up in the temples for success in war, recovery from sickness, escape from peril by sea, or for any remarkable prosperity or rescue in adversity. The Hebrew had a rule not to appear before Jehovah empty handed.[1]

437. *Of Fruits, etc.*—Early sacrifices in the Orient were, for the most part, of fruits, grain, and later, of flocks and herds. The earlier races do not seem to have had a keen sense of sin or any fixed standard of virtue. The distinctions between right and wrong were not marked, or very thin. In India sacrifices of animals among Buddhists were not practiced, no trees were cut down, but libations of milk, oil, and honey

[1] See Ex. 23 : 15.

were offered. In China and Eastern Asia the animals sacrificed were those used for food, as cows, sheep, hares, deer, and pigs. They were slain on the east side of the altar. The hair and blood were buried, possibly for the use of the spirits of the earth; the dead ancestors were invited to the feasts.

In the Acadian times there is a legend in which it is said that the father was required to give the life of his child for the sin of his soul—child's head for his head, child's neck for his neck, child's breast for his breast.

438. *In India.*—Many modern religious customs, the possible survival of ancient forms, are still current in Oriental lands. Thus, Dr. Allen tells of tribes in northern Madras, a province of India, who offer sacrifices of men and animals to the great earth goddess. She was believed to be the goddess of the seasons, sending rain, causing seed to grow, fields to be fruitful or barren, people to be in health or sick, just as it pleased her. There was no image made of her nor any temple built to her. Nor was she conceived of as having a fixed bodily form. She was thought to be able to assume any form at pleasure.

439. *Vicarious.*—The idea of vicarious sacrifice and suffering is strongly entrenched in the Oriental mind. All forms of offices and crimes are included in this idea. Even a human life can be thus paid for by some sort of vicarious sacrifice, either in money or some other form of substitutionary recompense. This illustrates the substitution of an animal for a human life, as in the case of Abraham offering a ram for his son Isaac.[1] These peculiar offerings, that is, the demand of a life sacrifice, to atone for some offense or act that had broken friendship, are widespread among all Oriental religions. The life of the animal was substituted in place of the life of the owner, as shown also by putting hands on the animal.[2]

440. *To Saints.*—Burckhardt tells us that sacrifices in honor

[1] Gen. 22 : 1–13.
[2] Compare Gen. 4 : 4 with 22 : 2–14; Lev. 4 : 4, 15, 24, 29, 33; 16 : 21; Deut. 21 : 6.

19

of saints at their tombs are common among nearly all Bedouin
tribes. Major Conder found that the influence of some great
leader or sheikh was supposed to extend for twenty miles
around his tomb. A hilltop out of Gaza, to which Samson
is believed to have carried the gates of that city, is still a place
for votive or religious offerings. The daughters of Israel went
yearly, four days a year, to commemorate the memory of
Jephthah's daughter in a similar manner.[1]

441. *Sacrifice, Covenant.*—Sacrifice is thus a common religious act, applying to many transactions and events of life. It
is more than simply a part of worship. Killing a lamb is an
Oriental act of hospitality to honor a guest, and is called
sacrificing. The most common way of confirming a covenant
and agreement between two parties, man and man, is to offer
a sacrifice, or have a sacrificial feast. Any occasion of unusual
joy or gladness is commonly counted poorly or imperfectly
celebrated, if not observed by a similar sacrifice of a lamb
or some clean animal. It is a universal custom to have such
a sacrifice in the Orient at betrothals and at wedding feasts.
The custom is widespread throughout all Oriental lands now,
and is as old as the history of the Oriental races.

442. *Meditation.*—The Hindu seeker after God gives himself up to days and weeks of meditation, being dimly conscious
in these states of something which the earth, the heavens, and
the power and grandeur of nature fail to reveal to the soul.
There is beyond these, and beyond the scattered glories of the
visible world, something real, though mystic, yet unspeakably
greater. It may lead him on to austere mortification of his
physical self, and through a conceived series of future penal
existences to an eternal blessedness, supposed to be attained
by absorption in supreme spirit. In contrast with this is the
meditation of the prophets and Hebrew psalmists, whose
blessedness is attained by a perfection of the individual soul
in communion with the ineffable and eternal Spirit.

The soul at such times, with its windows open toward heaven,

[1] Judg. 16 : 3; 11 : 39, 40.

full of hope and promise, and full of blessedness, is led to exclaim as the vision fades: "Surely the Lord is in this place;
and I knew it not. . . . This is none other but the house of
God, and this is the gate of heaven."[1]

443. *Conclusion.*—All the great religions of the world arose
in the Orient.   The Oriental may be a mystic, but no skeptic;
he may be visionary, but he never loses faith in God.   He may
be formal in worship, inconsistent in life, and debased in
morals, but he clings to the hope of an ideal, divine, and
invisible Being.   In radical contrast with the scientific and
severely practical Occidental mind, the Oriental clings to this
belief in God the invisible, and in his dominion over all human
events.   This characteristic consciousness of the reality of
an unseen power, this vivid conception of his universal presence,
this wealth of poetic portrayal, this idiomatic and figurative
expression of spiritual truths, through which the Bible came
to man, would seem peculiarly to fit the Oriental mind for
reinterpreting its marvelous revelation more accurately and
clearly to the whole human race.   This may come some day.

Meanwhile, the great lessons God would teach the West,
through this His supreme revelation of the supreme religion,
may be more accurately understood, and become more im-
pressively the Word of God to our souls, if we read them in
the light of the Oriental life out of which they came.

[1] Gen. 28 : 17; see Gen. 24 : 6; Josh. 1 : 8; Ps. 1 : 2; 5 : 1; 19 : 14; 49 : 3; 63 : 6;
77 : 12; 104 : 34; 119 : 15, 23, 48, 78, 97, 99, 148; Amos 4 : 13; Deut. 6 : 7; Ex. 13 : 8, 9, 14.

INDEX.